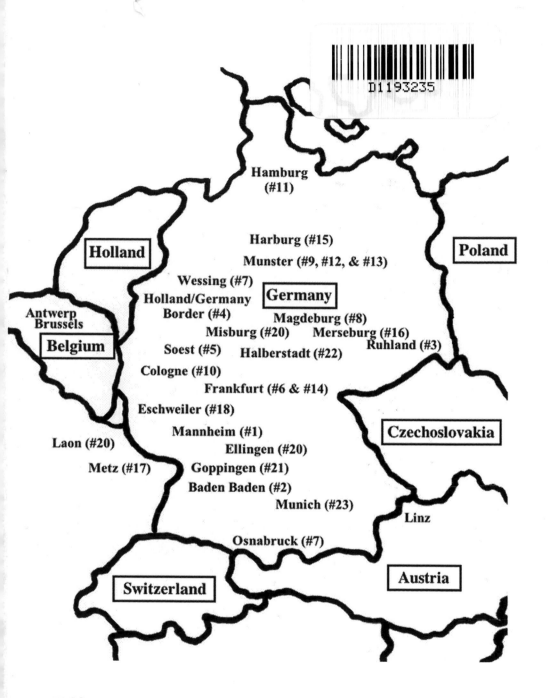

Hamburg (#11)

Harburg (#15)

Munster (#9, #12, & #13)

Holland

Poland

Wessing (#7)

Holland/Germany
Border (#4)

Germany

Magdeburg (#8)

Misburg (#20)   Merseburg (#16)

Antwerp
Brussels

Ruhland (#3)

Belgium

Soest (#5)   Halberstadt (#22)

Cologne (#10)

Frankfurt (#6 & #14)

Eschweiler (#18)

Czechoslovakia

Mannheim (#1)

Laon (#20)

Ellingen (#20)

Metz (#17)   Goppingen (#21)

Baden Baden (#2)

Munich (#23)

Linz

Osnabruck (#7)

Austria

Switzerland

Clifford B. Digre's 24 WWII Bombing Missions
September 1944 to April 1945

Into Life's School:
My World War II Memories

Clifford B. "CB" Digre
Veteran of the 457th Bomb Group,
8th Air Force

Library of Congress Control Number: 2008908484

ISBN   0-615-28229-6
ISBN 978-0-615-28229-9

1. World War II
2. Memoir
3. Minnesota
4. 8th Air Force
5. Bomb groups
6. B-17s
7. Military service
I. Title

First Paperback Edition

Printed in Minneapolis, Minnesota, USA, on acid-free paper.
www.intolifesschool.com

*To my wife, Bernice, the love of my life,
my children—their spouses and families,
and to the Robbie Robertson crew*

Table of Contents

Preface

What prompted me to write these memories of World War II?

It started with a small diary that I kept of my combat experiences. Years after the war, as our children were growing up, they were interested in reading about WWII history. When they discovered my diary, they found it extremely intriguing to read about their dad's personal experiences. By the time this small four-inch by six-inch spiral-bound book had survived our fourth child, it was tattered and torn and almost illegible.

With the interest our children had shown and with their encouragement, I decided to rewrite the diary to preserve this bit of personal history for my grandchildren and descendants. This account is a combination of the records in that diary, miscellaneous shipping orders, letters I had written and received, conversations with crew members, and my personal recollections.

I started writing this book over 10 years ago; it has taken a long time to come to completion.

I have elaborated on without embellishing what I recorded, and these, my recollections, join many books written about the 457th Bomb Group such as the three *Fait Accompli* books written by my good friend James L. Bass.

I know for certain some of my fellow crew members and others from the 457th Bomb Group will have recollections different from mine and I look forward to reading them when they write their memoirs.

For additional information, the 457th Bomb Group Association now has a web site: www.457thbombgroup.org. We have attended many of the reunions of the 457th Bomb Group, having the pleasure of meeting several people mentioned in this book and many more who have memories of this time in our country's history.

In this book I cover the time from the months after high school graduation, the pre-induction years, my military service, and the two years after the war—all significant years that made up my development to adulthood.

The title of the book, *Into Life's School*, is taken from my 1941 Hendricks High School class motto: "Out of school life, into life's school." The reason I chose this title was that I found out that most of the real lessons learned in life are not just from school and formal education but from life itself and the people you meet, the experiences you have, and relationships you form—Life's School.

The cover design is symbolic. The picture is of me standing in front of the 749th Squadron emblem that was displayed in front of the orderly room at the Glatton, our base in England. The emblem is that of the 457th Bomb Group. In my opinion, the B-17 bombers that we flew were the workhorses of the 8th Air Force. The back cover is a photo of my beautiful wife, Bernice, and me. The significance of these formative years is that they lead to my marriage to the love of my life, Bernice, and the wonderful, blessed life we have had together—from life's school to my whole life.

Acknowledgments

All of these pages and hundreds of words were written in my most horrendous longhand scribbling, and believe me, when I hurriedly write longhand, I scribble! Only a bright, dedicated secretary would have the patience to decipher and make sense of my longhand scribbles. I say, "Thank you a million" to a first-class secretary and my good friend, Shirley Kaiser, for initially typing this up. This was done, not on a word processor or computer, but on an old-fashioned Remington typewriter!

I thank the photo lab at the base for some of the photographs. Bernie Baines, the 457th historian, gave me pictures and information for this book. I thank Craig Harris for information about the Cliff Hendrickson crash. I thank William T. Robertson for his contribution of several photographs in this book, and for our lively discussions about many of these missions. Randall Stutman, son of Bernie Stutman, has our thanks for the photograph of his father. Thanks to Rosalie and Dennis Griebenow for photographs of my diary and typing assistance. Thanks to Russ Karl for history and photographs of the aircraft *You Never Know*.

I want to thank our 457th Bomb Group newsletter for information about planes, crew members, missions, and people. Loading lists and track charts are from Joe Toth and his daughter, Nancy Toth, secretary of the 457th Bomb Group Association.

I want to thank all of my crew members and friends for their support and contributions to the memories in these pages.

I also thank James Bass for his advice and counsel about writing the book.

I want to thank at Joe and Josh at the UPS Store on 50th and Xerxes in Minneapolis, Minnesota, for all of their personal assistance.

Thanks to Suzanne Filbin for her publishing assistance.

This book would not have been possible except for the expert computer assistance and skills of my niece Marcia Ellis and nephew Gary Ellis. Marcia scanned the typewritten pages, assisted with the layouts, and with the help of Gary, designed the cover and map. As you will see, the Ellis family plays an integral role in my early life development.

Acknowledgments

My thanks go to my niece Carol Johnson Mattson for her review of the manuscript and editorial assistance, and to David Mattson for his technical assistance.

My thanks go to my family for their encouragement that I write these memories.

My thanks go especially to my daughters, Kathleen Digre and Carrie Murphy, for their assistance in editing these pages. I must add that without Kathleen's persistence that I write this book, it never would have happened.

Above all I thank my wife, Bernice, for her love and continued support and encouragement to write these memories.

CHAPTER 1

Leaving School Life:
The Two Years Before
Military Induction

May 1941 to May 1943

From the day I graduated from Hendricks High School in May as a member of the Class of 1941 until I was inducted into the military in May of 1943, I was in a state of limbo, truly confined, knowing that I could not make any long-range plans. Every job, every relationship I had or would have, I viewed as being on an interim basis.

After graduation I had planned to attend St. Cloud State University and become a high school basketball/football coach. Our coach, Warren Freed, had lived in St. Cloud and attended college there. During my senior year, Coach Freed took my class teammate, Arnie Johnson, and me to St. Cloud for a few days. We stayed at his parents' home and had a tour of the campus, met with coaches, and got a commitment from the admission's office that we would have employment on campus to pay for our room and board.

During the summer of 1941, the war in Europe continued to escalate and the likelihood of United States involvement seemed imminent. I reasoned I would be in the military service long before I could complete four years of college, and so I put my plans to become a coach on hold. Arnie also made that decision.

I had worked at the Hendricks Creamery and Produce part time since I was in ninth grade. After graduation I worked full time picking up cream from the area farmers.

In the fall of 1941, instead of college I attended a trade school — The Minnesota School of Aircraft, located at 3030 Hennepin Avenue. Every aircraft manufacturer was hiring, but all required some schooling. While attending the school, I stayed at an honest-to-goodness boarding house on Pleasant Avenue owned and operated by a very short and a bit chunky Jewish lady — dear, dear **Mrs. Roth**. I never did know her first name. It was always just **Mrs. Roth**. That was what she asked us to address her as, and we did. When I say "we," it was my cousin Vernon "Buddy" Mathison, Orville "Rocky" Rockman, and I. We met Rocky the day we enrolled at the school and the three of us immediately hit it off. Rocky came from Marshall, a town only thirty miles from Hendricks, so perhaps that had something to do with it. Rocky was one great person and easy to get along with.

The three of us shared a big bedroom—six-foot-plus Rocky had his own bed while Buddy and I shared one. It was cozy! I could write several pages on Mrs. Roth and her house alone. It was a great experience. She had one other boarder who had been at her house for months and still addressed her always as **Mrs. Roth**. He was a machinist and worked at a machinery company on Pleasant Avenue just a block from Mrs. Roth's house. Oh how I wish I had taken pictures of her. She fixed us breakfast, packed us a bag lunch, and then in the evening we all sat in the dining room for dinner. She requested that we all come to the table with clean clothes, scrubbed hands, and clean fingernails. The three of us never got very dirty at work, but the machinist always changed clothes and came to the table looking neat. There was very little conversation at the table until Mrs. Roth broke the silence asking each, "Tell us about your day, Mr. Rockman, Mr. Mathison," etc. It was a bit formal.

I lived in Mrs. Roth's boarding house. Our room was to the right, on the first floor, and in the back.

Our high school class motto was, "**Out of school life and into life's school**," and staying at Mrs. Roth's boarding house was the beginning of "life's school."

At the Minnesota School of Aircraft, I became proficient in drafting, reading prints, sheet metal layout, fabricating, drilling, riveting—all valuable training I have used extensively throughout my life.

After completing the education requirements, we could have chosen to work at any of the aircraft manufacturers such as Boeing, Lockheed, or Martin Douglas, but one of our favorite instructors had worked at and recommended Consolidated Aircraft in San Diego, so that was our choice. I think he may have gotten a bit of a stipend from Consolidated for referring capable workers.

Our next project was to get to San Diego in the least expensive way. We checked the classified ads (rides/riders wanted) and found just the right ad—"Have room for three riders to West Coast," and with that came my next course in "life's school." We called, and yes, he would get us to Los Angeles; he even offered to pick us up in Hendricks en route West. He asked if it was okay to drive straight through, he and his wife taking turns driving. That was just fine with us—it would save motel money. They showed up in Hendricks exactly on time driving a newer two-door sedan, the back seat a bit smaller than the standard four door. Buddy and I agreed to take turns riding in the center seat, knowing that position would be very, very uncomfortable for the six-foot-plus Rockman. We were a cozy threesome for the 1,500 miles.

Somewhere in mid Wyoming, the driver made a surprise announcement. "By the way fellows, we will be in Salt Lake City sometime late tonight, and I will be leaving you there. I am going to Seattle, but I have made arrangements with a friend of mine to pick you up tomorrow morning in Salt Lake City and take you on to Los Angeles." The plan was his friend would pick us up at 10 a.m. at the visitor's center of the Temple Square at the Mormon Tabernacle. So far the driver and his wife had been straight shooters, and although I remember being anxious, we trusted him. **What else could we do?**

I remember well the first view we had of Salt Lake City valley in the dead of night—a sea of lights. I thought it was spectacular.

We were dropped off at the Salt Lake City bus depot where we found chairs and caught a few hours of shut-eye. We were at the

Tabernacle early enough for a visitors' tour, and just as promised, his friend and his wife picked us up at about 10 a.m., and we were off to California. The friend and his wife were a nice, honest couple. They took us to the Los Angeles bus depot and from there we took a bus to San Diego. We checked into a residence hotel, The Golden West, recommended by the instructor at the aircraft school.

Within a day or two we were on the production line at Consolidated, working on the new Navy Aircraft: PB2-Y-3 — *The Coronado*. I loved San Diego and honing my skills learned at the Minnesota School of Aircraft — another lesson from "life's school." The experiences of working at Consolidated have all been so important in my life's work.

One weekend, Rocky and I took a long, overnight Greyhound Bus ride from San Diego to San Luis Obispo, California. My brother, Gerhard, had been drafted and was stationed in the infantry (quarter masters). His wife, Alice, was there, living with him for a few weeks. By now my brother was somewhat familiar with his base, and the four of us took a tour of the base and surrounding area. It was a great weekend.

I am standing next to my sister-in-law, Alice, and my brother, Gerhard, at the San Luis Obispo USO traveler's assistance building.

We worked at Consolidated until the fall of 1942 when we decided to return home before our military draft numbers were called. About a month before we left San Diego, Buddy and I purchased a 1929 Model A Ford convertible from a friend and coworker at Consolidated. The price? A whole $200! This was Buddy's first car, and he fell in love with it, letting me know he was to be in charge of all maintenance. Buddy was very mechanical and this car became his passion. Within days after our purchase he let me know that when he had an extra $100, he would buy me out. "Fine," I said, and that is what eventually happened.

Buddy decided he wanted to spend time at home before the military called. Rocky and I weren't too sure that we wanted to leave. We both liked San Diego and our work, but we agreed we came together and we should go home together. Rocky and I felt Buddy was just itching to get his car on the road and drive the 2,000 plus miles back to Minnesota. As it turned out, it was the right time to leave for home.

We started out bright and early, and I was about to have more lessons in "life's school."

The route we had chosen to avoid the higher mountains was San Diego to Yuma, Arizona, to Phoenix, across New Mexico, the panhandle of Texas, Oklahoma to Missouri, and then straight north to Minnesota. Would the Model A we had nicknamed "Betsy" handle the mile after mile of highways? We were about to find out.

We were but 50 miles out of San Diego when the first of Betsy's problems showed up. It started with a bit of radiator steaming, but soon grew to a full-scale boiling. Had we forgotten to check the radiator water? Absolutely not, Buddy asserted, but he guessed that the cooling system was plugged and not circulating. Fortunately, we were near a roadside service station that carried a few groceries. So our improvising mechanic bought two boxes of baking soda, poured both into the radiator, and between the regular blow offs, which looked like Old Faithful, he added water, and lo and behold, this was just the tonic old Betsy needed. Soon she settled down, the water was going through, and Betsy was back purring. No more heating problems the rest of the way.

Rocky was not going to have luxury seating in the front, but he announced even before we left San Diego that the rumble seat was his. At least, he reasoned, he could sit at an angle with some room for his long legs.

Even though Buddy and I had a few disagreements, sometimes even heated arguments, Rocky was always good-natured, taking everything in stride, a fun guy to travel with.

We had no idea how cold the desert nights would be. We drove from Yuma to Phoenix in the dead of night, covering up with whatever we had. We put the top up and even put on the tattered side curtains, but still we sat on what seemed like frozen butts. We drove straight through to Phoenix and spent two days with cousin Joe, already in the service and stationed at Williams Air Force Base. Phoenix was our rest stop before driving across New Mexico where Betsy had a couple of flat tires. In the middle of nowhere in Oklahoma the muffler and tailpipe came off, but Buddy seemed prepared for all problems with his mechanical savvy and with a well-equipped toolbox. He made all the repairs. Besides doing all the fixing, Buddy did most of the driving, only occasionally asking me to drive. We had only a few more "Betsy problems" somewhere in Iowa before we crossed the Minnesota border. Then on to Marshall where Rocky left us, and Buddy and I went to our homes in Hendricks. In spite of those few car problems, it had been a fun trip as we traveled through areas we had never seen before.

Good Old Betsy

In spite of her ailments, she made the 2,000-mile trek and brought us safely home to Minnesota.

Rocky (left) and I in "Good Old Betsy."

Buddy at the controls of his pride and joy. Rocky is in the rumble seat where he rode for 2,000 miles. Al Ronning and Harvey Kosberg, Hendricks boys stationed at this army base near San Diego, stand outside of the automobile.

When I heard nothing from my draft board, and after loafing in Hendricks for a couple of weeks, I went to Minneapolis, stayed with my sister Gurine and her husband, Merton Ellis, on Columbus Avenue in South Minneapolis, and went out seeking work. I found that because of my 1A draft status, good employment was impossible to find, but Sears and Roebuck at Lake Street and Chicago Avenue was so hard up for help, they would hire anyone, if even for a few days. While working at Sears in shipping and receiving, I kept looking for a better job. I lucked out when I found work at the Heidbrink Division of the Ohio Chemical Company which was located between 26th and 27th Streets on 4th Avenue, just north of Honeywell's main plant. This was a great company that gave me a variety of experiences in machine shop operations. How I lucked out and got the Heidbrink job is a story unto itself.

Since I was now living and working in Minneapolis, I requested to have my draft registration transferred from Lincoln County to Hennepin County. First, I reasoned that the paperwork required to transfer records would likely delay my induction a few weeks, and it did. Secondly, I had noticed in the *Hendricks Pioneer* that many of the Lincoln County draftees, including my brother, Gerhard, had gone into the infantry. Whether this was just a coincidence or not, I don't know, but the infantry was one branch of the military I wanted no part of. I desperately wanted to go into the Army Air Corps and get to be a member of a flight crew, and blessed with good luck, this is exactly what I got to do.

Columbus Avenue was my second home. Mert and Gurine lived on the top floor of this duplex.

On May 1st, I received the "greetings" I had been expecting: "You are to report for induction into the military service at the Federal Building at 9 a.m. on May 11, 1943." I immediately quit my job at Heidbrink, spent a week in Hendricks, left there on May 10, and reported the next day as ordered.

May 10, 1943

On this date, I left Hendricks to report for induction in Minneapolis.

Picture taken in front of Uncle Carl (my mother's brother) and Aunt Carrie's home. Note the three vertical stars in the upper right pane of the lower window. These stars honor their three sons in the military: Joe, Clarence, and Buddy.

CHAPTER 2

Into Life's School
Induction and Basic Training

May 11, 1943

My 28 months, 25 days, and 29 minutes in the military started with induction at the Federal Building in downtown Minneapolis at 9:30 a.m. on May 11, 1943.

After a brief "Raise your right hand" swearing-in ceremony at the Federal Building, we boarded Army trucks for the short ride out to Fort Snelling. Even though I had lived in Minneapolis for some time and often driven by Fort Snelling, I had never before seen the barracks, the mess halls, the drill fields, etc., so now seeing this, and seeing men marching in formation made it real—"You're in the Army now; you are Serial Number 37561701." It was off with our civilian clothes and into Army uniforms.

I then became Private Clifford B. Digre—37561701.

May 11 to May 17, 1943
Fort Snelling, Minneapolis, Minnesota

During the week at Fort Snelling we had physical exams and aptitude testing. We could request the branch of the military we preferred even though it was made clear the military would assign us after testing to the branch of the service they felt we were most suited for.

During this week at the Fort we were free to go into Minneapolis every evening; for me it was on to my second home to be with my sister Gurine and her husband, Mert Ellis, and their children, Colleen and Gary.

I requested assignment to the Army Air Corps* and I got it. On May 16 orders came through that we would be shipping out at 1500 hours for the Army Air Corps base at Lincoln, Nebraska.

When I learned that three of my new-found friends: Arnold Engh, a 100% Norwegian from Sherwood, North Dakota, Arvid Eggenberger,

*Army Air Corps was part of the Army. It later was referred to as the Army Air Force. In 1947, it became its own branch of the military, known as the United States Air Force (USAF).

a 100% German from Lake City, Minnesota, and my favorite friend, Don Fernlund, a 100% Swede from Cross Lake, Minnesota, were also going to Lincoln, I was elated. So, as we boarded for the first of many, many Army train rides, I thought to myself, "So far this isn't too bad; Army life is going my way."

May 18 to July 15, 1943
Basic Training at Lincoln Air Base,
Lincoln, Nebraska

Train rides always had an intrigue for me, but the ride from Fort Snelling to Lincoln, Nebraska, was far from pleasant. It was hot! The train was crowded! The chow was poor! We had little or no sleep! As we were herded off the train like cattle and heard the barking of basic-training sergeants, I knew I was not at Fort Snelling; this was the Army I had been told about, and the Army I wasn't sure that I was going to like. The first commands we heard were, "You will take orders and when you leave here in July, you will be in the physical and mental condition the Army wants—Period!" Wow, what a welcome.

Lincoln Army Air Corps Base was recognized as the toughest basic training of all Army Air Corps bases and it was. To top it off, I was there during the hottest summer on record in Nebraska.

Our barracks' assignment, duties, formation marking, classes, and nearly every activity were arranged alphabetically by our names, so Digre was usually together with his new-found friends from Fort Snelling: Engh, Eggenberger, and Fernlund. We four became really good friends.

Below are some vivid memories of basic training at Lincoln.

A Punishing Sunburn...
On the second Sunday at the base I learned another lesson in life's school. Several of us got a first-hand lesson on Army rules and regulations and punishments. On this very hot, bright, sunny day, twenty or so of us from our barracks made up an unauthorized softball game. Soon our shirts were coming off, and after two or three hours in the blistering Nebraska sun most of us suffered **severe** sunburn, enough to require medical attention and keep us out of duty for three days. Since we did not receive these burns in the line of duty, and since we

had inflicted these burns to our bodies, we had broken Army rules and regulations. We were all convicted and were required to sign the 104th Article of War that carries a punishment. So somewhere in my military record, my punishment is stated as:

After your Army tour is completed you will be required to serve one week of duty without pay for each of the days you were confined due to the sunburn you inflicted to your body not in the line of duty.

When I was discharged 27 months later, this was forgotten, overlooked, or never recorded.

Physical Fitness...

Physical fitness was a primary emphasis nearly every day of basic training—calisthenics, hikes with full backpacks, obstacle courses, running tracks, some organized softball games, but mostly calisthenics until I hated them. Since I had been very active in athletics in high school only two years earlier, I was in good physical condition, and I kept up with the best. I remember a man perhaps 28-29 years old from Oklahoma we called "Pops;" this poor guy just couldn't keep up, and finally the instructor even gave up on him and he was transferred to permanent KP (kitchen patrol). He perhaps spent his military career scrubbing pots and pans.

Physical fitness was a part of our daily routine, and by the time we left Lincoln I was in the best shape of my life. The sergeant who met our train was right on. I was in the physical condition the Army wanted.

John Needed Scrubbing...

After a hot, dusty country hike, Fernlund and I were taking our daily shower when John from St. Paul came into the shower room. John's first comments were, "Gee, these showers are low; how do you get under them?" Suddenly it dawned on Fernlund and me that this was John's first time in the showers since we came here three weeks ago. That was it! The two of us wrestled John to the floor under the showers and with a GI scrub brush, scrubbed John until he was as red as our sunburns. He never, never again missed his daily shower.

Duncan's Dirty Ditch...

When it was built, Duncan's Dirty Ditch had been named with a bit of satire, I'm sure, for General Duncan, the commanding officer of Lincoln Air Base. The ditch was an open drainage ditch approximately twenty feet wide and twelve to fifteen feet deep. It was right in front of our barracks and ran several blocks through the heart of the base. Apparently it had been built to drain slough water, but now no water was running.

The bottom was covered with a mucky green slime perhaps two or three feet deep, which emitted a horrible stench and was said to be infested with rodents, lizards, and snakes. Well, this ditch became "center stage" on a hot, late June Saturday afternoon.

Here's the story: Usually on Saturday mornings we had a base parade, barracks' inspection, and then the afternoon off to write letters, read, or whatever. But on this Saturday for whatever reason, our barracks was singled out to report for duty in fatigues (work clothes). We were loaded onto trucks and taken to a grain field loaded with unwanted mustard. Our mission: pick each and every mustard plant out of the acres and acres of grain. After three hours of hot, dusty picking, we were loaded back onto the trucks and brought back to our barracks. Stumbling in, hot, tired, and looking forward to showers, we found three of our barrack mates all comfortably lying on their bunks reading or writing letters and smugly admitting they had hidden when the rest of us were loaded onto the trucks. That was it! Almost in unison the shouts came, "You're going for a dip in Duncan's Ditch." Two of the three quickly reasoned no way could they fight off this mob, and they went out in their shorts with a half dozen escorts and walked down the ditch embankment and were told to walk into the muck, sit down on it for five minutes. When they came out all covered with green slime, they were no longer smug or laughing as they ran to the showers.

The third guy was determined that he was not going into the ditch. He was a freckle-faced red head from the Minnesota Iron Range—tough as nails, a weight lifter, and a champion wrestler in high school. He was lying on his bunk hooking his arms and legs onto the bunk rails. He didn't say a word—just grit his teeth and hung on for dear life, as his red face got redder. It took seven or eight guys to tear him away from his bunk, with him kicking and clawing every inch of the way. They carried him down the ditch embankment and physically on the count of three threw him into the green crap. Coming back from the embankment, he was heaving his guts out and running for the latrines and showers. Never, never did those three, or anyone else in our barracks, goof off on another detail. It was a real lesson on, "Don't screw your buddies."

The Weirdo Dentist...

Going to a dentist is never pleasant, but we dreaded going to this particular examining dentist; we had been told about this weirdo since we arrived at the base.

He did the exam and barked out the treatments needed to his male assistant taking notes.

My Norsk buddy Arnold Engh and I were scheduled for our exams at the same time, and we were glad for the moral support we could give each other.

The examining room itself was unconventional. The dentist chair was in the center of an approximately twenty-by-twenty-foot room with chairs for his victims lined up on all four walls. There were perhaps twenty of us in the room watching and listening to this character shouting. We were called to the chair in alphabetical order so I was up before my friend, Engh. His first command to me was, "Open up and keep it open!" I assure you I did as he prodded with his pick and mirror. It was not pleasant, but I survived. I went back to my chair to wait for Engh whom he started on with the same, "Open up!" command and then went in with his pick. He apparently stuck Engh with the pick, and I saw Engh jerk a bit. The "Mad Man" pulled out the pick, put it on a tray, and with his fist cracked Engh across the jaw saying, "That will teach you to sit still, soldier!" He then went on with the exam.

The actual dental work we had some days later at the clinic was all together different; a very professional dentist, I think, did a good job.

A Hot Exam...

It seemed to me that basic training was designed to test us and make us as miserable as possible.

On another hot, hot day at Lincoln (and I believe that whole summer Nebraska had record temperatures) we were told to fall out in front of our barracks at 1400 hours. We were instructed the dress was to be shoes and rubber raincoats. That was all—no socks, no shorts, no hats, nothing—just shoes and rubber raincoats that didn't breathe. We marched in formation to a dispensary at least two miles away, all the time wringing wet with sweat. It was a relief when we could open our raincoats—pull *it* out and go through the famous "Army Short-Arm Inspection." *It* was inspected by the doctors of the base for venereal disease or other conditions, and during this inspection they shouted, "Pull it out and skin it back!"

On the way back to the barracks, our drill sergeant put us into a run for the last mile. This was too much for some who fell out with heat exhaustion and were picked up by a truck and the medics following us. Perhaps all this served a purpose, but just what purpose I don't know.

Not every day at Lincoln did we have the episodes of bad sunburns, scrubbing John, tossing guys into Duncan's Ditch, dentists, or the hot, short-arm inspections. Most days were pretty routine, starting with revelry at 5 a.m. and ending with taps and lights out at 9 p.m. In between those hours we were kept busy with some form of physical fitness, most often calisthenics, lectures, and films on everything from VD to buying GI life insurance, attending chapel services, formation marching, and tests both physical and aptitude. During those many weeks at Lincoln, I did not have a pass to go off the base. We were really restricted—"disciplined" they called it.

Shortly after we arrived at Lincoln, I made application for the Air Corps Cadet Program, so in addition to the aptitude and skills testing that was given to everyone, I took another series of tests, both written and personal interviews—requirements for the Cadet Program. My days were filled. I did well on all my tests, so I was certain that at the end of basic training I would be on my way to pre-flight school at the University of Montana at Missoula, but next came a series of physical exams and bingo, just like that, I was eliminated from the Cadet Program. I was diagnosed as colorblind. I had a hunch I might be, so the first time I was tested, as guys were in line for the test and one by one they repeatedly called off the same numbers—17, 29, 93, 81, etc., perhaps eight or nine numbers, I stood in the back of the room trying to be inconspicuous and memorizing these numbers. When I was sure I knew them, I got in line and read off the numbers as the pages were turned. The examiner marked my chart "passed," and I thought that would be it, but no—just a few days later I was called in for my Cadet Program physical which included another colorblind test, and this time I was alone. I tried and tried, but I absolutely could not see the numbers that are supposedly on those pages; I saw only colored dots.

That exam ended for me my hopes to be a pilot, navigator, or bombardier in the Air Corps. I had scored well in testing for Radio School in both code and mechanics, and I had decided if I didn't make Cadets, I would hope to attend the Radio Operators School at Sioux Falls, but being colorblind disqualified me from that, too.

Now my choice was to be an aerial gunner like my friends, Eggenberger and Fernlund. Fernlund's brother Kenny was already through gunnery school and assigned to a crew, and Don wanted to follow in his brother's footsteps. My Norski buddy, Engh, decided he wanted no part of flying and signed up for an aircraft ground mechanic's school.

Every gunner was given training in radio operation, aircraft mechanics, or armament so that in emergencies he could take over those positions.

On July 15, 1943, we had completed basic training, and while Engh was on his way to Texas, Eggenberger, Fernlund, and Digre were on a train headed for California and the Signal Corps Radio School at Camp Kohler, just north of Sacramento.

July 19 to November 20, 1943
Camp Kohler (Army Signal Corps)
Near Sacramento, California

The train ride to California was great—not a troop train, but a regular passenger rain with a dining car. After the miserable train ride from Minneapolis to Lincoln, this was sheer luxury.

Arriving at the Sacramento railroad station we were boarded onto US Signal Corps trucks for the ride to Camp Kohler. The camp was near the towns of Yuba City and Marysville, outside of Sacramento.

We had thought that leaving the plains of Nebraska we would be leaving behind the high temperatures, but not so. It was hotter here, and our first look at the camp was a depressing sight—not one blade of grass. The entire camp was sand and gravel. It reminded me of the deserts in Arizona and Nevada that Buddy Mathison, Orv Rockman, and I had driven through on our way home from San Diego in 1942. This camp was just like a desert. The barracks—the very crudest, tar-paper built on stilts. All of a sudden we realized it was not too bad at Lincoln. We even missed "Duncan's Ditch."

My two best buddies, together since induction at Fort Snelling: Don Fernlund (Cross Lake, Minnesota), left, and Arvid Eggenberger (Lake City, Minnesota).

I admit I was depressed as I was assigned to "A" barracks in Company "B" of the 4th Battalion of the US Signal Corps at Camp Kohler. I had a bit of good luck—Eggenberger, Fernlund, and I were still together with side-to-side bunks. After settling in, hanging up our clothes, and putting our few belongings in our footlockers, we were free to explore the camp and locate the two vitals—the PX and the mess halls.

The next morning after breakfast, we were assembled for orientation and a briefing on what to expect while we were at Camp Kohler. At this meeting, we were told that some of us were here on temporary assignment to the Signal Corps for radio school training. Those who successfully completed these courses and another Air Corps physical would return to the Air Corps and gunnery school training. However many of us would be transferred to the Signal Corps. Many who came with us from Lincoln did not qualify to attend radio school and were immediately made a permanent part of the Signal Corps. Some became truck drivers; others, like John, the fellow Don Fernlund and I had scrubbed in the showers at Lincoln, became a KP. I was told later he had been sent to a cook and baker's school—absolutely perfect for John, the "chow hound" to end all "chow hounds."

John, our good buddy and "Chow Hound." This is the guy who Don Fernlund and I wrestled to the shower floor and scrubbed beet red during basic training at Lincoln, Nebraska.

At this same meeting we learned of the history of Camp Kohler. Within days after Japan had bombed Pearl Harbor, an Act of Congress declared that Japanese Americans were considered a threat to American security, and Congress ordered that they be arrested and interned. The greatest number of Japanese Americans lived on the West Coast, particularly in San Francisco, so it was in this area that this crude camp with the barest of necessities was built to intern these people. It truly was a prison with sections of an eight-foot barbed wire fence still in evidence.

Many, many of the interned were model US citizens, and it was not long before pressure came to bear, and the government acknowledged the mistake and released the interned. It was then that Camp Kohler became a US Signal Corps base.

Just to keep us miserable, once a week we were on our hands and knees scrubbing the four-inch-wide pine board flooring! This was called a "GI PARTY."

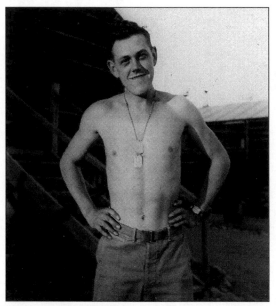

Skinny me after a GI PARTY. Here I weighed in at 135 pounds dripping wet but in top physical shape.

The Radio School...

The buildings housing the radio school were also crude, but the equipment and instructors were first class. About half of a class day was spent in code reading and the other half on mechanics and procedure. I later learned that the code and radio mechanics classes we had were far more extensive than the Air Corps schools, but the procedure classes and field training were strictly Signal Corps. In general the Signal Corps was much like the US Infantry, working closely together in combat since it was the Signal Corps' responsibility to provide radio and telephone communications for the infantry.

In the Field and Physical Fitness Training...

The physical fitness training we had at Lincoln was tough, but it was equally tough here. A part of each day was spent operating radio equipment in simulated combat conditions. With full field packs we operated radio transmitters, generating power by hand-turned generators. We hiked for hours with heavy backpacks. Calisthenics and obstacle courses were a part of most days. Since the Signal Corps field radio operators had to keep up with the Infantry, they had to be in top physical condition. I was in top shape!

This is the radio operators' manual I studied, cover to cover.

A Fifteen-Mile Hike I'll Never Forget...

It was an unusually hot day—the temperature I'm sure was in the 90s—when we took off with full backpacks on a fifteen-mile hike through hills on a dirt trail. After hours of hiking, and within sight of the camp, the sergeant stopped us and barked out that he didn't like the attitude of one of the guys in the back of the formation. He divided the formation directly behind my row, barked out an "about face" to that part of the formation, and assigned a corporal to take them completely back over the fifteen-mile route while he took us the few hundred yards back to the camp. As I turned around to see them leave us, I can see to this day the forlorn look on Fernlund's and Eggenberger's faces.

In formation ready to leave on a Friday fifteen-mile hike. I am the fourth person from the right in the first row.

Company B's Winning Obstacle Course Team...

Everyone in the four companies in the 4th Battalion had to run the obstacle course, one that was much more difficult than the one at Lincoln. The course started with about a fifty-foot run leading up to an eleven-foot-high wooden wall that we had to scale. The course ended with a fifty-yard sprint. In between there was a variety of obstacles that I vividly remember such as crawling on our bellies through a metal tunnel twenty feet long, three feet wide, and only eighteen inches high. Another obstacle was a thirty-foot-wide and three-foot-deep pond of water. To cross this pond we had to run or walk across the rocks that were placed two feet apart or slip; slipping meant a soaking. Another pond we crossed by broad jumping seven feet. There were also high jumps and hurdles—a real challenge.

In addition to everyone being required to run the course, each of the four companies had a team of seven who ran in competition against each other every week. I was on the Company "B" team, and our captain and trainer was Pvt. Horn, an instructor at the school. Horn was by far the fastest runner at the camp and he handpicked the members of his team. He had us finding time to practice most days. Week after week, our team was the winner. You see, there was a prize for the winning team. And what was that prize? A thirty-six-hour pass to San Francisco starting on Friday afternoon, and guess what? Pvt. Horn's home was in San Francisco. Most of the team, however, didn't even take advantage of the passes.

THE WESTERN SIGNAL CORPS MESSAGE

Thursday, September 30, 1943

Camp Kohler's Weekly Newspaper

4th BATTALION Flashes

Camp Kohler
Company "B" Undefeated Obstacle Course Team

Front to Back:

J.W. Stevens
Opkins
Digre
Horn (Capt.)
Kallejian
Grieff
(Not in picture:
Pvt. Richards)

Company A

By Pvt. Albert O. Marx

Pvt. John J. Saur has joined our cadre.

Sgt. Kenneth Olsen's "rolling shoulder" exercise makes him grit his teeth after a few minutes of action.

Our cadremen have acclaimed Sgt. Paul J. Guillot the happiest man in the company.

Tune in next week for details.

First Sgt. Davis looks mighty handsome in his new fatigues.

Nine men are enjoying furloughs this week, while 19 more are "vacationing" in the mountains.

We wish a happy New Year to all Jewish men celebrating the high holidays this week.

Company B

By Sgt. H. L. Campbell

Our softball team lost its first game of the season after having won the 4th Battalion title. The boys were knocked off by A-2, 9-0.

After six months of hard work and bucking, Marion Renswick made right guide at the USO formal dance Friday night at Sacramento Memorial Auditorium.

A practical joke backfired on yours truly. The thumb tacks I placed in 1st Sgt. Steele's chair were there when I sat down the next morning. I was soon standing at attention.

We have an obstacle course team that looks promising. Men on the team include Pvts. Digre, Opkins, J. W. Stevens, Horn, Kallejian, Grieff, and Richards.

Our day room is getting the once over. Also our orderly room, which is next in line.

Compliments of Pepsi-Cola...

Every Friday after a tough hike or hours of calisthenics or running the obstacle course, we showered and dressed into our suntan uniforms. We then marched to the parade grounds where we joined the other companies and the camp band for a parade. The formations passed the reviewing stands where we saluted the base CO and the other top brass of Camp Kohler. After the parade we marched back to the Company "B" area where our company clerk, Sgt. H. L. Cambell, was joined by a lieutenant for a personal inspection of each of us. The lieutenant and sergeant walked down each row. While we were standing at attention, Sgt. Cambell had his ever-present clip board and pencil making notes. The lieutenant was looking us over from head to toe, looking for something to criticize: your shoes don't shine, your tie is crooked, your shirt has a stain—any way to criticize—never, never a compliment. The lieutenant would make a comment and Sgt. Cambell would write it down. On this inspection when the lieutenant came to me, he looked me over carefully, asked for my name, and then told Sgt. Cambell to have me report to him after the inspection. I could not imagine what was wrong; I was cleanly shaven, my uniform was spotless, my tie was straight, shoes sparkled—what was it? Three other guys from Company "B" were also told to report, and as the four of us waited in the orderly room for Sgt. Campbell, we were all wondering, "Why?"

Then Sgt. Cambell came in with a smile and said, "The lieutenant decided you four guys are the best groomed in all of Company "B" and are in for a reward—a truck will be taking you four, as well as fellows from Companies A, C, and D, to the USO Club in downtown San Francisco, compliments of Pepsi-Cola, for a fun-filled evening starting with a dinner and ending with hours of socializing and dancing with gals as cute as you were well-groomed."

A Chapel Surprise...

Growing up in Hendricks I had attended Sunday school, Bible school, and church services since day one. It was just a part of our life, so when I was in the military, I often attended chapel, certainly not every Sunday, but I attended more often than most. I remember well when I left home to go into the military, my mother's last words were, "Don't forget to pray and go to church when you can." Those were her wishes, and I honored them.

The first Sunday I attended chapel at Kohler I couldn't believe my eyes when I saw that the chaplain's assistant was Jasper Swenson from Hendricks. Jasper had been two years ahead of me in high school, and though we were not close friends, I felt like I knew him well. I knew his parents, Sam and Anna, his brothers Selmer and Jonah, and his sister, Randina, born the same day as my brother, Gerhard. Jasper's family were members of our conservative Lutheran Free Church. After that first meeting at chapel, Jasper and I often got together for coffee to compare notes on our letters from home. After the war, Jasper went on to Augsburg Seminary and became a Lutheran Free Church minister. He died at a relatively young age and is buried at the East Cemetery next to our two Erickson ministers — Edward and M. A. (Magnus A.).

On another Sunday at the chapel Jasper introduced me to a doctor from St. Paul. His name I do not remember, but I do remember him as a very nice guy, and in the military, just being from the same state gave a feeling of kinship.

Sometime later I again met this doctor while I was on guard duty at the base dispensary. He remembered our meeting at chapel. I told him about my concerns of not getting into gunnery school because of being colorblind. He gave me his card and said I should ask for him when it was time for Air Corps physicals.

Attending chapel services brought two of the few highlights of Camp Kohler — meeting Jasper Swenson and the St. Paul doctor.

An Invite to Stay at Camp Kohler...

It was an everyday routine to check the Company "B" bulletin board for "What's Happening Notices." One day there was a notice that Clifford B. Digre, 37561701, was to report to Company Clerk Sgt. Cambell. He and I had hit it off well since the day I had arrived at the camp, so I wasn't too concerned about a problem.

We went into his small private office; there he suggested that I consider staying on at Camp Kohler. He knew I did well at the radio school and said I could become an instructor there and an assistant to him in the orderly room. I would have my own private quarters, and I would be promoted to corporal. The offer had a bit of intrigue. The chances were I would not go overseas and into combat; the promotion also would mean an immediate salary increase. Sgt. Cambell was a real nice guy, and I could see working with him. But the thought of being in the Signal Corps and a permanent part of Camp Kohler did not have much appeal. I would not be happy being a ground pounder in the Army Signal Corps. I had wanted to fly! I knew that going into combat as an aerial gunner increased the odds of being injured or killed; however, I still loved the glamour of the Air Corps and the much higher pay that flying would bring. I left Sgt. Cambell's office thanking him for the offers and telling him that if I failed my Air Corps physical, I would give his proposal a lot of consideration.

The End of Radio School...

As the radio school was winding down, we were given a series of tests to determine just where we would be placed. Of those who had failed the courses, some were assigned to the motor pool as mechanics or drivers, some to the MPs (Military Police), and others to the medics as orderlies. I scored well in radio mechanics but best in radio operations, so I knew if I passed the Air Corps physicals, it would be a cinch to go to an Air Corps gunnery school. If I didn't pass, I had Sgt. Cambell's offer to fall back on.

Time for the Physicals...

School was over, and for those of us who had passed the courses, it was time to take the physicals many of us had dreaded. My buddies, Fernlund and Eggenberger, had both passed the school courses, but they, too, had concerns about the physicals. Don Fernlund had a weight problem and had worked at it and had lost some weight. Don more than anyone wanted to be a gunner like his brother, Kenny.

When I went to the dispensary to take my exam, I presented the card given me by the St. Paul doctor, so it was he who gave me my physical. I passed everything with flying colors, but when he pulled out the colorblind book, I again reminded him that I had washed out of the Cadets because I could not read the numbers in the book. Bless him! He put away the book and pulled out a box of colored yarns. He said, "If you can pass this yarn test, you can go back to the Air Corps and on to gunnery school, but you can't get back into the Cadet program." Even though I wanted the Cadets, I would be glad to be an aerial gunner. I had absolutely no problem picking out bright red yarn, black yarn, white, green, yellow, etc., and so I passed.

I immediately went to see Sgt. Cambell to tell him I had passed and would be going on to gunnery school.

Eggenberger had passed his physical, too, but Fernlund didn't make it because of weight. There were only the two of us now going to gunnery school who had been together since induction at Fort Snelling, but we had made other new friends at radio school like George Larson and Bob Suing from Oregon, Dick Wiercowski from Chicago, and John Jackson also from Minnesota, all of whom would also be going on to gunnery school.

So it was a happy group going back to the Army Air Corps and the 180-mile truck ride to the staging center at Hamer Air Corps Base, Fresno, California.

My good friend, Sgt. H. L. Cambell, our company clerk. Sgt. Cambell asked me to transfer to the Signal Corps to become his assistant and an instructor at the radio school.

November 30, 1943 to January 31, 1944
Air Corps Staging Center, Hamer Field,
Fresno, California

The five-hour truck ride from Camp Kohler to Hamer Field was uneventful—a couple of restroom stops and a stop for lunch.

Coming through the gates at Hamer Field was an immediate boost for the morale—back in the Air Corps, grass lawns, trees, two-story permanent-style barracks. It was a far cry from the depressing feeling we had had as we arrived at Camp Kohler.

Eggenberger and I were again assigned to the same barracks, and we chose bunks next to each other. We were happy we were together, but we both missed Don Fernlund. Don was always dreaming up something to do, always liking a good time.

After settling in we were free to explore the base. Hamer Field was three times the size of Camp Kohler; we needed a directory and a map to find our way around to the PX and mess halls.

The day after we arrived we had an orientation and briefing on base rules and regulations. At this meeting we were told that all of us from Camp Kohler would be going on together to one of the several gunnery schools in Arizona, Texas, or Nevada. As of that time they did not know which school or when we would be leaving. They estimated it would be two weeks. We were told that we would all be going as a group. It was good news knowing we would be with friends for this time at Hamer Field and the six weeks of gunnery school. In addition to our group from Camp Kohler's radio operators' school, there were also fellows from mechanics and armament schools. So again, we began to make new friends.

The Two Weeks We Expected to be in Hamer Field Turned into Two Months...

We really had no purposeful training here other than putting together a pool of guys for the gunnery school, and I think they had to dream up things to keep the 50 of us busy.

There were physical fitness activities such as calisthenics, short hikes, training films, and *always* KP and guard duties.

I have only a few memorable highlights of my two months at Hamer Field.

A Memorable and Miserable 30-Mile Hike...

About a week after arriving at Hamer Field, the bulletin board had all fifty of us scheduled for the thirty-mile hike up to Mt. Owens with full backpacks. The first day we hiked about half way and then put up camp—pup tents for sleeping and our first experience eating K-rations we had all been issued. The food was in a tightly sealed box which was completely waterproof. Inside was canned meat, sealed packs of crackers, cookies, and bouillon cubes to be heated in our canteen water cups. I must admit I didn't find the K-ration food too bad.

The next day we continued up the mountain to a semi-permanent camp with canvas-top tents over wooden floors and sides. We slept four men in each of these.

The main purpose of this camp and hike was just to keep us busy for the two weeks we were gone from Hamer Field. There was a field kitchen with cooks preparing typical GI chow. The food was not too bad until the last night we were there. Our dessert that night was bread pudding. About an hour or so after settling into our tents for the night, every one of us who had eaten the bread pudding came pouring out of the tents heaving our guts out, sick as we could be. It seemed to hit all of us at the same time. It was a sight to behold. I can see it to this day. The next morning, still feeling the effects of food poisoning, we packed up for the thirty-mile hike back.

Christmas 1943...

Since I had had such a good relationship with Sgt. Cambell at Camp Kohler, I made it a point to become acquainted with the orderly room clerk here at Hamer Field, too. His name I don't recall. Every time I went to the orderly room to check for mail or check the bulletin board for "What's Happening," I made it a point to visit with him. Well, on December 21 when I was again at the orderly room, he asked if I had anything planned for Christmas Eve, and when I told him, "No," he said his wife was coming to spend some weeks in Fresno, and he, of course, wanted to be with her. He asked if I would take over some of his duties. For the next two days, he gave me an excused absence for everything I was scheduled for, and I spent the time with him learning some of the orderly room clerk duties—answering the phone, typing up duty rosters, waking up guys for KP and guard duty. When I had nothing to do, I could listen to the radio or write letters. I even had permission to call home on Christmas Eve. He had the authority and made me the assistant orderly room clerk. From that day on, just a little calisthenics to keep me in shape, but no more KP, no more guard duty, and best of all, no more long hikes up to Mt. Owens. I had it made!

A Gallon of Tomato Juice (TJ)—Courtesy of Libby McNeal and Libby...

One day while on duty at the orderly room, I took a call from the canning company Libby McNeal and Libby, now called just Libby's. They asked that we post a "help wanted" notice on the bulletin board for part-time days, nights, or just any time. I now had the time, and, of course, I could always use the money, so I went to work at Libby's in a warehouse loading onto trucks cases of canned fruits, vegetables, and tomato juice (TJ). One night a case containing four one-gallon cans of TJ broke open. I told my foreman that I just loved TJ and asked if I could have some. "Take a whole gallon if you like," he said, and I took him up on it. At break time I opened a gallon and went to work on it. By the end of my shift I had polished off nearly the whole gallon of lukewarm TJ. It was just way too much; I got sick, very sick! Surprisingly, in spite of the vivid memory of that night, to this day I have a **fondness** for tomato juice.

Finally! We're Shipping Out...
I continued my orderly room duties, and I also worked part time at Libby's. I was at the orderly room the night the orders came through — our group had been assigned to the gunnery school at the Army Air Field, Las Vegas, Nevada, and we were shipping out on February 1.

I now had such a good deal at Hamer Field that I almost hated to leave.

The night before we left, Eggenberger, John Jackson from Minneapolis, and I went into town for a few beers — a farewell to Hamer Field.

Footnote: The way scheduling was supposed to be, when we finished radio school at Camp Kohler we would have gone directly to gunnery school. I then would have started flying combat missions two months earlier than I did.

The missions I flew were tough, but two months earlier they were tougher still. Just perhaps the two months at Hamer Field that I considered a waste were meant to be. What a difference those two months may have made. Was it fate? Predestination? Or just what?

January 31, 1944 to April 8, 1944
Las Vegas Army Air Field (Gunnery School)
Las Vegas, Nevada

As the crow flies, it is about 300 miles from Fresno to Las Vegas, but the route we took was perhaps twice that distance. For whatever reason, we took a train from Fresno to Los Angeles where we had a five-hour layover before we took a train to Las Vegas.

Las Vegas Army Air Field (LVAAF) was out in the middle of nowhere in the desert. As we were coming through the main gate, the sandy grounds with no vegetation reminded me of the grounds at Camp Kohler. But that is the only thing that was similar to Camp Kohler. We immediately sensed the air of excitement here. I knew at once I was going to like it here at LVAAF. Today this airfield is the Las Vegas International Airport and is in the middle of a huge city, but the day I arrived, Las Vegas was a small town.

Since I had been inducted at Fort Snelling about eight months ago, this was the first time we had heard the drone of the aircraft engines, with planes constantly taking off and landing. At last I felt like I was in the Army Air Corps.

The first week we all had KP duties and a lot of razzing from students about to graduate. The second week was spent on various orientation sessions on basic rules and regulations, and a lot of typical military training films and briefings on what the schooling would consist of.

When we knew we were going to Las Vegas, we were all excited about the prospect of weekend passes to enjoy that city's night life, but at an orientation meeting we learned that was not to be. During our time at LVAAF we had **one** six-hour pass and that was to be after the fifth week of school.

The third week was spent with more testing and a very extensive physical examination. Thankfully the doctor who had given me the colorblind test at Camp Kohler made a special note that I had passed the yarn test and that I was qualified to be an aerial gunner, so these new examinations gave me no problems. We also took additional psychological exams—would we crack up under combat conditions? Many failed these tests; by the end of the week of testing, ten or twelve who had come with us from Hamer Field were transferred out, some back to the Signal Corps we were told.

School is Underway...

Our class was divided into two groups. While half the class was getting the field "hands on" training, the other half was in a classroom setting, and then we would alternate on a daily basis.

The 50-Caliber Machine Gun...

The classroom training started with an introduction to the 50-caliber flexible machine gun with which both the B-24 and B-17 bombers were equipped. Our training began by learning the nomenclature of every part of the gun we disassembled time after time. At the end of the six weeks, as a final exam we were required to disassemble and reassemble the gun blindfolded. I passed that exam with flying colors, perhaps because in my childhood in Hendricks on hot summer days just for something to do, I spent many hours taking apart every piece of my bicycle, even the new departure coaster brake with all the many washer-shaped discs. I would wash all the parts in kerosene and then put it back together again. I was good at that, too, and made several nickels fixing other kids' bikes.

The Ball Turret...

It was also in the classroom setting that I was first introduced to the ball turret. When I knew I would be an aerial gunner on a bomber, I was certain I would be a ball turret gunner. Why? I was perfect for that position—5' 9" tall, a lean 130 pounds, and in the physical condition to readily get in and out of the ball through the very small door.

In the classroom we had an operating ball turret; we could visually see how everything functioned. The ball was truly a ball shape except for the two protruding 50-caliber guns and the flat, small, round window we viewed our targets through. The turret rotated 360 degrees in azimuth (horizontally) and 90 degrees vertically. Since I knew my responsibility on a crew would be the ball turret, I wanted to learn everything possible about it. By the end of our six weeks of school, I knew the functioning of it as well as the two guns the turret employed.

On every mission I needed the ball turret skills I had been trained for, but on my 7th mission, September 26, 1944, and on my 20th mission, February 23, 1945, my knowledge of the ball turret became particularly essential.

At this stage of our training we did not know if we would be flying in B-17s or B-24s, so we were given some information on both. On both aircraft the ball turret was located on the underside—the belly of the plane about midway from back to front. Because of this belly location, it was often times referred to as the "belly turret." The turrets were basically the same on the B-24s and the B-17s but were mounted differently on the B-24s. The turret was lowered and raised into the waist of the plane hydraulically. On the B-17 the turret was permanently affixed with half of the sphere inside the aircraft and the other half on the outside.

In the classroom turret I had my first experience of getting in and out of the ball. Although it was cramped with no room for a parachute, I fit into the turret well and felt I would be comfortable flying in the ball. I also had no problem with the claustrophobia that washed out some more from our class.

Again I passed all the "Belly Ball" turret tests and moved on to aircraft recognition.

Aircraft Recognition...

We were given a lot of training during the six short weeks of gunnery school. These were all crash courses, and aircraft recognition was no exception.

For a young, small-town Minnesota kid who had never flown on a plane and had seen only a few in his life, it was somewhat overwhelming to be expected to recognize at a glance the fifty or more American, British, German, or Japanese planes we might encounter in combat. Before this course started, I was lucky to know the difference between a bomber and a fighter, but after the few hours of aircraft recognition training, I could within seconds identify an American P-51 from a German ME-109, two fighters that had similar appearances. Not being able to tell instantly the difference between these two aircraft could be a disaster.

The course started with an instructor showing pictures and explaining the different designs of the fuselage, the wings, and the tail assemblies. These were the sections of the aircraft the gunners would see. We were also given a book to study that showed silhouette views of aircrafts. We watched films of planes in flight. The films would then be turned off and on work sheets, we were to identify the make and model of the aircraft. It took many hours of training before we were scoring correctly most of the time.

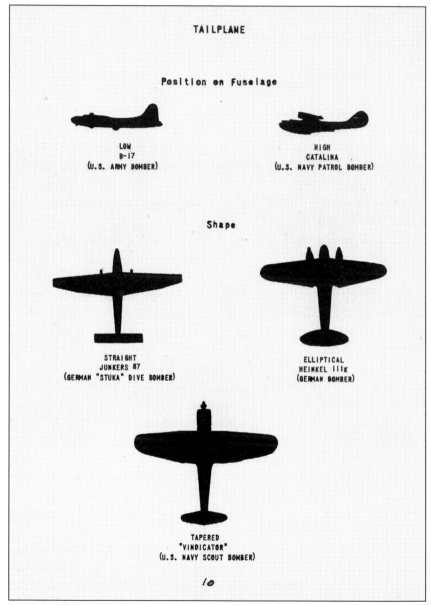

We studied these silhouettes until we could identify them easily. This is a page of our aircraft identification books. We had to study all views and learn to recognize the profile in seconds.

At the end of the course, we were tested by film shots of all the planes in our books. If we didn't pass, we weren't washed out, but we did spend our free time studying and then took the tests again and again until they were passed.

I passed the test on the first round of testing. I knew aircraft recognition was important, and I worked hard at it, but it was not my favorite course at gunnery school.

Jam Handy Training...

When we arrived at LVAAF back on January 31, the first thing we heard about from the graduating class was the **Jam Handy Training**. At that time those words meant nothing to those of us just coming in.

By the time we knew what Jam Handy Training was all about we had spent hours of in-the-field and hands-on training. We had been on the skeet range. We had fired guns from the back of moving trucks. We had experienced some air-to-ground firing but had not started air-to-air firing, so when Jam Handy Training started, we were somewhat checked out on position sighting and leading targets visually, but we knew very little about the use of the Sperry automatic computing sights with which the two turrets were equipped.

What was Jam Handy Training? It was the 1940's version of the modern-day computer-type pin ball and the firing games you see in the shopping center arcades. In a small sound-proof room set aside for the trainer, there was a screen, two movie projectors, flexible 50-caliber guns, and a turret with two guns equipped with the Sperry automatic computing sights. As we fired the guns, a beam of light was projected from guns striking the screen exactly where bullets of live ammunition would hit. Projected onto the screen were actual combat films of German fighters attacking bombers. There were also American P-51s, P-47s, and P-38s in pursuit and dog fighting with the German fighters. Learning to fire accurately at a plane thought to be attacking us made the aircraft recognition class supremely important.

This training served several purposes. It was to show the shooting skills we had been taught. It tested our aircraft recognition knowledge, and it gave us a bit of the feeling of what combat would be like. To make it even more real, the sounds of guns firing were also reproduced. I looked forward to the times I was scheduled to be in the **Jam Handy Training** sessions.

Hands-on Training...

From the first day of gunnery school a part of each day was spent in the classroom setting and a part in the field, "hands on." There was a lot to learn in the classroom in such a short time, and I don't say these sessions were boring, but it was the "hands on" that had the excitement.

Growing up in Hendricks in the heart of Minnesota's pheasant country, I should have been good with a shotgun, but not so! We were poor and owning a shotgun, considered a luxury to us, was out of the question. My brother, Gerhard, never owned a gun, but I remember he borrowed one from an older gent in town named Haldo Fjeseth. I never hunted with Gerhard, but I heard he was a good shot. I remember one Saturday in the fall of 1940 when Gerhard, Carvell, and Mert went hunting and came home with a bit more than a limit. With Mert supervising, the three guys cleaned up many birds, and with mother in charge of the pan-frying, we had a feast.

As for my hunting skills, I had none. I perhaps hunted only three or four times, and on those occasions I had borrowed a single-shot 20-gauge gun my brother-in-law Carvell had bought for my sister Clara. I do remember once hunting at grandpa's farm and knocking down a bird in tall slough grass. We looked and looked, but couldn't find it. Oh, I felt bad. If I could go back in time, I would have been an ace at pheasant hunting after spending hours on the skeet range.

Skeet Range Training...

On the first day on the range, the instructors gave us no instructions — just had each of us come up to the stands, call out "pull," and fire two shots from each of the five positions at clay pigeons coming out of the trap at what seemed to be at least 100 miles an hour. Many, many of the guys were really good shots and knocked down all ten. Right then these guys were checked out of the class and went to the skeet range only for recreation. **I was not one of them**. I remember well I was completely lost; on my first ten shots I only got a small chip off one of the clay pigeons, and that with a 12-gauge gun. I was bad, but I was not alone; there were many in my league, too. Several in the group had never fired a gun before, so the instructors had their work cut out. It started with group training; then they worked with us individually. Many of us had to spend time on the range with instructors until we regularly were scoring eight or nine out of ten. The skeet range was one the fun times at gunnery school. After the war I didn't go pheasant hunting for several years, and like everything you do, **use it or lose it.**

From the skeet range we moved on to firing 12-gauge shotguns at moving targets while standing on a moving flatbed truck. That, too, was tricky, but with instructions and a lot of practice, we became good at that, too.

Off We Go—Into the Air...

Finally the time came that we had been looking forward to for months—the excitement of flying.

Again, many of us had never been in a plane. From takeoff to landing, that first flight was nothing thrilling—just a half hour of flying over the desolate, deserted Nevada desert in war-weary B-24s and B-17s. On the same day we had that first plane ride, we went back into the planes, but this time they were equipped with the 50-caliber guns we knew inside and out from our classroom training. On this part of the training we fired at stationary targets on the ground, flying at low, low altitudes. After several air-to-ground firing sessions, we moved on to air-to-air firing. Flying in the same old tired bombers that still had life enough to climb to a higher altitude, we fired at targets that were towed at what was supposed to be a safe distance behind the small towing aircraft. Yes! The target we were to shoot at was supposed to be a safe distance behind, but that was not always the case. I personally never saw a tow plane hit, but we were told many, many stray bullets did hit the towing plane in spite of the instructors constantly yelling, *"Hit the targets, not the tow plane!"*

The towing plane consisted of a pilot and a person responsible for letting out and retrieving the targets. Obviously, not too many pilots or helpers volunteered for those jobs. Passing the air-to-air training was the climax and signaled the end of gunnery school.

Our Last Week at LVAAF...

Our last week at LVAAF was a busy one, starting with the one and only pass during the weeks there. We were supposed to have had this pass after our fifth week, but for whatever reason, it was postponed. We had looked forward to going into this "Sin City" since the day we came here, but for me the evening turned out to be a disappointment.

I got all dressed up in my class-A dress uniform, shoes all shined, cleanly shaven, and as I boarded the crowded truck, I had expectations of that great night at the Pepsi Center in San Francisco. I envisioned beautiful Las Vegas show girls to go dancing with, but that was not to be. As we approached the city center, the glitter of the casino lights was spectacular, and as it turned out, to me that was the *highlight*. As our trucks were unloading in front of Harold's and the Frontier Club, we were again reminded, "Be here at midnight or you will miss the trucks and be counted as AWOL (absent without leave)." That I did not want. As I entered the casino, all I could hear was the constant ringing of the slots, something that had very little appeal to me. Sure, I dropped a few nickels, less than five bucks I'm sure. For many in our group gambling was their passion, and they were in seventh heaven. Poker playing was a big part of military life but not for this conservative Norwegian. At midnight as we were herded back on trucks like cattle, I was almost glad.

The Graduating Ceremony...

The graduating ceremony was bigger than I had expected. Like at Camp Kohler, it started with a parade with our class in dress uniforms and marching in formation behind the band. As we passed in review, we saluted the colors and the officers that included the commanding officer (CO) of the base. A short speech by the CO and then each name was called and we stepped forward to receive a handshake and our gunner's wings.

We were proud to receive our gunner's wings that we wore on our dress uniforms.

On this graduation day, I also received my promotion from private to corporal—a few extra dollars.

To many the graduation exercise was a big thing, and their wives or sweethearts were there for the event. It was a nice ceremony, but not like the movies I had seen of fighter pilots receiving their wings as a group of fighters flew overhead. That is what I had envisioned when I applied for the Cadet Corps.

A Call for the Chaplain's Help...

When we were inducted into the service, the first thing we were issued was a heavy-duty pillowcase with a tie string called "the duffle bag." We shoved all our clothing, shoes, boots, and shaving gear—just everything we owned into this bag; it was the traveling companion for all enlisted men in all branches of the US Army including the Air Corps with **one exception**—those on "flying status." When we graduated from gunnery school, we too would be automatically on flying status.

After our graduation, we were to be issued a state-of-the-art traveling bag with zipper pockets on each side; when the bag was opened, it could be hung up. There were hangers for coats and trousers—truly deluxe. Called the B4 bag, it was a far cry from the duffle bags we had used. We looked forward to receiving our B4 bags as much as receiving our gunner's wings and the 50% pay increase the flying status brought.

The day after graduation when we were supposed to receive our bags, the whole class went en-masse to the quartermaster building where we were to pick them up. Here we were told they did not have enough to supply the whole class, so the quartermasters had made the decision not to issue any bags, and we were told we would be issued the bags at our next station. This went over like a lead balloon, but thankfully, we had some assertive guys in our class, most from New York City. From the quartermaster building, these guys went directly to see the orderly room clerk, but that got them nowhere. From the orderly room, they went directly to the base chapel and the chaplain's office where they pleaded with both the Protestant and Catholic chaplains, and you know what? The divine intervention paid off. Somehow, somewhere, the quartermasters came up with enough bags for the whole class.

That same day my friend Coakley from Michigan, with his flare for art, painted gunner's wings and my name on my treasured B4 bag. The next day, April 8, with our bags neatly packed, we boarded a train bound for Chicago and our first furlough since entering the military eleven months ago.

This is my B4 Bag today—on the front you can see my name and serial number.

April 8 to April 24, 1944
Home for My First Furlough

With our classy Air Corps B4 bags packed and wearing our gunner's wings with pride, it was a happy bunch of guys who boarded the Chicago-bound train on the afternoon of April 8. The schedule for those of us going to Minneapolis was to arrive in Chicago on the morning of April 10, a two-hour layover, and then get a train going back west to Minneapolis, arriving there at 1600 hours.

Our Chicago-bound train was a regularly scheduled passenger train. Even though we didn't have sleepers, we felt we were traveling first class in the deluxe reclining seats by big windows. We were all in a car reserved for military personnel so we had no more than gotten on board when out came the cards and poker games were underway—for many, all the way to Chicago.

Cards were not for me. I got a nice window seat to watch the ever-changing scenery starting with the deserts of Nevada and Utah, on to the mountains of Colorado, and back to the familiar plains and farmland of Nebraska. I loved every minute. Perhaps my enchantment for the train went back to one of my favorite childhood books, *Jack, The Runaway*.

When it was too dark to enjoy the scenery, I was a casual observer of the poker games but stayed away from the sharks from New York.

As we were approaching Omaha, Nebraska, at about 2200 hours on the second night, Eggenberger and I got what we thought was a brilliant idea. We reasoned that Omaha was only about 400 miles from Minneapolis, and if we could get an overnight train from Omaha to Minneapolis, we would be home before this train gets to Chicago. We checked with the conductor, he checked the schedules, and said, "Yes," there was an overnight train from Omaha to Minneapolis, but he said it would be a slow, slow milk train, stopping at every small town—a freight train with a coach car—very uncomfortable. He also cautioned we would arrive in Omaha only minutes before the train to Minneapolis left, and if we miss it, we would spend the night in Omaha. "Eck" and I thought it would be worth the chance. When we pulled into Omaha, we picked up our bags and ran like mad to the station—but too late; we had missed the train. With the help from the USO in the station, we got a room in a sleazy hotel near the station.

We were a couple of "Sad Sacks" who caught another milk-run train in the early morning arriving in Minneapolis at 1900 hours, three hours after the train from Chicago. Even worse for Eck was missing his train to Lake City, so he contacted some friends living in Minneapolis and stayed with them, while I took the Chicago-Penn streetcar to my second home—Gurine and Mert's on Columbus Avenue. As Eck and I parted that night, we agreed our great plans had backfired; we just plain goofed.

After spending two days in Minneapolis, I took the evening bus to Marshall where Clara and Carvell met me. It was nice to be home with mother and my sister Pearl, but the weather that April was not nice. We even had snow, something I had not seen for more than a year. A bit of good luck—my classmate and good friend, Arnie Johnson, was also home on furlough. We spent a lot of time together, but we had trouble finding fun things to do—no dances at Bohemian Hall, the

Blue Moon, or the Show Boat. None of our old Ivanhoe girlfriends were around. We went to a couple of movies in Canby and spent some afternoons playing pool at the "Den of Iniquity"—**The Hendricks Pool Hall.**

I was glad to spend some days with my classmate and good friend, Arnie Johnson, in Hendricks; we even had an April snowstorm.

It was nice to be home, but the timing was not great. Most of the guys were in the military and the gals were off to colleges or to the big cities working. We even had a big April "Welcome Home, Cliff" snowstorm.

The *Hendricks Pioneer* was doing a series of articles on local men and women in the military and asked me for a picture and a write-up of my life in the service. I had a picture taken by photographer William Digre, no relative, but a fine gentleman who took and printed the pictures at no charge.

Knowing I would soon be having interesting experiences coming up, my sister Clara gave me a diary. Her schoolteacher-like assignment and orders were, "I want you to start recording your experiences, starting when you are assigned to a crew, and your experiences in combat." So, given these orders from an older sister, I started my diary.

On April 23rd I was back on the bus for Minneapolis. I spent one day there before Eck and I boarded the train for Tampa, Florida, and the next phase—crew assignment at Plant Park, near Tampa.

My formal portrait in dress uniform by William Digre Photography.

April 24 to April 27, 1944
En route to Florida

I boarded a train in Minneapolis—a transfer in Chicago, and then on to Tampa and Plant Park for the next phase—**crew assignment**. I remember well that long train ride. My mind was constantly thinking of what would be the makeup of our crew. "What would the mix of guys be?" "Would we get along?" Particularly I thought of the pilot. "Would he be a fresh young punk just out of cadets?" As you read on, you will see my concerns were all for naught!

Crew Assignment and Training

April 27 to May 3, 1944
Memories of Crew Assignment—
Plant Park, Tampa, Florida

Nearly a year had passed since I had been inducted at Fort Snelling—a year full of new experiences, eight exhausting weeks of basic training, a stint in the US Signal Corps at an excellent radio operators' school, six exciting weeks of gunnery school, and now expectations of the most important so far—**crew assignment**.

My orders were to report to the 3rd Army Air Force replacement depot—Plant Park near Tampa, Florida, for assignment. Plant Park was the home of the Florida State Fair.

Plant Park was one of the assembly locations for making up bomber crews of pilots, navigators, bombardiers, and gunners with their skills as flight engineers, armament, and radio operators.

My stay at Plant Park was short—less than a week—just long enough to undergo another series of tests, physical and psychological, and final testing to determine if I was physically fit and mentally stable enough to cope with the strain of combat flying.

Having passed these tests, next was the suspense of being assigned to the right crew, knowing that the skills of my pilot and the other crew members could likely be a matter of life or death.

Most crews were put together with clerks pulling out the names of pilots, copilots, navigators, etc., in a random manner more or less—just the luck of the draw. But this was **not** to be the way our crew was put together.

One day, returning to the barracks after playing a baseball game in the field that was used as a training field for the Cincinnati Reds, I found a note on my bunk that a Lt. Robertson had stopped to see me and that he would be back at such and such a time. I had no idea what it was all about, but I was certain I was not in trouble since I was a conscientious soldier, always playing by military rules.

So I waited, and almost exactly at the time noted, he came back and introduced himself as First Lt. William T. Robertson, bomber crew pilot. He explained he was **not** taking a clerk's list for his crew. Instead, he had reviewed the records of at least two persons for each position who would make up his crew, and then he was personally interviewing them. I remember him saying, "I don't want just an ordinary crew; I want the **best**!" He visited with me for about a half an hour, asking a lot of questions — where from, about my family, hobbies, likes, dislikes. I could tell he was sincere and a good listener. I was impressed, and when he left, I was hoping he would choose me to be on his crew.

Two days later, posted on the bulletin board, was a listing of the newly assigned crews, and there I was, Clifford Digre, ball turret gunner on the First Lt. Wm. T. Robertson crew. Included on the crew listing were the orders that we were to assemble the next afternoon at the parade/ball field area where we would meet each other for the first time.

Only Lt. Robertson had met all of us, so of course he made the initial introductions. He then asked that we each give a brief personal profile — name and nickname we wanted to be addressed by — marital status — where from, etc.

As we were introducing ourselves, **everyone** was all ears and sizing each other up. We were all going to be very important to one another. These were guys we would be going through "Hell and High Water" with, living and perhaps dying with, so each person's skills and attitudes were important to everyone.

The following is my profile of each of the members of our crew; in my opinion, the best crew ever in the Army Air Corps.

The Wm. T. "Robbie" Robertson Crew

Pilot Wm. T. Robertson—Robbie

Orlando, Florida — married — wife, Rose, and baby daughter, Grace. Robbie had been in the military service five or six years before Pearl Harbor and had flown nearly every military aircraft as a flying sergeant. From our very first meeting we all knew this man was in charge — an exacting person — competent — a bit "cocky," radiating confidence and the very image of a self-assured bomber crew commander.

Our Captain, Pilot William T. "Robbie" Robertson.

Copilot Clifford Hendrickson—Cliff

Jasper, Indiana—single—very handsome—a "woman's man." Cliff had been a P-51 pilot in the Canadian Air Force before joining the US Army Air Corps and training in B-17s. Cliff let it be known he was perfectly happy to be Robbie's right hand man as copilot and let Robbie be in charge.

Navigator Elmer L. Mankin—Elmer or Luke

Alexandria, Virginia—single. Elmer was the shortest on the crew—a charming Southern accent—soft spoken—very kind person showing a personal interest in everyone. Elmer would have made a great chaplain—a wizard at navigation. Robbie said he was the best.

Bombardier Charles W. Carbery—Charlie or C. W.

Long Island, NY—single. C. W. had a dignified and distinctive voice—perfect enunciation. I felt C. W. must be truly an upper class New Yorker—dark hair—good looking—another "lady's man," I assumed, since he often was with Hendrickson on passes.

Engineer/Top Turret Gunner
Earl A. Rinehart—Pops

Romney, Indiana—married—wife, Ruth, pregnant with first child. Earl was the tallest at 6'1" and the oldest at 28 years, just starting to show signs of balding. It wasn't long before we dubbed him "Pops"—a good athlete having played semi-pro baseball as a pitcher. As an engineer, I doubt there was anyone better. Robbie said he was the best engineer he had ever known and knew the B-17 better than he.

Radio Operator/Gunner Bernard Stutman—Bernie

Philadelphia, PA—single. It seemed to me, Bernie came from considerable means and continued to have a business interest in Philly even while in the service. In the evening while the rest of us wrote letters, he was attending to his financial interests. He had washed out of the cadet program; not having a commission really bothered him. His abilities as a radio operator were outstanding, and before signing up to fly a tour of combat, he had been an instructor in a radio school. My Signal Corps radio training was equal to or better than his in code and mechanics, but I learned much from Bernie on Air Corps procedure. In spite of Bernie's aloofness and independent ways, which didn't sit well with many on the crew, I really liked him and considered him my good friend.

Waist Gunner Julius Kornblatt—Korny or Julie

New York City, New York—single—a Russian Jew right out of New York City with the Jimmy Cagney accent, "Yous Guys," and every other image I had ever associated with New Yorkers—a street fighter—rough and tough   but very savvy—bright and a good gunner. When I first met Korny, my first opinion was that he was too arrogant—we'll never be pals, but he grew on me, and I actually learned to like him.

Tail Gunner John F. Brown—John

New York, New York—single—just John—the youngest at age 19—skinny—at 5'10" he weighed in at 120 pounds. John, whose real name was Baranowski, was right out of the "Dead End Kids" from the streets of New York. Not until the day Uncle Sam put John on a train had he ever been out of New York City. He thought he had heard of Minnesota, but had no idea where it was. John was a very friendly person eager for our acceptance.

Armament/Waist Gunner
Stanley P. Szydlowski—Sid

Ludlow, Massachusetts—single. Sid and I were about the same height and weight. Some think he looked like the actor, Van Johnson. "Sid" was as Polish as I was Norwegian—100%. He had the Polish dialect mixed with the Massachusetts accent. He came on as somewhat brazen and initially he was not my favorite on the crew, but before long, I learned to know the real Sid—genuine and generous, but "whoa" to the person who crossed him up. He could be vindictive. He and I developed a true friendship—the very best friend I had or ever would have. There was absolutely nothing we wouldn't do for one another. We both knew this was the relationship we needed—we could be facing death together.

Ball Turret Gunner Clifford B. Digre—
Cliff to the Officers; C. B. to the Enlisted Men

Hendricks, Minnesota—I was the only one on the crew from west of the Mississippi—Minnesota. "You still have Indian wars, don't you?" was a common joke. Only Robbie and Bernie had ever been in Minnesota, but it wasn't long before I was promoting our 10,000 lakes and Bernie Bierman's Golden Gophers.

The makeup of the Robertson crew was truly a mixture of diverse personalities: Robbie and Mankin, our two Southern gentlemen; Carbery, our *classy* New Yorker, contrasting Brown and Korny right off the streets of New York City; Stutman, a loner, the successful entrepreneur from Philadelphia; the two Hoosiers, Hendrickson and Rinehart; Cliff, planning to make the Air Corps a career; while Earl was counting the days until he would return to Indiana and to his wife, Ruth, and their first child to be born that fall. Rinehart and I were the two from small town USA (Hendricks, population about 700 and Romney less than 30) and last, but by no way least, Szydlowski, the "cocky" self-assured Polack was from central Massachusetts who spoke absolutely fluent Polish and was proud of it.

Yes, we had diverse personalities, but we had one thing in common—we were ten young men ranging in age from 19 to 28 years, all dedicated to making our crew outstanding—**and we were!**

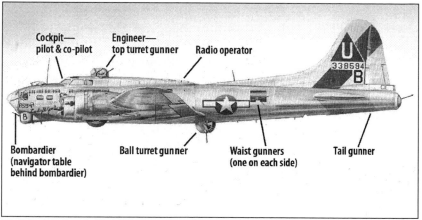

Of all the bombers in World War II, we hoped to be assigned to the B-17—which we eventually did indeed fly during our time in England. The markings on the plane include the bomb group symbol, in our case the triangle U (the marking of the 457th Bomb Group) located on the tail section. Below that is the serial number—in this case 338594. Most planes were named; in this case, the name of the plane is *Lady B Good*, and the name usually was placed in the front of the aircraft. The position of the crew members is indicated on the drawing.

Replacement Crew Training
May 2 to July 20, 1944

The day after we met as a crew, we packed our duffle and B4 bags, and we were off for our first journey together. We were still sizing each other up as we rode in a truck together for the ride to Drew Field just a short distance from Plant Park.

We had hardly settled into the temporary tarpaper exterior barracks, built on stilts, identical to those at Camp Kohler, when our crew was told to pack up again—we were being transferred to McDill Field.

Drew and McDill were just a short distance apart, but what a **big**, **big** difference in the two bases. McDill was a permanent Air Corps base built before Pearl Harbor. All facilities—the barracks, the PX, the NCO Club—everything was **first class**. Besides being a training base, McDill was also the headquarters for the 3rd Army Air Force. This was a great place for officers such as Robbie, planning to make the military a career, to see and be seen by high-ranking officers. It was not unusual to see full colonels and even generals walking or riding through the base in staff cars.

We wondered were we just lucky to be transferred to McDill, or did our boy Robbie engineer the transfer? Whatever, we all realized already how lucky we were to have been assigned to the Wm. T. Robbie Robertson crew.

Our replacement crew training began the second day after arriving at McDill. We were told right off that there was a big push to get us trained and on to our mission, which was to replace bomber crews that had been lost in combat and crews who had completed their tour of missions.

Several of the instructors we had were veterans of a complete tour and some had injuries that prevented them from flying any longer as a combat crew member. These guys gave us not only the benefit of their practical experience, but also firsthand stories of what combat was all about, sometimes, I think, with a little embellishment.

The first day of training was set aside for our pilots Robbie and Cliff shooting touch-and-go landings and takeoffs. We had an instructor aboard to observe their abilities and assist when further training was needed. Our engineer, Rinehart, was in the cockpit area with Robbie, Cliff, and the instructor. Rinehart told us that after Robbie had made four perfect landings and takeoffs, the instructor asked Robbie to taxi back to the hanger area where he, the instructor, got out of the plane and told Robbie, "You don't need me—I can't improve on your skills—your copilot needs some help, so you can work with him as well as I can." The rest of that first half day was spent with Robbie and Cliff making takeoffs and landings, so Cliff got his training from the best.

We knew from the very first day we were going to have intense training—six days a week for twelve weeks—a portion of each day flying and a portion in ground school. Each day was something new to give all ten of us the training we would need for the real thing—combat—such as navigation exercises for Mankin, and camera and sandbag bombing to improve Carbery's skills. Rinehart was always busy and got much of his training from Robbie and Cliff. Stutman was an absolute perfectionist in his duties as radio operator. He kept a flawless log. When I was not involved with gunnery exercises, I would sit in the radio room with Bernie, and he would teach me the Air Corps procedure I had not had in the Signal Corps. One day Bernie got sick with the stomach flu or food poisoning, quite common in hot and humid Tampa, and Robbie asked if I could take over as radio operator, which I did and had no problems. I liked it. Szydlowski had additional training on the latest improvements in 50-caliber guns, bomb bay racks, bombs, and bomb pins. Even as the war was going on, there were constant improvements and changes with the equipment.

The gunners had gunnery exercises on a daily basis. Much of our ground school was spent on aircraft recognition. It was *imperative* that we would be able to instantly identify all aircraft—both friendly and enemy.

By the third week we were starting to fly formations with other B-17s. This was a new experience, and we soon realized how valuable the pilots' skills would be as they flew wing tip to wing tip. Our crew had no bad experiences, but collisions were not uncommon. McDill Field was right on Tampa Bay, and it was also not uncommon for planes to ditch into the deep waters of the bay on takeoffs or landings. "**One a day in Tampa Bay**" was a common phrase around the base.

Replacement Crew Training— Memories of McDill Airfield in Tampa (The ones that stand out the most)

Flying the "Memphis Belle"

One afternoon after a ground school session, Robbie called us together to inform us, "No leave tonight—we are going to take a special flight." That's all he told us except when and where to meet.

A truck took us out to a plane parked some distance from all the other training planes. We could see immediately it was a plane that had battle scars, but not until we got out of the truck and got a look at the nose art did we know it was the ***Memphis Belle***, the first B-17 with its original crew still intact to complete twenty-five combat missions with the 8th Air Force. The plane and the crew were already famous, and their mission now was to tour the USA in the *Memphis Belle* promoting "**Buy Bonds**."

It was just dusk when we took off for the flight that took us up to southern Illinois and back. Robbie seemed to know just how famous the "*Belle*" would someday be; he wanted to fly it. Not only did Robbie and Cliff Hendrickson fly the "*Belle*," but he had each of us come up into the cockpit, sit in his seat, and take ten minutes or so at the controls. He wanted each of us to say, "**I flew the *Memphis Belle*.**"

The Treatment for Athlete's Foot—A Real Treat!

The weather in Tampa during the summer was **hot** and **humid** and this summer was worse than ever, so we were told.

Combining the hot weather and hundreds of guys using the shower stalls are the right conditions for an outbreak of athlete's foot, and I had a miserable case of it that sent me on to sick call. The doctor's prescription? Take two days off all duty, take a bus to St. Pete's beach, spend eight hours a day with bare feet, alternating time in the hot dry beach sand and rinsing off in the salty gulf waters. In two days it was much, much better. From then on I changed socks at least once a day and religiously rinsed my feet in the pan of formaldehyde mixed with water just outside the shower stalls. It worked—no more problems.

Danny's and Doc's Jewel Box
(Our favorite watering hole)

Tampa was a mid-sized city with plenty of bars, but the majority of all flight crews gathered at one place—**Danny's and Doc's Jewel Box**. Perhaps it was the friendly atmosphere with the owners greeting us as we came in, or the nightly floor show—not burlesque, just a clean show with the MC combining as a singer and comedian, or the female vocalist singing our favorites, or the modest-priced drinks. Whatever the reason, Danny's & Doc's was **the** gathering place. When we went there, we knew we would likely run into buddies way back from basic training or radio school or gunnery school. The crowded bar was primarily made up of flight crew members, a few sailors, but virtually no civilians. If you were thinking of meeting girls, forget it!

This was not the place for that. If there were girls in the bar, the ratio of men to gals would have been 50 to 1. No, Danny's & Doc's was just a fun-filled gathering place.

Danny's and Doc's Jewel Box, Tampa, Florida. Left to right: Arvid Eggenberger, Arvid's brother, Arvid's friend from Lake City, Minnesota, myself, and Don Fjeseth (my Hendricks friend and classmate since first grade).

One night as I came in, the first person I saw was my good friend from Hendricks, Donnie Fjeseth. We had been classmates since first grade when his mother, Sadie, was our teacher. We had played on football and basketball teams together—real good friends. Donnie and I joined another good friend of mine, Arvid "Eck" Eggenberger, from Lake City, Minnesota, whom I had been with since our induction at Fort Snelling. Eck was with his brother and his brother's Navy friend, also from Lake City. The five of us had a good time over a few beers and swapping tales.

Donnie was also a gunner on a crew and had now completed his replacement crew training and was soon to ship out for overseas and combat, so this was the only time we got together. What fun my chance meeting with Donnie was—and that was just what made Danny's & Doc's Jewel Box so special. Every time we went there, we could count on a **fun time**!

Our replacement crew training ended on July 20th, and on the 21st we were all off to our homes for a 15-day furlough.

Photo taken on May 6, 1944 at Danny's and Doc's Jewel Box, Tampa, Florida. Together since November 1943, Hamer Field, Fresno, California. Left to right: Eggenberger (Minnesota), Wiercioch (Illinois), Larson (Oregon), Jackson (Minnesota), Scarffe (Michigan), Digre (Minnesota), Coakley (Michigan), Williams (Michigan), and Suing (Oregon).

July 21 to August 5, 1944
A 15-day Furlough

Some Memories of that Furlough

My good friend since radio school, George Larson, a 100% Norwegian from Oregon City, Oregon, decided it would take him 10 or 12 days of round-trip travel time leaving very little time at home, so George came to Minnesota with me. George was a very congenial person, fun to be with, and he fit in great with the Hendricks' Norwegians.

Our train ride to Minneapolis was miserable. The hot, humid weather of Florida was with us all the way. To make it even worse, the train was a combination troop and milk train, stopping at every **podunk** town en route. It was more than a two-day ride to Chicago with a several-hour layover before another ten-hour ride to Minneapolis, and a night in Minneapolis before the four-hour bus ride to Canby where my sister Clara and her husband, Carvell, met us. The traveling time was not pleasant. By the time we got to Hendricks, we both had had enough, and George was glad he had decided not to go home to Oregon.

Our days in Hendricks were relaxing, nothing super exciting, activities such as old-fashioned picnics by the lake, one with Clara and Carvell and another with my sister Pearl.

Clara and Carvell were always there to pick me up when I returned to Hendricks for leave. They picked me up in either Canby or Marshall. In this picture, I was on leave before going overseas. Standing left to right are: Carvell, Clara, me, my mother, my sister Pearl, and my dog Spot whom I'd had since I was six years old; he lived to be nineteen.

George and I rowed Carvell's big heavy wooden fishing boat across the lake. Each afternoon it was coffee time with mother and Pearl in the back yard, playing with my dog, Spot—just small-town pleasures.

One hot, hot afternoon A. P. Johnson, Carvell's dad, cornered us on Main Street. He said with all the young men in the service it was hard to get farm help, and asked if we would come out to one of his farms and shock grain. In four solid hot hours, A. P., George, and I shocked a big field of oats. A. P. gave each of us a $5 bill—enough for a few beers out at Bohemian Hall the following Sunday night.

Much of the time was spent visiting with and saying goodbyes to friends and relatives. My final goodbye with Mother was hard—knowing that in a month or so I would likely be in combat. I couldn't help but wonder—would I ever be home again?

Again Carvell and Clara took us to Canby where we got the bus to Minneapolis, spent a day with my oldest sister, Gurine, and left Minneapolis on August 2 for the long trip back to Tampa.

On the way back I got sick! sick! with an extremely high temperature. I was so miserable that the train ride was worse than ever. We arrived back at the base on August 5; I went directly on sick call and was immediately put into the base hospital. I was there until August 8, the day we again boarded a train—this time for Savannah, Georgia.

George Larson and I having coffee in our back yard with my sister Pearl and mother, Carrie Digre.

Above is the diary I received as a gift from my sister Clara in which I recorded my experiences in the 8th Air Force during World War II.

On to Combat

August 8 to August 12, 1944
Processing at Hunter Field, Savannah, Georgia
to Go Overseas

Although I was not feeling 100% on the morning of August 8, I insisted on being discharged from the hospital. I knew we were going to ship out that day, and there was no way I wanted to take a chance of going into combat with a crew other than the Robbie Robertson crew. Rinehart and Sydlowski came up to the hospital to help me, and when we got back to the barracks, they had packed all my gear. What friends! We all boarded a train that evening for the overnight ride to Hunter Field, Savannah, Georgia.

From the minute we arrived at Hunter Field, we were kept busy. We could tell there was a big push to complete the processing and get us on our way. Within the next twenty-four hours we had another physical and films and a lecture on psychological warfare. We were issued our combat gear — flight jackets, heated flying suits, Mae Wests (life jackets), and even a Colt 45, a sidearm weapon.

Before going to Hunter Field, we knew our final destination was to be England, and we knew that some crews went to England by an unpleasant six- to seven-day ship voyage while the lucky ones were assigned brand new B-17s to ferry over. *Again*, we were *lucky*. On August 11 we learned we would be leaving the next morning, and late that afternoon we became acquainted with our shining new B-17, serial #43-38374, which we took on a one-hour test flight. Before that short flight, the plane had been flown a total of only eight hours, most of that the flight from the Boeing factory in Seattle to Savannah.

On the evening of August 11th there were no passes issued for us to go into Savannah, but knowing this could be the last night in the USA, there were many parties planned at both the NCO and Officers' Club. Knowing we would have a big day with an early wake-up call, most of us played it cool that night and all of us were at our shining B-17 at the designated time of 0500 hours — all, that is, **except** Carbery and Mankin.

Robbie was getting a bit impatient when they showed up fifteen minutes late. In the back of the Jeep that brought them was a good-sized easy chair. After apologizing to Robbie for being late, they told us **The Tale of the Chair**:

"Yes, they had been at the Officers' Club last night, and, yes, they had partied a bit. The club had been packed wall-to-wall with people. When the two of them had been in the lounge area visiting, suddenly a fellow next to them was somehow pushed and fell into a chair, breaking one of the chair legs and an arm. The blame was put on to Elmer and Charlie, and even though they denied any involvement, the club manager immediately told them they had to pay for the chair or he would call the MPs. They had no choice and between them split the cost.

After leaving the club, they started to think about it and reasoned that since they had paid for the chair, it belonged to them; they wanted to take it to their barracks in England, so this morning they stopped by the club, found the chair out by the garbage, and now they are here, ready to load **their chair**."

Their plan was to put the chair in the bomb bay, but Robbie quickly zeroed out that idea and told them that if they couldn't get the chair into the plane through the side door, they wouldn't be taking it along. They tried every which way, but no way worked; the chair was just too big. Admittedly, it would have given their barracks a touch of comfort and a memory of the last night in the States, but it was not to be.

They loaded it back on to the Jeep, and the driver said he would take care of it. No doubt it ended up in *his* barracks.

Within minutes of the chair episode, we were all aboard and airborne en route to England.

RESTRICTED

HEADQUARTERS THIRD AIR FORCE STAGING WING   G-ALT-h
Office of the Commanding Officer

SPECIAL ORDERS)   Hunter Field, Ga.
NO.   225)   E X T R A C T   12 August 1944

                   *   *   *

2. Following B-17 Repl Crews are asgd Shipment FD-900-BJ (Project 92805R) and WP fr Hunter Field, Ga, immediately by air to Dow Field, Bangor, Me, rptg to CG ATC for temp duty pending further dispatch to overseas destination.

FD-900-BJ-10	P	1091	Capt JOHN B WALLACE	0433616	Ap No. 43-38335
	CP	1051	2nd Lt HERBERT A LAWYER	0713805	(B-17-G)
	N	1034	2nd Lt OLIN G WELLBORN	02058598	
	B	1035	2nd Lt WILLIAM T WILBORN	0760086	
	EG	748	Sgt Peter Credidio	32461025	
	AEG	611	Sgt Grant A Hanson	20272128	
	ROG	757	Cpl Jerome Grossman	13080728	
	AROG	611	Pvt William R Biggie	39275120	
	AG	612	Sgt Ferdinand G Rupanian	32494784	
	AAG	611	Sgt Edwin B Hartley	14076773	
FD-900-BJ-11	P	1091	2nd Lt CLARENCE R STOTESBURY	0558056	Ap No. 43-38338
	CP	1051	F/O STUART L WHITE	T62337	(B-17-G)
	N	1034	F/O JOHN W MELCHER	T126486	
	B	1035	2nd Lt ROBERT H OLSEN	0712305	
	EG	748	Cpl Barnie K Fondren	34713696	
	AEG	611	Cpl Fred G Collins	32767290	
	ROG	757	Cpl Roland W Hamilton	33565274	
	AROG	611	Cpl Homer Carrol Jr	34816403	
	AG	612	Cpl John V McCarthy	39120060	
	AAG	611	Cpl Edwin H Sisk	17098698	
D-900-BJ-12	P	1091	1st Lt WILLIAM T ROBERTSON	0523177	Ap No. 43-38374
	CP	1051	2nd Lt CLIFFORD HENDRICKSON	0812261	(B-17-G)
	N	1034	2nd Lt ELMER L MANKIN	02057973	
	B	1035	2nd Lt CHARLES W CARBERY	0712271	
	EG	748	Sgt Earl A Rinehart	15083847	
	AEG	611	Cpl Julius Kornblatt	32689450	
	ROG	757	Sgt Bernard Stutman	13052839	
	AROG	611	Cpl Clifford B Digre	37561701	
	AG	612	Sgt Stanley P Szydlowski	20108024	
	AAG	611	Cpl John F Brown	12151503	
D-900-BJ-13	P	1091	2nd Lt HOMER M PASSMORE JR	0798350	Ap No. 43-38373
	CP	1051	2nd Lt RUDOLPH PROKOP	0558154	(B-17-G)
	N	1034	2nd Lt JEROME W PAGE	02056457	
	B	1035	2nd Lt MILTON R LONG	0712184	

RESTRICTED

All of the crew members listed on this sheet were well known to all of us. For example, Jerome Grossman was a particularly good friend of Bernie Stutman. William Biggey from the same crew was a good friend of mine since gunnery school. From our serial numbers, one could make some form of identification. Officers' numbers started with an "0." Volunteered enlisted men had the number 1. Two meant some form of previous military experience, such as being a member of the National Guard. Three meant one was drafted. The second number referred to one's congressional district. So for example, my number starts 37, meaning I was drafted and from the seventh congressional district.

SO #225, Hq 3AFSW Hunter Fld, Ga, 12 Aug 44 (Cont'd):

    a. See Annex "A" to this order.

    b. This shipment will use APO 16403-BJ (suffixed by individual crew no. to which asgd i.e. 16403-BJ17) c/o Postmaster New York, N.Y.

    c. Pers will be clothed and equipped in accordance with List H, Individual Clo and Equipment, 15 Nov 43 as amended. Acft will be equipped and loaded in accordance with List C.

    d. O baggage not transported by air may be shipped to New York P/E for movement by water to destination.

    e. TDN 501-31 P 431-01, 02, 03, 07, 08 212/50425.

    f. Autht Ltr Hq AAF 370.5 (22 Jul 44)PUB-R-AF-M subject: "Movement O, Shipment FD-900" dated 24 Jul 44.

    #   *   *

By order of Colonel FITZMAURICE:

                         DAVID S CARTER,
                         Capt, Air Corps,
                         Adjutant.

ARTHUR L TSCHEPL,
Capt, Air Corps,
Asst Adjutant.

DISTRIBUTION: 5-CO ATC Dow Field, Bangor, Me (airmail)
                 plus regular combat crew distribution

Shipping orders sending us from Savannah, Georgia, to Valley, Wales.

August 14 to August 19, 1944
On to Our Base in England

Our first stop after leaving Savannah was Bangor, Maine. The flight was smooth and uneventful. Not much chatter on the intercom other than comments from the cockpit as to our location. We had a glimpse of the New York City skyline which was interesting.

Our stop at Bangor was a bit over an hour—just long enough to fuel the plane and feed the crew. Bangor was a popular fueling stop, so planes were constantly landing and taking off, most bound for the European Theatre of Operation (ETO).

Our next fueling and food stop was Goose Bay, Labrador (Newfoundland). Again, another smooth and uneventful flight, and even less intercom chattering; we were flying further and further from the USA.

Since Goose Bay is another common fueling stop, air traffic was heavy with a lot of B-17s being ferried to the ETO. Everything was so well organized that even the mess hall was on the flight line; their mission was to get the planes fueled, crew fed, and out in the shortest possible time. Our stop here was just over an hour, and we were in the air again; the next stop was to be Reykjavik, Iceland. When we were about forty-five minutes out of Goose Bay, we had a **complete** electrical power failure—no lights in the aircraft, no navigation lights, no lights period. Rinehart knew immediately what to check to determine if he could make the repairs while we were in flight. When he determined he couldn't, we made a 180 and started our return to Goose Bay. Knowing we were out over the cold North Atlantic without navigation lights made it a long, scary forty-five minute return to Goose Bay. Again, Mankin's skills as a navigator and Robbie's skills as the pilot brought us back safely to Goose Bay. Even though it didn't take the ground crews long to make the repairs, we stayed on the ground for four hours to give Mankin, Robbie, and Cliff a time to rest before taking off again. After this, the longest leg of our flight went smoothly and with no more problems.

Our first look and impression of Iceland was not too appealing. Again and again I would hear guys commenting, "I'm glad I'm not stationed here."

The weather in Iceland was not great, and the crew needed a good rest, so we were at the Reykjavik Base for just over two full days. For whatever the reason, each crew had to have a member assigned to guard duty at their plane, so Sid and I volunteered for the hour or so of first shift. At dusk we settled into our sleeping bags, and after darkness, it was daylight again—our first experience with the midnight sun.

During those two days, most of our crew went into the city of Reykjavik, but since I was still feeling the effects of the flu, I chose not to go along. They all came back with glowing reports about the friendly people and the great local brews. The crew knew I understood and spoke a little Norwegian so they thought I might have been of help with the language when Sid couldn't score with the girls speaking Polish.

On August 15 we took off on the final leg of our flight to Valley, Wales, a city located at the far northwest coast of Wales. At Valley we left our B-17. Here the plane would be made combat ready and then assigned to a bomb group. Since this plane had brought us safely from Savannah to Great Britain, we hoped it would be ours; we had developed a special attachment to the B-17G with serial number 43-38374.

On August 20 we boarded a train in Valley for the long, slow train ride to Peterborough, England, the largest city near the base to which we were assigned. Trucks met us at the railroad station to transport us to the 457th Bomb Group located about 10 miles south of Peterborough on Highway A1.

The first stop was at the base headquarters where Robbie met with the group commander, Colonel James R. Luper.

While Robbie was meeting with Col. Luper, several veterans of one or more missions, (knowing we were a replacement crew just arriving) stopped by to give us the typical, "You'll be sorry," and razzing with remarks like, "More fresh meat," "We lost six crews yesterday," "Ball turret and tail gunners are usually washed out with high pressure hoses," "Hey, that's a neat jacket; can I have it when you go down?"—a real welcoming committee. Fortunately, we had been briefed to expect such a reception, but the razzing had its effect. It was just another reminder we were getting closer to the real thing—**combat**.

After Robbie's meeting and the friendly razzing, we again boarded the truck for the short ride to our squadron area and our new home, Hut #20.

Footnote: Sometime after the war, I asked Bernie Baines, the 457th historian, to trace the serial number, 43-38374. He found that it had been assigned to the 748th Squadron of the 457th Bomb Group.

I think it completed its tours successfully and returned after the war to the USA.

August 21 to August 24, 1944
Settling in and Getting Acquainted
8th Air Force, Station 130
The 457th Bomb Group

"The Fireball Outfit"

The 457th Bomb Group was called "The Fireball Outfit." The 457th is made up of four squadrons: 748th, 749th, 750th, and 751st. The base was located in the small village of Conington, 60 miles north of London on Highway A1, also known as "The Great North Road," the main route from London to York. Our base was known as Glatton, named for a small village just west of there. I am not certain why we were not known as Conington, but I was told it is to prevent confusion with another bomb group in a village with a name similar to Conington.

Group/Squadron Insignias

748th Squadron

749th Squadron

750th Squadron

751st Squadron

Each 8th Air Force bomb group had their own individually designed group and squadron insignias. Most of us wore these patches on our A-2 leather jackets.

We were assigned to the 749th Bomb Squadron. Located somewhat in the center of the base, it was convenient to everything—the mess hall, the Officers' Club, the NCO Club, Headquarters, and the flight lines. In our opinion the location was the best of the four squadrons, so again we felt lucky when we were assigned to the 749th. The squadron area was made up of several huts—prefab corrugated metal buildings set on concrete slabs. There was absolutely no insulation, so come winter we knew it would be cold with only a potbelly stove in the center of the hut to heat the eighteen of us, three crews, in our Hut #20.

Since arriving we had no duties, only a couple of meetings to acquaint us with leave policies, the base, and base facilities. Sid and I walked into the small village of Sawtry and had beers at a couple of different pubs. Our favorite was "The Oddfellows Arms" owned by Frank and Rose Warren. I was sure we would be visiting them often. Soon we would start ground and more flight training, and then **the real thing**.

August 25 to September 9, 1944
Final Training Before Combat

Our training started with a meeting of the new replacement crews. Some had arrived a day or two before we did and other crews arrived with us. One of these was the crew of Capt. John Wallace. We had been with the Wallace crew since we started training at McDill. Now we would be flying combat together. They, too, had a quality crew. At that meeting we were told we would have ground school and air flight training when weather and available aircraft permitted. Most of the air flight training would concentrate on formation flying. Many new techniques had developed since our training at McDill.

August 28, 1944

Sid and I bought bicycles from a crew in the hut next to ours who no longer needed them; they had completed their tour and were going home. I paid nearly four pounds ($16), about the price of a good bottle of Scotch, for an old beat up but usable bike. Some years ago I had sold my classmate, John Midtaune, a bike in very good condition for three dollars. Bikes were at a premium there. Our bikes would make our trips to Sawtry easier, so I was sure we could be there more often.

September 6, 1944

On this day we were told that we had completed all flight training, and we were now combat ready so we could expect to be on a loading list for our first mission any day. We knew we were not scheduled for a mission the next day, so to keep our minds off what was coming up, Sid, Korny, Brown, and I went to a dance in Sawtry. We asked Rinehart to go, too, but he said he had letters to write. Earl wrote to his wife, Ruth, almost daily. Earl definitely had a fatalistic attitude, while Sid and I kept trying to keep up our optimism, thinking positively. We said, "We wouldn't be here if we didn't think we would make it."

September 8, 1944
The Eve Before Mission #1

Just a short time ago we learned we would be flying our first mission the next day. Now it was for real—no more practice missions. All the crew members were in the barracks tonight—even Kornblatt and Szydlowski, even though they were not flying tomorrow. Everyone had been writing letters tonight, even Korny whom I had never before seen write a letter, and Sid wasn't even going out for a beer.

You may wonder why Kornblatt and Szydlowski were not flying. We were trained as a crew of ten members with two waist gunners. Since our training, the Air Force decided to reduce the number of waist gunners from two to one—thus eliminating one position and making a crew of nine. On a crew's first mission, they always flew an experienced crew member.

I hoped that the next night I would be writing up Mission #1.

Me with my $16 bike.

Glatton

STATION 130

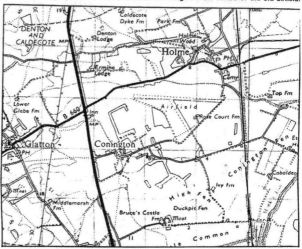

Top: Lieutenant Winfred Pugh eases his B-17G on to the SE-NW runway at Glatton with Rose Court Farm in the background. 42-97571 'H' of the 457th Bomb Squadron was attacked by a German jet during a raid on Weimar on Thursday, August 24, 1944. The aircraft broke from the formation, spiralled down and exploded in mid-air. *Above:* Our comparison photograph with Rose Court Farm unchanged in the centre of the old airfield.

Known locally as Conington, which is the parish in which most of the airfield was built, Glatton lies in the county of Huntingdonshire between the A1 road and the main rail link between London and the north. Glatton village lies to the west, on the other side of the A1 and this name was chosen because the name Conington might have caused confusion with the existing airfield of Coningsby, in Lincolnshire.

The airfield was built during 1942-43 to the standard heavy bomber layout with three runways, encircling perimeter track and fifty hardstands and temporary buildings by the 809th Engineer Battalion (Aviation) of the US Army and was due to be completed by January 1943. Its layout was unique in that the three runways surrounded Rose Court Farm which continued to operate in the centre of the airfield. Like other airfields commenced late in the building programme, two T2 hangars were erected with other technical and administrative buildings built in concrete, brick, steel and asbestos. Living accommodation for 2,900 personnel was dispersed in the countryside around the village of Conington to the south-west of the airfield.

Glatton was first occupied by a combat unit on January 21, 1944. The last B-17 Fortress group assigned to the 1st Division, the 457th, became operational in mid-February and remained at Glatton until June 21, 1945, having carried out 237 missions. Total number of sorties was 7,086 with nearly 17,000 tons of bombs and 142 tons of leaflets being dropped.

Map reproduced from Ordnance Survey 1:50,000 Sheet 142 (Crown Copyright).

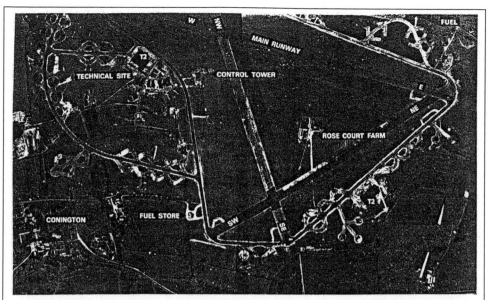

The need for large quantitites of hardcore during the post-war modernisation of the A1 resulted in some early demolition of the runways and perimeter track at Glatton. However parts of two runways have been retained and Glatton now operates as Conington Airport. The 457th Bomb Group has a memorial dedicated to the men who lost their lives flying from Glatton in Conington churchyard.

There have been two light aircraft crashes at Conington, the first on February 21, 1973 when a Beechcraft Queen Air G-ARFF swerved violently to port as the nosewheel touched the runway during landing, the aircraft ending up through a wire fence. The second accident occurred on February 15, 1974 when the pilot of a Beech Baron made the off-repeated fatal mistake of failing to lower his undercarriage before landing. The

Above: Unfortunately the RAF sortie over Glatton on October 16, 1945 failed to cover the whole airfield and the mission was not reflown (Crown Copyright). *Below:* Glatton, or more correctly Conington Airport, today. The road to Holme now uses a strip of the old NE-SW runway.

aircraft G-AYKA successfully performed a belly landing and no-one was hurt.

Mission Number: 1 (One)
Mission Date: September 9, 1944
Mission Length: Seven hours, thirty minutes—plus
To: Mannheim, Germany
Target: Marshalling Yards
Results: Unknown
Plane: *You'll Never Know,* **#42-32086**

Mission Highlights

The biggest highlight—**we made it!** We were awakened at 0300 hours. First on to breakfast, then by trucks to briefing. At briefing we learned what the target would be, the routes to and from the target, that we should expect moderate to heavy flak, that we could expect German fighters to attack us after "bombs away," that there would be a heavy cloud cover in the target area, and that the length of the mission would be just over seven hours and thirty minutes.

After briefing, Protestant and Catholic chaplains held a short prayer and benediction service; I attended.

Next it was on to the equipment room where we picked up parachutes, heated suits, and flak suits. But no flak suit for Cliff. No room in the ball turret for such a luxury. Next was another truck ride to the plane assigned to us for this mission—#42-32086. The plane was named, *You'll Never Know.* "How true," I thought, as I saw this painted on the nose.

Takeoff, the assembling of our boxes into the group, and then into the wings went with no problems.

As we approached the initial point (I.P.) we had our first look at flak, and it looked *very heavy* to us first timers. After the mission we were told it was a heavy concentration of light flak. The flak attack followed all through the bomb run and even after Carbery shouted, "Bombs away."

The return to England was smooth going—no more flak and no fighters were sighted.

After the return and landing we were all anxious to get out and examine the damage since we knew we had been hit. We found eight holes, the largest being large enough to put my fist through. The ground crew said the damage was not bad, and they would have the plane ready for tomorrow's mission. This plane was good to us today, and we were hoping we would be assigned *You'll Never Know* again the next day, but I was sure we would not have any say in the plane assignment.

Our next stop was the equipment room to return chutes and suits and then on to a debriefing where we told what we had observed. They were particularly interested in the results of the bomb strike. Since there was cloud coverage over the target, the results at this time were unknown.

During debriefing we were all offered a good strong shot of Scotch. It proved just the thing to relax us before we went on to a big steak dinner.

Today's routine would be pretty much duplicated each day, so on my future mission write-ups, I skip a lot of these details and write up the mission number, the date, length of the mission, mission destination, the target, the results, and, of course, the mission highlights and the name of the plane we flew. Our crew that day was:

Pilot:	Robbie Robertson
Copilot:	Cliff Hendrickson
Bombardier:	Charles Carbery
Navigator:	Elmer Mankin
Waist Gunner:	Alexander McDermott (veteran)
Eng/Gunner:	Earl Rinehart
Radio Op:	Bernie Stutman
Tail Gunner:	John Brown
Ball Turret Gunner:	Cliff Digre

The waist gunner was a veteran of 20 missions. A seasoned combat crew member was always flown with a crew on their first mission. After the mission he commented that we had a quality, cool crew. He could hardly believe this was our first mission. We did have a good crew, and one thing is for certain—Robbie was one of the best to ever fly with the 457th bomb group; I predicted before his tour was over, he would be a lead pilot.

We knew we were scheduled to fly tomorrow so it was early sack time.

Mission Number: 2 (Two)
Mission Date: September 10, 1944
Mission Length: Seven hours, forty minutes
To: Baden Baden, Germany
Target: Secret weapons factory
Results: Fair
Plane: *Rattlesnake Daddy*, #44-6088

Mission Highlights

First and most important, our Lt. Carbery was hit by a piece of flak just after we had reached the I.P. and were on the bomb run. After he had shouted, "Bombs away," he added, "I was hit by flak a few minutes ago." Robbie asked Rinehart to check on Carbery and take care of his wound. Rinehart said it was a bloody mess but not very serious. He will no doubt be out of flying for a week or so.

You'll Never Know, the plane we flew yesterday and hoped to fly today, went down over the target today. Fate and luck were with us. It just wasn't our time.

The flak today was very heavy and very accurate. We had eight large holes in the plane—bigger than yesterday's.

Szydlowski flew his first mission today. Sid and Kornblatt were our waist gunners.

"Minnesota Swedes" was painted on the tail of our plane.

Charles Carbery. Home: New York. Injured by
flak on Mission #2, September 10, 1944.

Aircraft Serial No. 42-32086—
You'll Never Know

This is the aircraft we flew on our first mission September 9, 1944. The next day September 10, 1944, on this aircraft's 45th mission, it took heavy hits just after "bombs away" and was severely damaged. Two of the crew members bailed out. One was killed and the other taken as a P.O.W. and executed by the Nazis on November 25, 1944. The rest of the crew stayed on the aircraft and made a safe belly landing near the village of Senan, France, a small town that had been liberated only two days before.

The photos and crash information I received from my friend, Russ Karl, the radio operator on this crew.

> **Mission Number: 3 (Three)**
> **Mission Date: September 12, 1944**
> **Mission Length: Nine hours, fifteen minutes**
> **To: Ruhland, Germany**
> **Target: Synthetic rubber plant**
> **Results: Good**
> **Plane: *Rattlesnake Daddy*, #44-6088**

Mission Highlights

This was one day I shall **never** forget—no doubt the saddest day of my young life. Our engineer top turret gunner, Earl A. Rinehart, died of anoxia when his oxygen hose was cut by shrapnel from flak. We were perhaps thirty to forty minutes from the target when we were first hit by light but accurate flak. When we passed the flak pocket, Robbie called for an oxygen check starting with: tail gunner—OK, waist gunner—OK, ball turret—OK, radio operator—OK, but then no answer from top turret. Earl's intercom had been intermittent so Robbie asked that he turn the turret if he was OK. Still no response, so copilot Cliff Hendrickson left his seat and went back to Earl. He was still standing upright in his turret position, but when Hendrickson gave a slight tug on his trousers, he slumped down. He was completely unconscious; when Cliff saw the severed oxygen hose, he knew what had happened. Cliff, with Elmer Mankin's help, brought him up to the nose. They loosened his clothing and put him on pure oxygen. While Elmer was working on Earl, we were struck by a fierce fighter attack consisting of an estimated fifty fighters (ME-109s and FW-190s) as well as new jet-propelled fighters. At one instant I saw three B-17s hit and going down end over end in flames, and from those three planes I saw only three parachutes open. It was a horrible sight, one I'll never forget. Our group lost a total of twenty-eight men that day, either killed or missing in action.

When we returned to Glatton, we were given priority landing and medics met our plane. Immediately, they put Earl on a respirator and rushed him by ambulance to the nearest hospital. Later that evening they reported to us that he was dead. Earl was one super person and an extremely capable engineer. He knew his aircraft. On occasion he would make suggestions regarding the engines to Robbie and Robbie listened. He was good and had the utmost respect from all of the crew members. Earl was the "Pop" to our crew—the oldest at age 28. Earl's hometown was Romney, Indiana. Earl, I'll forever remember you.

We are off to a rough start—yesterday Carbery was injured by flak; today Earl was killed. What's ahead? You never know.

Earl Rinehart, flight engineer. Home: Indiana. Born: December 28, 1916.
Killed: September 9, 1944.

September 14, 1944
Today's Mission Scrubbed

Our crew wasn't scheduled to fly this day. Guess they thought we should have a day off after our rough one two days ago when Earl died.

The other crews were awakened at 0330 hours. They went on to breakfast and briefing and then sat in the planes for two hours before the mission was scrubbed (canceled) due to bad weather. The target was to be the big "B"—Berlin—always a dreaded target. You can count on heavy flak and fighter attacks. The target was to be a Focke-Wulf (FW) aircraft factory. We hoped that the RAF would do the job that night.

On this day, I learned that Sgt. James Fauls of Detroit, Michigan, had been killed on his second mission. I had been with Jim for a year ever since radio school in Camp Kohler. Jim was a grand buddy. I'll always remember him.

September 15, 1944

Today Robbie came to our barracks to tell us we had a new engineer/top turret gunner to take Earl's place. Robbie told us this fellow had had some personality clashes with his previous crew, but that he thought he was a very capable person; if he could do a good job, that was the main thing. He would be moving into our barracks in a day or so. His name was Louis Dahle and he hailed from Chicago. He would have big shoes to fill taking Rinehart's place.

September 16, 1944
Today's Mission Scrubbed

Again we had a scrubbed mission. Our planes were all loaded and ready to taxi for takeoff when we were told the mission was called off. We weren't told if it was because of the weather or for other reasons. The mission was to be low-altitude bombing German gun emplacements (a platform or a position where a gun is placed for firing) at the front lines in Holland where our infantry troops were fighting. It would have been an easy mission and might actually have been fun. We were disappointed when it was scrubbed. Our plane today was to have been *Slow But Sure*, #42-31706.

Mission Number: 4 (Four)
Mission Date: September 17, 1944
Mission Length: Five hours, forty-five minutes
To: Front Lines
Target: Gun emplacements and tanks
Results: Good
Plane: *Remember Me? Georgia Peach*, #43-37828

Mission Highlights

Today we bombed the target we were supposed to have bombed yesterday, German gun emplacements and tanks in a grove of trees at the front lines on the Holland-German border (The Battle of the Bulge). Our box* was hit with very little flak, but the lead box was hit hard and the group leader's plane and another plane in that same box went down, too. We encountered no enemy fighters. We were all conscious that this was our first mission without Earl; it was just like part of our aircraft was missing. Our new engineer, Louis Dahle, flew with us today.

Today's mission was Julius Kornblatt's first, so this was his first look at flak and seeing planes shot down. Julie was one of our waist gunners and would be alternating the waist position with Szydlowski.

A box is a formation of 12 aircraft. There are three boxes in a group—a lead box, a high box, and a low box.

Louis A. Dahle—"The Head"—our flight
engineer after Rinehart's death. Home: Illinois.

Mission Number: 5 (Five)
Mission Date: September 19, 1944
Mission Length: Seven hours, fifty-five minutes
To: Soest, Germany
Target: Marshalling yards
Plane: *Remember Me? Georgia Peach*, #43-37828

Mission Highlights

The mission itself was a milk run—no fighters, no flak, but on our return we ran into heavy fog over the Channel which became worse as we approached England's coastline. We were told Glatton was closed; we would need to find an alternate field. With visibility near zero and running dangerously low on gas, sweating it out in the waist (the midsection of the plane) with Korny and Brown was as bad as sweating out flak. Then, suddenly, faint red flares led us safely to a field at Snederton Heath, some fifty miles from Glatton. After feasting on GI chow, a few bitters and milds (a popular beer in British pubs), and a sleeping bag bunk, we returned to Glatton the next day safe and sound.

The Two From the Streets of New York

Julius Kornblatt, waist gunner.
Home: New York.

John Brown, tail gunner.
Home: New York.

September 18, 1944

Today we flew a practice mission, camera bombing the marshalling yards at Nottingham. The purpose of the mission was to try out a new formation. We were in the air for four hours.

September 22 to September 24, 1944
My First Visit to London

We left Peterborough at 7 p.m., Friday, September 22, and arrived in London at 10:30. We took a subway to Piccadilly Circus, went to the Red Cross and got rooms. Four from our crew went down together—Sid, Brown, Korny, and I.

We teamed up in pairs—Sid and I, Korny and Brown. On Saturday until about 4 p.m., Sid and I window shopped and just bummed around seeing the sights of the Piccadilly Circus area. At 4 p.m. we hired a cab for a two-hour sightseeing tour. First we saw Buckingham Palace, the Changing of the Guard, and toured through Westminster Abbey. That was really a beautiful sight and its historical background was, of course, the main point of interest.

Men of fame were buried here: Rudyard Kipling, Edgar Allen Poe, Charles Dickens, and many other great authors and poets. Kings and queens were buried here, too—the latest man of fame was Neville Chamberlain.

From Westminster we went over the London Bridge to the economic (banking) center of London where the blitz of December 29, 1940, was concentrated. As far as the eye could see were **nothing** but ruins, most done on that one day. The German plan was to disrupt England's economic system.

From there we went to St. Paul's Cathedral and saw the famed Whispering Gallery. The dome was 365 feet high. Of all the hundreds of bombs dropped on London, only one made a hit on the Cathedral and that damage was very minimal.

Leaving St. Paul's we toured and saw the famed gates of Scotland Yard, the home of Winston Churchill, the Lord Mayor's Home, and an ancient bookshop created by Dickens in his writing called *The Old Curiosity Shop*. We next toured sections of London damaged by the flying bombs. What a mess!

Saturday night at the Red Cross, I met a buddy I had gone through gunnery school with, "Red" Horner. His crew went down over Germany on their 11th mission, and they had walked back through the lines into France; they were now going back to the States. I also met Dick Wiercioch's crew and a swell fellow from Chicago, Sgt. George Whitmore. I also had a long and interesting visit with three Norwegian officers. They told us of a Norwegian exhibit called, "Before We Go Back." After Sid and I visited that on Sunday morning, in the afternoon we went to a movie and then rejoined Korny and Brown for our trip back to Peterborough and the base. Truly a memorable two-day pass.

Mission Number: 6 (Six)
Mission Date: September 25, 1944
Mission Length: Seven hours, forty-five minutes
To: Frankfurt, Germany
Target: The city
Results: Unknown
Plane: *The Murderous Witch*, #43-38540

Mission Highlights

Each plane carried twelve 500-pound bombs. We were supposed to have bombed the marshalling yards, but because of the heavy cloud cover, we bombed the city itself. The flak was very heavy, but fortunately we weren't hit. A plane in the group next to ours went down when it got a direct hit and the tail section was completely blown off. This sight really shook me up since I was flying for the first time as tail gunner, and I did not like it one bit. If I can help it, I won't fly in that position again. Our tail gunner, John Brown, somehow pulled guard duty this week. Sid flew my ball turret position, and Korny was in the waist.

Our bombardier, Carbery, flew today for the first time since his flak injury of September 10.

This was the very first mission for the plane we flew today.

> **Mission Number: 7 (Seven)**
> **Mission Date: September 26, 1944**
> **Mission Length: Six hours, forty-five minutes**
> **To: Osnabruck, Germany**
> **Target: Marshalling yards**
> **Results: Good**
> **Plane: *Rattlesnake Daddy*, #44-6088**

Mission Highlights

Another rough one. Over the target there was a heavy concentration of heavy flak. On the bomb run our navigator, Lt. Elmer (Luke) Mankin, was hit in the leg by flak. Today I flew in the waist gun position. During the bomb run when Elmer was hit, a piece of flak went through the waist only inches from me, breaking a three-inch hole through the plane's fuselage—a bit of a scare.

On our way home, just when we thought we were out of the flak areas, a call came on the intercom—flak at 12 o'clock; just then one burst under our plane and just seemed to throw the plane out of control; we were going down. I seemed to float through the air, landing at the waist door with Kornblatt on top of me. Korny and I were both struggling to locate and put our chutes on.

Sid was flying in the ball turret, my position, and I could see the ball was not moving. Sid called on the intercom, "I've lost power; the ball won't move."

There is no room for a parachute in the ball, and the ball entry door was out of the plane. The ball turret was my normal position, and I knew everything about the turret. Within seconds I had the emergency crank and mechanically cranked the ball so the door was in the plane, allowing Sid to get out. Korny handed Sid his parachute, but about the same time, our boy Robbie had the plane back in control. We had all had visions of going down or at best ending up in a German P.O.W. Camp.

Rattlesnake Daddy seems to be our jinx ship; on all three we have had rough missions. First, Carbery was hit by flak, second, Rinehart was killed, and today Mankin was hit in the leg. We have had enough of *Rattlesnake Daddy*.

P.S. Szydlowski and I had been buddies since we met back in Florida, and it was just taken for granted that we would be there for each other when help was needed. On that night, Sid gave me a beautiful red ruby ring that was special to him. He insisted he wanted me to have it. We were special buddies.

Stanley Szydlowski, armament and waist gunner. Home: Massachusetts.

Myself, Clifford Digre, ball turret gunner. Home: Minnesota.

September 27, 1944
Six Hours, Forty-Five Minutes

Today's mission was to Wessing, Germany, in the Ruhr Valley or "Happy Valley," so called because of the many flak guns there.

I didn't fly today; Brown flew in my place. I spent the day sleeping. Guess I needed the rest after yesterday's rough one.

Today's mission went without incident even though the plane was *Rattlesnake Daddy*.

Life in Our Hut #20

Back in the States our living quarters were known as barracks. Here in England we lived in huts. Webster defines a hut as "a make-shift shelter or dwelling" and that is just what they were. They were made of prefab metal on a concrete slab with absolutely no insulation and heated by a potbelly coal-burning stove rationed to one bucket of coal a day. During the winter of '44 and '45, it was mighty cold. I was not in England during the summer, but I am sure that on hot days the huts were equally miserable.

Elmer Mankin, navigator. Injured by flak Mission #7, September 26, 1944. Home: Virginia.

Bernie Stutman standing by Hut #20. Home: Pennsylvania.

The hut had a front and back door with small windows on both ends. The front entry had a vestibule perhaps four feet by six feet. My bunk was on the right side of this vestibule entry, so I had the closest to a private room with walls on three sides. The trade off for this semi-privacy was that it was the farthest from the stove and next to the entry, so it was **cold**, very cold. I was, however, used to sleeping in the cold; my room in Hendricks was in an unheated, uninsulated upstairs where the chamber pots under our beds froze at night.

When we knew we would be flying a mission the next day, the evenings were usually spent in our huts. Before lights out, I would be sitting on my bunk writing letters or writing up the day's mission events for my diary, while Korny and Art Astor were planning their next forty-eight hour pass to London. John Brown would be either writing a letter or playing solitaire, Szydlowski and "The Head—" Louie Dahle, had no problem finding something to argue about, and

Bernie Stutman, the financier, would sit on his bunk and count his *pounds*—his many, many pounds. The dean and "Pops" of our original crew was Earl Rinehart. Before Earl was killed, he firmly called lights out, and then turned off the single 60-watt bulb that hung on a cord from the ceiling in the center of the hut. Our wake-up calls were usually between 0330 and 0400 hours.

On evenings when we knew we would not be flying the next day, we spent very little time in Hut #20 except to sleep. On those nights we were often at the NCO Club or taking a truck to Peterborough or, for Sid and I, it was taking the short three-mile bike ride to Sawtry and to our favorite pub, The Oddfellows Arms.

I have many, many memories of life in our dear Hut #20.

Stand Down, Stand By, Alert, and Loading Lists and Track Charts

Every evening before a crew member would even consider riding his bike or taking a truck to his favorite pub, he would check the orderly room for the status of the next day's mission.

When the "Stand Down" card was displayed, that meant no mission for tomorrow and away we would go to our favorite—The Oddfellows Arms pub—where the owners, Frank and Rose Warren, always gave us a hearty greeting. When the "Stand By" card was up, that meant no decision about a mission yet, check back later; weather condition was often the reason for the stand by. If we still rode our bikes to Sawtry, we played it cool, maybe having one bitters or milds and back to the base early. When the "Alert" card was up, that meant there is a mission scheduled for tomorrow. If the crew member still went out and partied, he paid a price the next day when he was awakened at three or four hundred hours.

When the "Alert" card was up, crew members next checked the "Loading List." The list showed the names of the crew members who would be flying. This also showed the serial number of the aircraft they would be flying. When I saw "Clifford Digre" on the loading list, I seldom if ever went to a pub. I was very disciplined and hit the sack early, waiting for lights out.

At briefing the morning of the mission, the commanding officer of the base would greet us with "Good Morning, Gentlemen." He would make a few comments and he would raise a curtain that covered a chart of the upcoming mission. This chart had a map of the target, key locations, the flight plan, and the I.P. (initial point). The commander then turned the briefing over to the leads of navigation, bombardment, weather, and others involved in the planning of the mission.

I have the loading lists for all my missions, a real keepsake. I have written up the drama of the December 23, 1944, mission.

I've included here the loading list for my first mission and my twentieth mission when I was the radio operator for the infamous, one and only, Thomas P. (Tommy) Thompson III flying as the pilot for the Don Sellon Crew.

I have also included the "track charts" that are a summary of each mission. Track charts are summaries of missions developed after returning from the mission. It describes the target, the briefed route, and the actual route flown; these routes were often different. The report described the enemy fire and bombing results, depending on cloud coverage. Bomb strikes were photographed and the lead plane crew was also often photographed after return to the base.

Footnote: See Appendix C, starting on page 245, for a complete collection of loading lists and track charts of the missions that I flew.

Mission Number: 8 (Eight)
Mission Date: September 28, 1944
Mission Length: Eight hours, twenty minutes
To: Magdeburg, Germany
Target: Krupp machine works
(A manufacturer of tanks and anti-aircraft guns)
Results: Unknown
Plane: *Rattlesnake Daddy*, #44-6088

Mission Highlights

This was one rough mission! I am really going to have a tough time writing this one up. We lost five good pals today—our Hut #20 mates—just five of the nicest guys I've ever known: Sgt. Griffith, engineer from Illinois; Dethloff, radio operator from New York; Anderson (Norski), gunner from Washington; Dooley, tail gunner from Texas;

Loading List, September 9, 1944. My Mission #1.

SHIP	086			
P	P	ROBERTSON. WILLIAM T.	1st Lt	O-523177
CP	CP	HENDRICKSON. CLIFFORD	2nd Lt	O-812261
N	N	MANKIN. EIMER L	2nd Lt	O-2057973
B	B	CARBERT. CHARLES W.	2nd Lt	O-712271
E	TT	RINEHART. EARL A.	Sgt	15083847
RO	RR	STUTMAN. BERNERD	Sgt	13052839
	BT	DIGRE. CLIFFORD B.	Sgt	3756
	WG	MCDERMOTT. ALEXANDRA	T/Sgt	12064088
	TG	BROWN. JOHN F.	Sgt	12151503
SHIP	154			
P	P	BURGESS. OLIVER. G. JR	2nd Lt	O-764870
CP	CP	TEUTSHELL. ALBERT V. JR	2nd Lt	O-767685
N	N	PIKE. LOUIS	2nd Lt	O-720004
B	B	EIWOOD. JOHN E.	2nd Lt	O-769021
E	TT	MOLESTATORE. ALDO	T/Sgt	33102264
RO	RR	PARSONS. GEOIGE A. JR	T/Sgt	31319167
	BT	DURKE. ROBERT J	S/Sgt	32401099
	WG	DOLLAR. HERBERT.	S/Sgt	38509207
	TG	VEVIER. ROLAND	S/Sgt	11088710
SHIP	079			
P	P	WHITMAN. HARRY J	2nd Lt	O-761230
CP	CP	GILBERISON. ALBERT O JR	F/O	T-68919
N	N	PATRICK. HAROLD	2nd Lt	O-718409
B	B	STONER. LEONARD.	2nd Lt	O-772767
E	TT	MELLY. HOSEPH	T/Sgt	11119454
RO	RR	MUNGER. HOWARD.	T/Sgt	17150565
	BT	SITEK. BERNARD	S/Sgt	31284358
	WG	SCHARNHORST. WILLIAM	S/Sgt	37571842
	TG	MCGRIFF. KENNETH	S/Sgt	39704936
SHIP	034			
P	P	MCCALL. WILLIAM R. JR	2nd Lt	O-756295
CP	CP	GREGORY. THOMAS L	2nd Lt	O-823592
N	N	LIVINGSTONE. ARTHUR M	2nd Lt	O-712618
B	B	PLAGIANOS. LEON M	2nd Lt	O-708040
E	TT	PERRY. GEORGE W.	S/Sgt	7001463
RO	RR	HAYES. ROBERT J	S/Sgt	20952240
	BT	WILLS. LINVILLE	Sgt	35872572
	WG	COOKE. GEORGE	S/Sgt	6975178
	TG	BATTISTI. LARIDO	Sgt	16127713
SHIP	088			
P	P	HEDRICK. RAY D. JR	1st Lt	O-742715
CP	CP	DUNDAS. BASIL R. JR	2nd Ltm	O-770978
N	N	PARKER. JOHN B.	2nd Lt	O-722930
B	B	HENSON. EDWIN B	2nd Lt	O-706671
E	TT	SNYDER. PHILIP H. JR	S/Sgt	12176625
RO	RR	GRAVELLE. DONALD H	S/Sgt	36597044
	BT	SWEENEY. JOHN J	T/Sgt	11042459
	WG	MCGILLIAN. JOHN F.	Sgt	20250794
	TG	RAY. HARVEY G.	Sgt	33564680

This is an example of a loading list. The ship is designated by the last three numbers of the plane's serial number. Each position was listed as well as each serial number of the man flying. F/O is a flying officer.

and Simpson (Red), ball turret from Utah. Another gunner of this crew, Art Astor from California, wasn't scheduled to fly today; tonight Art is alone. It's tough on all of us, particularly on Art. The officers were very special too: pilot, Lt. Kenyon Clarke, copilot Hovland, navigator Sundling, and bombardier Smith (Smitty).

Smitty and I would often play together in touch football games. Lt. Clarke's crew was one of the six crews the 457th lost today when fifty-plus German ME-109 and FW-190 fighters hitting our low box attacked us. The fighters came up from six o'clock low out of a cloud. From my position in the ball turret, I saw them coming and coming. It seemed there would be no end to their numbers. I was plain scared stiff. They passed to our left, to our right, and below us going into the sun. As they passed, I got in a few shots and then sat waiting for them to strike again. They then came in bearing down on the low box. The forts were pealing off and going down like flies. It was an awful sight. As I sat in the ball seeing planes going down in flames, exploding, it was as if I were watching a movie and saying to myself, "This can't be real." One of the planes went into a steep dive and only three chutes came out. Then the plane exploded. I knew then that at least six men were instantly killed.

After the FW-190s and ME-109s made two passes at our group, our escort mustangs (P-51s) came to our rescue, or we may have all been shot down. As our mustangs were breaking up the attack, one of the FW-190s, I swear, was no more than 50 yards below my ball turret, so close I could see all the plane markings—swastika crosses and even the pilot in the cockpit. I had gotten in only a few shots when I saw a mustang on his tail and within seconds the FW-190 went down in flames. I am positive some of my shot had struck him, too, but at debriefing I was not certain, so I didn't claim the kill. When the fighter attack ended, we were over the target and being hit hard by flak—large pieces just barely missed Sid in the waist. Brown was missed by four large holes in the vertical stabilizer, and the nose was hit just missing Carbery. We had many holes in the wings and bomb bays. One hole in the Tokyo Tank (a larger, spare gas tank for long missions) was big enough to stick my hand into.

This evening we learned the 457th had a total of 60-plus killed or missing, many of whom it is believed are alive and are prisoners of war (P.O.W.). Hopefully Clarke's crew was one of these.

Loading List, February 23, 1945. My Mission #20.

```
Crew #165   SHIP #570
P      Thompson    Thomas      P. Jr.   0820104    2nd Lt.   P
CP     Jett        Murry       V.       0782294    2nd Lt.   CP
N      O'Brian     Anthony     A.       02068297   2nd Lt.   N
B      Kenyon      Ralph       S.       02068101   2nd Lt.   B
TT     Nose        Daniel      W.       13144290   T/Sgt.    AEG
RO     Digre       Clifford    B.       37561791   S/Sgt.    ROG
WG     Elliott     Thomas      C.       11116955   S/Sgt.    AAEG
BT     Johnson     Bennie      W.       18138428   S/Sgt.    AROG
TG     Nowak       Walter      C.       36903497   S/Sgt.    AAG

Crew #170   SHIP #190
P      Burk        Marion      K.       0777576    2nd Lt.   P
CP     Harris      Cecil       C.       0828790    2nd Lt.   CP
N      Freese      John        T.       02068645   2nd Lt.   N
TOG    Cunningham  Clifford    N.       15325502   Sgt.      AG
TT     Clark       Herbert     K. Jr.   39147908   Sgt.      AAEG
RO     Keyon       Earl        R. Jr.   31291423   Sgt.      Rog
BT     Buhrow      Harold      E.       37560669   Sgt.      AROG
TG     Floerke     Joe         E.       17136907   Sgt.      AAG
Ga     McDuffie    Frederick   A.       33539698   Sgt.      AEG

Crew #164   SHIP #072
P      Southwood   Duane       E.       0775169    2nd Lt.   P
CP     Keran       Lyle        BE.      0782301    2nd Lt.   CP
N      Reed        Wallace     (NMI)    02068747   2nd Lt.   N
TOG    Van Wagner  Raymond     D.       35556610   S/Sgt.    AG
TT     Parmeter    Warren      H.       38404201   T/Sgt.    AEG
RO     Clark       Orville     D.       35148605   T/Sgt.    ROG
WG     Radakovich  George      N.       33421864   S/Sgt.    AAEG
BT     Kelley      R.          B.       38548440   S/Sgt.    AROG
TG     Maira       Santo       V.       42086554   S/Sgt.    AAG

Crew #143   SHIP #506
P      McChesney   Ben         W.       0828726    2nd Lt.   P
CP     Manspeaker  William     C.       0835796    2nd Lt.   CP
N      Siler       William     W.       02064343   2nd Lt.   N
TOG    Byoff       George      S.       18142965   S/Sgt.    AAG
TT     Gubino      Joseph      H.       33603906   T/Sgt.    AAEG
RO     Madsen      Chester     C.       37555990   T/Sgt.    ROG
WG     Saylor      Wilbert     M.       37566366   S/Sgt.    AG
BT     Young       Robert      H.       39215688   S/Sgt.    CG
TG     Wilt        Charles     A.       35870639   S/Sgt.    AAEG

For the Squadron COMMANDER:
```

EDWARD B. DOZIER,
Capt., Air Corps,
Operations Officer.

In front of Hut #21 (next to Hut #20).

Clowning with Sid.

Footnote: At the Reno reunion, November 12-15, 1995, I was reading in the memorabilia room with my wife, Bernice, discussing what a rough mission September 28 had been, describing to her that I had seen this plane take a direct hit, that I had seen three parachutes coming out, and then the plane exploded into bits so I knew six men were dead. Bob Christofferson, accompanied by his wife, Grace, tapped me on the shoulder and said, "I was one of those three that you saw." Bob Christofferson told me that he was the only one who survived the jump—the other two were killed or didn't make it. Before he even jumped from the plane, his foot had been shot off and was badly bleeding. After he landed in a farmer's field, unable to move because of his foot, the farmer came up with a pitch fork and spit on him but did not harm him. In a few minutes the farmer's wife came and folded up his parachute and placed it under his head as a pillow. Later the military police arrived and took Bob to a German hospital. There an Austrian surgeon repaired his wounds and later fit him with a German prosthesis. The surgeon said, "We have done a good job on your foot, and it should be good; don't let anyone touch that when you get back home." After he was healed, he went to a prisoner of war camp where the food was terrible, but then no one had good food. He became friends with the guard; the guard even let Bob examine his gun one day to see the workings. We have kept in contact with Bob and Grace since that time.

Me in the ball.

Me with my 45.

Arthur Nubar Astor

Art was "orphaned" when his crew was shot down on September 28, but he continued to live in our Hut #20. He was put into the spare gunner's pool, flying with several different crews—filling in for gunners who became sick or injured. Although he never flew with our crew, we made him an honorary member of the Robertson Crew, and we became good friends.

Art was a handsome Armenian who hailed from the Hollywood area. He relished telling of his movie career as a bit-part player in two movies—*Gunga Din* and *Five Graves to Cairo*.

Art Astor. Home: California.

Art Astor.

Me and Art Astor.

```
Mission Number: 9 (Nine)
Mission Date: September 30, 1944
Mission Length: Six hours, fifteen minutes
To: Munster, Germany
Target: Railroad junctions
Results: Unknown
Plane: Rattlesnake Daddy, #44-6088
```

Mission Highlights

We encountered no fighters but the flak, although moderate, was very accurate. Over the target the deputy lead plane directly ahead of us got what was apparently a direct hit. The plane pulled out of formation and exploded going down in flames. No one was seen bailing out so apparently all were killed. Stutman saw the whole episode: the hit, the plane leaving formation, and the explosion. Bernie said, "It was gruesome; I'll never forget it." Stutman had a bad day all around. Shortly after takeoff, his electric suit failed so he had no heat the entire mission with temperatures at perhaps 45 to 50 below zero. It was mighty cold. As I was sitting there on the edge of my bunk, writing up this mission, Bernie was sitting by the potbelly stove in the barracks rubbing his legs. No doubt he suffered some frostbite— hopefully not too severe.

Footnote: Three or four years after the war, Bernie Stutman contacted me. He was having problems as a result of the frostbite and was going to have a leg amputated. Since he did not go on sick call, there was nothing on record. Thankfully I was able to verify the incident, and he established that it was service connected.

In 1972 Bernice and I visited Bernie and his wife, Marge, in Philadelphia. Sometime after that he had his other leg amputated.

Ironically, forty-seven years after Bernie's worst military day, on September 30, 1991, his grandson, Benjamin Stutman, was born.

Bernard Stutman, Radio Operator

Bernie suffered frostbite to his legs on Mission #9 when his heat suit failed. Home: Pennsylvania.

October 1, 1944

Just a note to remind me that on this day, Sid and I had to sign the 104th Article of War acknowledging our violation for riding our bikes without lights. As Sid and I were coming back from The Oddfellows Arms pub in Sawtry, the MPs pulled us over on the road, asked for our IDs, and gave us a citation for not having lights on our bikes. They confiscated our two bikes, put them in their Jeep, and we had to walk back to the base. Later, we appeared at the MP office to reclaim our bikes. The penalty never materialized. What a joke!

October 3, 1944

Today we flew a practice mission, camera bombing the city of North Hampton. Flying with us was a gunnery instructor, Bob Byers. Bob had been an instructor in Texas with my high school classmate, Bob Morseth. I later met Byers when he was the chief of police in Ohio.

> **Mission Number: 10 (Ten)**
> **Mission: Date: October 5, 1944**
> **To: Köln (Cologne), Germany**
> **Target: Marshalling yards/Ford Motor plant**
> **Results: ???**
> **Plane: *Rattlesnake Daddy*, #44-6088**

Mission Highlights

This mission turned out to be nine days of super highlights with un-believable adventures I'll *never* forget.

Here's the story...The day started out routine enough with our wake-up call at approximately 0400 hours, on to breakfast, next to briefing, and on to our planes. Takeoff and assembling over England went without incident. We entered the continent at the Belgian coast, heading to our target, Cologne—a dreaded target; always a heavy concentration of flak.

We were about fifty miles into Germany and our armament gunner (Sid) Szydlowski had just come out of the bomb bay after pulling the bomb pins when the number-four engine started to run rough, and Robbie had to "feather" it. With a near maximum bomb and gas load, there was no way we could keep up with the formation. Robbie came on the intercom and said, "Fellows, we have no choice—we will have to turn around and go for home alone without fighter escort, so be alert." He added, "We don't dare to drop our bombs since we are not certain where the front lines are."

Our navigator, Elmer Mankin, had been wounded on September 26, and our bombardier, Carbery, was flying as a combination navigator/bombardier. Carbery's navigation training was very minimal, particu-larly on instruments.

Within minutes, number-one engine was running rough and had to be feathered, too. Now with only our two inboard engines, we were losing altitude at 700 feet a minute and we were not certain of our location. Were we in enemy territory? We did not know!

Robbie alerted us that we might need to abandon the plane and bail out, or we might need to prepare for a belly landing. In either event, he told me to come out of the ball turret and take over the waist gun position while Sid went back into the bomb bay to put the pins back in the bombs so they could be dropped without detonating.

Suddenly Carbery burst out, "There's an airfield at 10 o'clock." It was just on the edge of a city. Robbie said, "What's the city, Carbery?" I can still hear C. W.'s joking response, "God, Robbie, I don't know; it could be Paris, maybe Brussels, but my calculations say it is Antwerp." He was right on—it was Antwerp, Belgium.

When we flew over the field, we could see it was a fighter base with a short runway. We also saw near the city center a body of water—an estuary of the North Sea; here we safely dropped our bombs.

By getting rid of that bomb load we were able to maintain our altitude that was then down to only 300 feet. We returned to the field we had seen and spotted German planes parked near the runways and two fighters taking off which we could not immediately identify. Robbie lowered the landing gear signifying we were surrendering and landing. The landing was on a fighter plane runway (very short). As we were making our approach to land with only the two inboard engines, number-four engine burst into flames. Stutman, Brown, Sid, and I positioned ourselves in the radio room for a possible crash landing. But our boy Robbie made a perfect landing. He was great. In the crew's opinion, the very best!

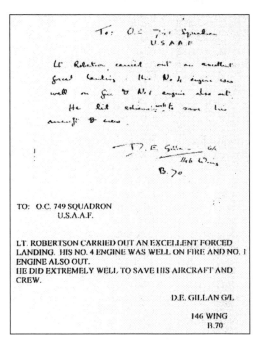

TO: O.C. 749 SQUADRON
       U.S.A.A.F.

LT. ROBERTSON CARRIED OUT AN EXCELLENT FORCED LANDING. HIS NO. 4 ENGINE WAS WELL ON FIRE AND NO. 1 ENGINE ALSO OUT.
HE DID EXTREMELY WELL TO SAVE HIS AIRCRAFT AND CREW.

D.E. GILLAN G/L

146 WING
B.70

When the plane came to a complete stop, we scrambled out and ran for fear of an explosion, but the base fire fighters soon extinguished the fire and our concerns.

We were first met by the base CO, not the German Gestapo, but an RAF Colonel. It was then we learned that the Canadian First Army had captured the field just three days before our landing. The German planes we had seen had been left behind as they retreated. This field was the Antwerp Airport located on the south side of the city, and at this time there was still intense street fighting on the city's north side.

When it was apparent our plane's engine fire was out, and it was safe, several officers and enlisted men came out to our plane to get a close-up view of a combat B-17. The colonel came to congratulate Robbie on his spectacular landing with only two engines working, a third (non-working engine) on fire, and all of this on a very short runway.

When the group gathered, Robbie called Sid Szydlowski to join them. Some in this group were Polish pilots and Sid Stanislaw Pavol Szydlowski was needed to translate. Sid felt honored.

When all the handshakes and praises were over, we were escorted to the base mess hall for a meal. After typical GI chow it was on to a truck and into the city of Antwerp. We stopped in front of a luxury hotel, The Century, but we soon learned this was to be for the three officers—Robbie, Hendrickson, and Carbery. We, the enlisted men, were taken to the Antwerp city jail. Bernie Stutman looked over the crude cots and said in Bernie's definite mannerism, "To hell with this noise," and decided right then no way were we going to be put up in a jail while the officers were in the luxury Century Hotel. Off Bernie went, and in a short time he was back with Robbie, who looked it over and said, "Come on fellows," and we were off to the Century Hotel. Robbie said to the desk clerk, "We want the best rooms you have in the hotel."

We were told this hotel had been home for the most elite German officers; this was to be our home for the next nine days and nights. Sid and I shared a room, with Dahle and Brown in the adjoining room; Bernie had a room of his own. After the day we had been through, those plush baths and beds looked inviting, so it was an "early to bed" night.

The next morning Robbie called a crew meeting telling us the engines were in worse condition than was thought; it could be several days before the plane would be ready to fly. He also gave us permission to open our money packs. On each mission, crew members are issued a sealed package that contained currency to be opened only in an emergency. This, Robbie declared, was such an emergency. He said, "You're all on your own—just check in with me each morning." He added, "Have a good time," and so started nine days of adventurous experiences I wouldn't trade for anything. Below are a few of the highlights.

The Luxurious Century Hotel

On the hotel marquis just below the Century Hotel were the words "The Hotel of the Ambassadors," and indeed it was. This was truly an elegant hotel in every detail. The lobby area was wide open and spacious with thick plush carpeting, big easy chairs for lounging, and small tables and leather-upholstered chairs on casters. Each afternoon between 1500 and 1600 hours a string ensemble, all dressed in tuxedos, played soft classical music, typically European. This time was much like the British "Tea Time." People were served tea, coffee, light snacks, but mostly wines, brandy, and a drink called calvados (we had never heard of it, but boy it was good). The lobby was so exciting during this time that we made it a point to be there—to sit, lounge, sip on a small calvados, and people watch. Here we were only a few miles from the combat actions, and we were living the life of kings.

October 5-14, 1944
Antwerp, Belgium

The nine days we were in Antwerp were **the** highlight of the ten months I was in Europe. How I wish I could have captured the events I have written about with photos, but we had no cameras. Our friends, the Van Gastels, owners of the Normandy Bar, did take a couple of photos for us. In spite of the war, Antwerp was beautiful.

October 5, 1944

The rooms at The Century Hotel were something, too. Luxury! With plush carpeting, drapes, and overstuffed chairs—this was really living at its best. The bathrooms were big! and fancy, two double sinks, a

Our luxury Century Hotel was immediately to the right of this picture, overlooking this beautiful city, Center Park. The railroad station was in the center of this photo.

bathtub, and a separate shower. The toilet stool was standard enough, but next to the stool was another porcelain commode that looked like a larger stool without a seat. We reasoned it was not a urinal even though we used it for one. Even Szydlowski and The Head (Dahle) who both knew everything, did not know what this device was. Our curiosity got the best of us. Checking with hotel employees, we found out it was a woman's douche bowl. We had no idea what it was or how it worked. A typical Sid comment, "Beat's me." But with all this fancy stuff, there was not a single bar of soap! With everything so elegant we thought this was just an oversight, so I called room service and requested they send up a bar of soap. Within a few minutes came a knock on the door, and there was a cute little gal holding a silver tray with a bar of soap perched in the center. This I thought was super class and called for a generous tip, so I pulled out one of my USA dollar bills I kept for such special tips. She looked shocked; at first I thought it was because of my generous tip, but soon she made it known this was an insult since the cost of the soap alone was five times my tip. I tried to bargain with her and have it charged to the room, but no dice, so I paid her with our precious francs. It was obvious soap was a very scarce commodity. More about our precious bar of soap later.

We Meet the Frateurs...

One evening Sid and I were having a snack at a small cafe near our hotel. At a table across from ours sat an elderly couple and a very beautiful brunette about eighteen or nineteen years old. This girl was so striking we just couldn't help it; we just stared. Our gazing obviously got through to them. The gentleman came over to our table, introducing himself as Mr. Frateur. He spoke perfect English and gave Sid and me a pear to share. We asked if they would like to join us for a beer. He said they would be delighted to, and he then introduced us to his wife and their daughter, Nannette. Neither could speak a word of English. Nannette just smiled while Mr. Frateur (Jules) interpreted. We were the first Americans they had ever met, and he went into a big speech on how grateful they were that we had come to liberate them. They were very genuine people. When they got up to leave, Jules asked if we would like to come to their home for dinner the next evening. With Nannette still smiling at us, how could we refuse?!

Nanette Frateur, Sid's friend.

Sid and me.

Dinner at the Frateurs...

On the way out to the Frateurs, Sid let me know he was going to make a move on Nannette, and in spite of a language problem, was going to ask her out to a movie. I had my own plans, but just said, "We'll see."

We arrived at Frateurs at exactly 5 p.m. as Jules had asked us to. Nannette met us at the door with a big smile. She was the "knock out" we remembered. While Mrs. Frateur was making the dinner, Jules came and visited with us, telling about the German occupation with photos, painting a painful time for the people in Belgium.

Just before we were to sit down to dinner, the door opened and in bounced a vivacious blonde who introduced herself in pretty good English as Nannette's older sister, Nelly. Wow! This gal was a beauty. I swear these two sisters were the most beautiful in all of Belgium. It didn't take me long to tell Sid, "Go ahead and make your move; I'm making mine on Nelly."

Considering that food was in short supply, Mrs. Frateur served a fantastic dinner—meat, potatoes, vegetables, dessert—the whole bit. After dinner it was more visiting, pictures, coffee, and brandy. At midnight another lunch, and at 2 a.m., we caught a bus back to the hotel. This was a very special family who treated Sid and me like royalty with such sincere appreciation that the dangers of combat seemed worth it.

Sid, me, Mr. Van Gastel, and The Head (Louie Dahle).

Maria Van Gastel, The Head's special friend.

A Collaborator Pays a Horrible Price...

One morning while taking a walk alone near our hotel, I heard a commotion at a major street intersection where a crowd of people was gathered. From the shouting I could tell it was some form of a riot. I soon learned the crowd had taken from police custody a downtown businessman, a known German collaborator. All of his fingernails had been pulled out with pliers, and with a gun to his head he was cleaning the street with a toothbrush. He was bleeding and screaming. I took one look and turned away. It was gruesome!

Almost on the Front Lines...

One night Sid and I were out exploring the residential areas of Antwerp and hailed down an Army truck thinking it was going to the City Center. We climbed in the back and the truck took off. After riding for ten minutes or so, we started to realize we might not be going into the city. We pounded on the window of the cab. The truck stopped, and we then learned the vehicle was bringing supplies to the troops on the front lines. It didn't take us long to decide we didn't need that excitement. We climbed out, and after walking for an hour, we got to a bus line and back to our hotel.

A Little Wheeling and Dealing...

Brown bought a bottle of cognac for 300 francs, and then fifteen minutes later sold the same bottle back to the same person for 1,000 francs. Brownie was really proud of his dealing until he discovered he had given up 300 francs of solid "invasion currency" for 1,000 francs of pre–invasion money which was practically worthless.

Sid had a passion for collecting guns, having started a collection before entering the service. One night he paid a Belgian civilian 300 francs for an old, beat-up 32-caliber pistol. The next night one of his new-found friends, a Polish pilot, gave Sid a 25-caliber automatic in mint condition.

An Exciting Evening at the Follies...

One afternoon I met Nelly for teatime in the Century lobby. She suggested we go to the "Follies" that evening. Even though my finances were getting a bit low, I didn't say, "No." Nelly seemed to know the right people and got a table front and center. The show was quite an extravaganza of dancing girls, comedians, vaudeville acts—a very classy show—not like the back-home American burlesque shows.

At the table next to ours were two signal corps officers with girl-friends. After a little chatting, they suggested we push our tables together and join them. They had a wad of invasion money and said there was a lot more if we needed it. Knowing this was Uncle Sam's money, I didn't feel bad when they picked up the tab for the rest of the evening.

At closing time the signal corps officers said they had a staff car and would take us to Nelly's home. As we came to their car, we saw a

Canadian soldier in the car and another standing by a broken window. We were trying to hold them while we called for the MPs. When the one we were holding pulled out a handgun, we let go and they both took off. We reported the break-in and the gun episode to the MPs, and then took the three girls to their homes and then back to the Century Hotel where the officers were staying, too. One unforgettable night!

The Belgium Railroad Reroutes for Stutman...

Bernie Stutman, Mr. Money Bags of our crew, always carried a wad of money and always in English pounds. It was no exception on this mission. I'm sure he had several hundred dollars in the highly negotiable English pounds.

Bernie often bragged about his finances saying, "I've got pounds — many, many pounds." His boasting annoyed many, but not me. I respected his good business savvy.

Here in Belgium Bernie soon saw a money-making opportunity. Although Antwerp was the diamond capital of the world, Bernie thought he could do better dealing in Brussels, fifty miles away. After being with the rest of the crew for a couple of days, Bernie asked Robbie for permission to go to Brussels to check out the diamond market.

Robbie gave his okay with a firm stipulation that Bernie would call him every morning at 0900 hours. So for the next five days, Bernie called Robbie precisely at 900 hours and got permission to stay in Brussels another day. On October 13 when he called, Robbie said we might leave around noon. Bernie and his new-found girlfriend rushed to the railroad station hoping to catch the transit leaving Brussels at 0930 hours and arriving in Antwerp at about 1130 hours, but they missed the Antwerp-bound train by minutes. Bernie's friend went directly to the train master's office pleading that her American Air Corps friend absolutely must be in Antwerp by noon. The train master made a few phone calls and agreed to reroute a train leaving at 1000 hours to get Bernie to Antwerp by 1200 hours.

Bernie did arrive back in Antwerp by noon only to learn we would not be leaving that day, but the next, October 14, without fail. Bernie was really proud that his girlfriend had convinced the train master to reroute a full passenger train just for him.

Our Final Day and Night, and Our Precious Bar of Soap...

Knowing for certain we would be leaving the next day, Sid and I spent most of our last day visiting and saying our goodbyes to our Belgian friends—The Frateur family and the Van Gastels, owners of the Normandy Bar where we had enjoyed a few beers and socialized. We also got a goodbye hug from Maria Van Gastel, daughter of the owners, and Louie Dahle's—The Head's—special friend.

That evening Sid and I decided we had partied enough and we wanted to enjoy a leisurely night in our luxurious Century Hotel room. Dahle and Brown had other plans—a last-night party at the Normandy. We knew The Head had spent his last francs last night; we couldn't imagine he could party too much. However, Dahle could always find a way to party. Knowing we would soon be back at our base and the dingy, cold shower stalls, the one thing Sid and I wanted to do this night was to enjoy our plush, plush bath/shower suite. But our precious expensive bar of soap was **missing**!

We scrounged our room and Brown and Dahle's room, too, but no soap in either. We knew soap was a precious commodity, but it seemed unlikely anyone from the hotel staff would have taken it. So we had to settle for soapless showers.

We had just settled into our beds when we heard The Head and Brown coming down the hall singing at the top of their voices. Obviously both had partied. Perceptive Sid said, "C. B., here comes our missing soap." They stumbled into our room full of beer and stories of their last party at the Normandy. It didn't take much prodding before The Head admitted he had taken our soap and traded it for a choice bottle of cognac. He didn't apologize—he was just proud of his negotiations.

The next morning we were up at 0700 hours, had breakfast at the hotel, and at 0900 hours an Army truck picked us all up at the hotel entrance for our fifty-mile ride to Brussels. Here we picked up a patched B-17 to fly back to England. The plane wasn't in top condition, but with Robbie at the controls, we had no concern.

We flew back over Antwerp, tipping the wing as a final farewell to Antwerp and the many friends we had all made.

A pair of P-51s flew escort for us back over the channel.

Except for our morning check-ins, we had seen little of Robbie, Hendrickson, and Carbery during these nine days. On the flight back they told us about some of their highlights. Hendrickson ended their report by saying, "Fellows, we now have made sketches of a design for our crew jackets. We'll be called 'The Shack Rats.'"

Nine exciting days I would remember forever. I swore someday I would revisit Antwerp.

Footnote 1: When we returned to our base and to Hut #20, anxious to tell our buddies about our fabulous experiences in Antwerp, they were far more interested in telling us about what we had missed — **the mission to Politz**.

Apparently fate had been with us again when we had made the scary, engines-on-fire, forced landing in Antwerp on October 5.

On October 7 while we were living the lives of kings, the 457th flew one of the roughest missions ever. The target was the synthetic oil plant at **Politz** in Eastern Germany. Our group had put up a total of forty-eight planes on that mission. Of those forty-eight, six had been shot down, including our group commander, Colonel James R. Luper, thirty-eight planes sustained damage and only **four** of the forty eight planes received no damage. More than sixty men were either killed or missing in action or at best P.O.W.s.

Had we not made that forced landing in Antwerp, the chances were 100% that we, too, would have been on that mission. Then what would have been our fortunes? Again, we were spared! Was it just plain luck that we were forced to land in Antwerp? **I don't think so!**

Footnote 2: What happened to Aircraft #44-6088, *Rattlesnake Daddy*, the plane left in Antwerp? The engines were replaced or repaired and then returned to the 457th.

And then? See the narrative of January 10, 1945.

Our Crew's Jacket Design

Name and design originated after Mission #10, October 5, 1944.

Mission Number: 11 (Eleven)
Mission Date: October 25, 1944
Mission Length: Seven hours, thirty minutes
To: Hamburg, Germany
Target: Oil Refineries
Results: Unknown
Plane: *Lady B Good*, #43-38594

Mission Highlights

This was our first mission since the nine fun-filled days and our luxurious stay at the Century Hotel in Antwerp. It was rough to face combat again and we were hoping for a "milk run"—but it wasn't to be.

At briefing we were told to expect very heavy flak attacks—perhaps 240 guns in range at the target area. We were also told to be on the lookout for enemy fighters. Briefing officers predicted a rough mission. With such a gloomy forecast, we knew our losses could be heavy.

After most briefings the Protestant and Catholic chaplains held short devotions that I always attended. When a mission was expected to be a "milk run," an easy mission, there were only a few of us at the devotions. When a tough mission with heavy losses was anticipated, we expected a full house at devotions, and that was exactly what we had on that day—standing-room only. As I was going into the room set aside for the devotions, one of the two Jews on our crew, Julius Kornblatt, came to me with a serious request, "Digre, how about putting in a good word for me?" I asked Julie to come in with me, but he said something to the effect, "I'd rather not—you just speak for me." I, of course, assured him I would. This was Kornblatt's air medal sixth mission, and he would be flying as chin turret gunner—a new position for him.

Takeoff, assembly, and the flight into Germany went without incident, but as we approached the target area, we could see it was going to be heavy. From the ball turret I had perhaps the best view of anyone, a panoramic view of everything in line with the underside of the aircraft. Since the ball turns 360° and 90° in elevation, I could look straight back, straight down, and straight ahead, and that was where the flak was—ahead, over the target. Since there were no enemy fighters reported yet, I had my guns faced straight ahead; then suddenly through my small round window I saw an absolutely solid wall of flak ahead of us. I thought, "240 guns—no way; there must be at least twice that many." I couldn't imagine that we had a chance of getting through that wall. A helpless feeling came over me. Since we were now on the bomb run, we had to keep a direct steady course with no evasive action. The closer we got, the more solid the wall appeared to be. I knew that if the flak ahead was at our altitude of 25,000 feet, our losses would be heavy.

As we got closer to the target area, I could see flak at our altitude, but the heaviest concentration was going to be a few hundred feet below us. **We had made it through**. Today the Germans manning the flak guns were inaccurate. Was that due to the ten-tenths cloud coverage or answers to our devotion prayers? The latter, I think.

Mission Number: 12 (Twelve)
Mission Date: October 28, 1944
Mission Length: Six hours, thirty minutes
To: Munster, Germany
Target: Marshalling yards
Results: Fair
Plane: *Rampant Punch*, last three numbers 034

Mission Highlights

The railroad yards at Munster were again the target. Although our bombing altitude was only 22,000 feet, **it was cold**!—minus 36 degrees Fahrenheit. Again, briefing must have underestimated the guns at the target area. They had reported forty guns, but again as on Mission #11, I would say there were at least twice that number. Unlike our mission to Hamburg just three days ago, the flak today was very accurate, and of the thirty-six planes from our group, twenty-seven planes were damaged—some had severe damage. Lt. Lloyd Gray's crew, now in Hut #20 with us, reported twenty holes scattered through their aircraft. Fortunately, there were no injuries. Again, we were lucky; one of nine out of thirty-six aircraft in the group with zero damage.

Above is a photo of the little red *New Testament* that my mother gave to me before I left. She wrote, "Please read a few verses each day. This is the wish of your Mother." I followed her wish every day.

My Faith Was *So* Important

Since my early childhood, our church was the core of our lives—both spiritually and socially. I think I must have been only five years old when we had an hour of Sunday School and then sat through boring sermons in both English and Norwegian. During the summer public school vacations, we had two- or three-week Bible school to attend. We memorized much of the Bible as well as gospel songs.

On every mission I had my small, red *New Testament* that my mother had given to me before I left home. I carried it in a small pocket in the upper left portion of my flight suit. To me this was as much a part of my flight gear as was my parachute.

As the flak became intense and a plane next to ours was suddenly blown out of the sky, an old gospel hymn we had memorized, "Through every day along life's way, God will take care of you" would ring over and over and over in my head. I would recite the many Bible verses I had memorized very often such as the Twenty-third Psalm, together with my prayers, and prayers I knew my mother was saying for me every day. Even though I was scared stiff, I had a peace and comfort that many didn't have. Yes, my faith was important then, as it is today.

My oldest cousin was an infantry soldier in WWI, and he would tell us of his experiences. He would always say, "There were no atheists in the fox holes." I would add to that, cousin Julius, "Nor on combat aircraft in WWII."

Mission Number: 13 (Thirteen)
Mission Date: October 30, 1944
Mission Length: Five hours, forty minutes
To: Munster, Germany
Target: Marshalling Yards
Results: Unknown
Plane: *Lady Luck*, #42-32051

Mission Highlights

Before we went on today's mission, I said it was Mission #12B, but after we came back, okay, it was Number 13. Again, we bombed the Munster marshalling yards. It would seem they hardly had time to put out the fires of the bombing on October 28. We must have destroyed many of the gun emplacements two days ago, too. Here we were bombing the same target in the same city as we did just two days before when the flak was super heavy and accurate. Today the flak was very light and very inaccurate, bursting way under us.

Brown had a bad cold and a pain in his side so he spent the day in bed. A fellow named Snyder flew in Brown's tail position.

The temperatures at the bombing altitudes had been extremely cold, and today was the coldest yet. Reports said minus 52° F. This I know because Sid said when he took a leak and missed the relief tube, his pee *froze* the instant it hit the floor. That's **cold**!

November 2, 1944

The target today was the synthetic oil plant at Merseburg—a very rough mission.

Our crew had flown only three missions since returning from Antwerp, so we certainly couldn't claim battle fatigue. But for whatever reason, Operation decided the Robertson crew wouldn't fly today, and for that all of us were thankful.

This was one of the fiercest air battles that the 457th had encountered. Several minutes after bombing the target, our group was attacked by reports of forty or more FW-190s and ME-109s. We lost ten of the thirty-six planes in our group—a total of eighty or more men killed or missing in action.

One of those lost was the Capt. James B. Wallace crew. Reports said an FW-190 crashed into their plane; it is unlikely there were survivors. We had been together since our Florida training days. We even came here the same day. A big loss for all of us—**great guys**!

Our Ground Crew

Left to right: Bill Nicklus, Joe Poppell, Homer Hasel, and Gab Ludds.

These men were so very important to us. We depended on their mechanical skills to keep our planes flying. Robbie said our ground crew was the best in the 457th Bomb Group.

Mission Number: 14 (Fourteen)
Mission Date: November 5, 1944
Mission Length: Six hours
To: Frankfurt, Germany
Target: Marshalling Yards
Results: Excellent
Plane: *Remember Me? Georgia Peach*, #43-37828

Mission Highlights

The flak today was light but very accurate. We had six small holes in our plane. Never before have I seen so many planes hit one target. The bomb loads were six 1,000 pounders. Reports say the results were excellent! This was the first mission for my good buddy, Art Astor, since his crew went down September 28. Art had a rough one today. With an engine on fire, there were anxious moments when the pilot alerted the crew to prepare to bail out! But fortunately the fire was extinguished.

Mission Number: 15 (Fifteen)
Mission Date: November 6, 1944
Mission Length: Seven hours, fifty-five minutes
To: Harburg (near Hamburg)
Target: Oil refinery that produced half of Germany's synthetic oil
Plane: *Remember Me? Georgia Peach*, #43-37828

Mission Highlights

Light flak, fighters in the area, but none hit us. About 1,100 forts (B-17 planes) with great fighter protection, 800 P-51s and P-47s. Power failed to open our bomb bay doors. While Dahle, The Head, our engineer, was manually cranking them down, his 45-caliber pistol fell out of his holster and became a souvenir for some lucky German.

> **Mission Number: 16 (Sixteen)**
> **Mission Date: November 8, 1944**
> **Mission Length: Six hours, twenty minutes**
> **To: Scheduled for Merseburg, but recalled**
> **Plane:** *Remember Me? Georgia Peach,* **#43-37828**

Mission Highlights

This mission was to be to Merseburg, where on November 2, just six days ago, our group lost nine planes, one of the roughest missions to date for the 457th. Takeoff went okay, but a heavy, overcast sky and cloud coverage prevented the group from assembling, so the individual squadrons crossed the North Sea with plans to assemble in clear skies over the continent. We crossed the North Sea into Holland but still no clear skies were to be found, and so we were recalled.

Shortly after we had turned around and again crossed the North Sea heading for home, two planes immediately ahead of us, clearly within my view, collided, causing one of the planes to be virtually cut in two at the waist about in line with the ball turret. The tail section went down mostly intact, but the front section shattered and went down in bits. The other plane, though badly damaged, was able to return to England, where I am told they made a safe crash landing. The plane that went down was called "Haf n Haf" or "Arf n Arf"—so named because the silver tail section of one battered fort and the olive-drab front section of another had gone into making up this plane.

I knew most of the fellows on "Haf n Haf"—a grand bunch of boys! They had been in about twenty-seven missions. Rough!

The Story of "Haf n Haf" or "Arf n Arf"

This one-of-a-kind aircraft was known by both these names, but on the nose art was "Arf n Arf," so to me that was the official name. In the British pubs, when a person wanted the popular beer drink of half bitters and half milds, they called out for an "Arf n Arf;" thus this name.

This unique plane was made from two battered forts that were individually beyond repair. The OD (olive drab)-colored plane with the front portion intact was welded to the silver, natural-metal-finish tail section of the other plane.

HAF N HAF received its name when a natural metal finish tail section was welded to the forward part of its fuselage after a ground accident, 23 July 1944. (457th)

November 8, 1944—Mission #16. From my ball turret position, I clearly saw *Arf n Arf* collide with aircraft #44-8418 called *Bad Times Inc. Arf n Arf* split in two about where the two plane halves had been connected. The silver tail was somewhat intact, but within seconds after collision, the front half exploded and shattered as the two sections plummeted into the North Sea. It was a horrific site. There were no survivors.

> **Mission Number: 17 (Seventeen)**
> **Mission Date: November 9, 1944**
> **Mission length: Seven hours, thirty minutes**
> **To: Metz, France**
> **Target: Front lines near Metz**
> **Plane:** *Remember Me? Georgia Peach,* **#43-37828**

Mission Highlights

Truly a milk run—no flak, no fighters—a mission in support of General Patton's new drive. Reports say 1,300 forts and liberators with 500 fighters participated.

November 12, 1944

Bad News, but Good News, Too

Today I received bad news, but good news, too. In a letter I received from my good friend Bob Suing, Bob wrote that John Jackson and Joe Cooke were both missing in action. I had been stationed with both for several months during training in the States. Jackson was from Minneapolis; he and I went home together on furlough last spring. Both John and Joe were good buddies whom I shall never forget.

The Good News!

Today we learned that Lt. Kenyon Clarke's crew who went down on September 28 were all P.O.W.s. We all welcomed this news, especially Art Astor, a member of that crew who didn't fly that day.

More Good News!

In a letter from my mother I received today, she told me the good news that Perwin Knutson (nicknamed Knute), an 8th Air Force gunner whose parents had previously been notified that he was missing in action, was now officially listed as a P.O.W. Knute was a couple years older than I, but we were in good ol' Hendricks High School at the same time. Knute had been on the football team and was a tough competitor; I was sure he would survive the rigors of a P.O.W. camp.

Just two months ago today, on September 12, this war became very real when our crew experienced its first casualty when Rinehart was killed. Earl, I promise I'll forever remember you.

Mission Number: 18 (Eighteen)
Mission Date: November 16, 1944
Mission Length: Six hours, fifteen minutes
To: Near Eschweiler, Germany
Target: Front lines in support of General Hodge's
    1st Army and General Simpson's 9th Army
Results: Very successful
Plane: *Remember Me? Georgia Peach*, #43-37828

Mission Highlights

We carried 7,800 pounds of anti-personnel bombs. Reports say this mission was very successful. We hope so and would like more milk runs like this one.

Mission Number: 19 (Nineteen)
Mission Date: November 29, 1944
Mission Length: Seven hours, five minutes
To: Misburg (near Hanover), Germany
Target: Oil refineries
Plane: *Remember Me? Georgia Peach*, #43-37828

Mission Highlights

At briefing we were told the Germans had 750 fighters in this area, so we were expecting a fighter attack, but we encountered none. Our escort support was excellent with 1,000 P-51s, P-47s, and P-38s. We were one of the first twelve bombers into Germany today. The 749th was a screening force with our bomb bays loaded with chaff (a tinsel foil to jam enemy radar).

November 29, 1944

After today's mission we were told our boy, Robbie, had been promoted to a 749th bomb squadron lead pilot, so this was the last mission several of us would be flying with him.

Since the ball turret had been replaced with "Mickey" radar equipment, my position would be eliminated. Others who would no longer be flying with Robbie included: copilot Cliff Hendrickson, bombardier Charles Carbery, and waist gunner Julius Kornblatt. As of now the status of our navigator, Elmer Mankin, and gunner, John Brown, was uncertain. What's ahead? Who knows? As of today we were orphans; the uncertainty was not a pleasant prospect. We would all miss the feeling of security we had with Robbie in command. He was one of the best.

November 30, 1944 to December 18, 1944

A few days after Robbie was chosen to be a lead pilot, Robbie and Cliff Hendrickson came over to our Hut #20 to tell us a new crew was to be formed—*The Cliff Hendrickson Crew*. The core would be the orphans from the Robertson crew—Cliff as pilot, Carbery as bombardier, possibly Mankin as navigator, Brown and Kornblatt as gunners, and me. The copilot, engineer, and another gunner had not yet been chosen.

Cliff asked if I could check out as radio operator. I assured him I could and wanted to. Although I felt a strange security in the ball turret, it was not the most comfortable position. By comparison, the radio room would have the comforts of the luxury suite at the Century Hotel in Antwerp. Most importantly, the radio operator position meant I would have one more stripe and the rank of technical sergeant; this translated into **more money**!

That same day I went to talk to the communications officer to inquire what would be required for me to be reclassified from a AROG-611 assistant radio operator gunner to an ROG-757 radio operator mechanic gunner—the classification I needed to fly as the crew's radio operator. After checking my Signal Corps school records, he said that since my training had exceeded Air Corps requirements, he was certain I could test out of code and radio mechanics. He also said I could come into the radio shack and an instructor would give me assignments and work with me on Air Corps procedure and additional Air Corps Q-signals. Within two weeks I tested out of code and mechanics and passed both the written and oral test with perfect scores.

Back on November 29, the day I learned I would no longer be flying with Robbie, things looked bleak and the future uncertain. It was depressing! But now, things really had turned around as we looked forward to flying as The Cliff Hendrickson Crew. To be sure, no one looks forward to flying combat missions, but knowing I must, I wanted to fly with a crew in which I had confidence. Cliff had flown hundreds of hours as Robbie's copilot; he had had the best instructor, so we all had the ultimate trust in Cliff's flying skills.

Our new crew flew practice missions almost on a daily basis to hone each individual's skills. Not only did we have a great pilot in Cliff, we had quality in every position.

December 18, 1944

The weather the past few days has been horrible—very heavy fog, drizzle, light snow—typical winter in England. Because of the weather, the 8th had not put a plane in the air for the past two days, and our ground forces were paying the price as the Germans were mounting an offense in the Ardennes forests in Belgium.

We learned this afternoon a slight clearing was expected tonight, and if so, a mission tomorrow was a certainty. Cliff said today, "If there is a mission tomorrow, we will definitely be flying, so all passes have been cancelled."

Late that evening I checked at the orderly room, and yes, there was a mission scheduled, and yes, our crew, the Cliff Hendrickson crew, was on the loading list, and there was listed "Clifford Digre, radio operator"—so it was early to bed!

December 19, 1944

It had been almost four weeks since I had flown my 19th mission, and today was to be my first as a radio operator, so I was wide awake when I heard the orderly room clerk walking around to the huts waking up crews. I was half dressed when he came into Hut #20. His first words were, "What are you up for Digre; you're not flying today." Since I had personally seen the Hendrickson crew, and my name on the loading list, I was certain he was wrong, and told him so. Kornblatt and Brown, though, took him at his word and were glad to get back into their sacks. But not me. I finished dressing, and cutting my way through the fog, walked up to the mess hall for breakfast with Sid, The Head, and Stutman who were flying with Robbie.

It wasn't until I met Cliff at the briefing room and he told me we were not flying, that I admitted the OR clerk did know what he was talking about.

Cliff explained, "For some reason, in the middle of the night someone in operations decided that I should fly as the pilot for a **new** crew on their very **first** mission." Cliff was certain, though, that the Cliff Hendrickson crew would be flying the next mission.

The fog lessened somewhat as the sun started to rise, but I was still certain the mission would be scrubbed, so I stayed on, thinking I would ride back to the 749th and Hut #20 with Sid, The Head, and Bernie.

To my surprise, taxi and takeoff flares were fired and planes proceeded to take off. I knew the planes Robbie and Cliff were flying; within minutes both were airborne. I stayed on to watch about twenty planes take off. When the fog really got heavy, the field was declared closed to takeoffs and landings.

Those twenty planes that had taken off did join other groups in the 94th wing and flew on to the designated target, Gemünd, Germany.

By mid afternoon, when it was time for the planes to be back, Kornblatt and I went down to wait for them. The fog was still very heavy and just a few planes, four or five, landed, when again the field was closed. All other planes, including Robbie's and Cliff's, were diverted to southern England. We checked with operations and were told none of the planes would be back tonight.

Knowing we would not be flying tomorrow, Korny & I went back to Hut #20 and picked up our bikes for a ride to Sawtry and to our favorite pub, The Oddfellows Arms.

December 20 to 22, 1944

Weather conditions continued to be horrible with heavy fog, a mist, and at times a light snow. I had been walking to the mess hall rather than riding my bike for fear of running into something or someone. Certainly the weather was not fit for flying. Each day we checked to see if our group was returning, and each day same answer—we doubt it. The evening of December 22 showed some signs of the fog lifting, so maybe tomorrow they will return.

December 23, 1944

Another unforgettable date, like September 12, the date Rinehart was killed. Late this evening we learned that our Robertson crew copilot and most recently my new crew's pilot, Lt. Clifford Hendrickson, had been killed when he crashed near Oxford.

It just didn't seem real. We were truly in a state of shock. This was to have been the first mission for our new Cliff Hendrickson crew. My name with the others was on the official loading list, until someone, for some reason decided Cliff should fly as the pilot for a new crew on their **first** mission. Why was the change made? Was it fate? Predestination? Answer to prayers? I'm sure I'll never know, but for certain, it just wasn't my time to die.

As of that time we did not know the official cause of the crash, but this is what we knew:

After the mission on December 19, our group had been diverted to a base at Portreach in the county of Cornwall in far southwest England. This morning the weather in Portreach was not bad, and the planes took off without incident.

Robbie and Cliff had decided they would fly somewhat together. They were in radio contact, and Cliff was flying off Robbie's left wing at an altitude above the clouds. As Bernie Stutman described it, "We were both in clear blue skies, when suddenly we lost radio contact—then slowly, but seemingly in control, Cliff's plane descended into the clouds and out of sight, and continued to be out of radio contact."

Robbie's crew assumed Cliff was having malfunctions that included radio transmitter failure, and that Cliff had decided to descend and visually find a field where he could land and get necessary repairs.

Robbie continued on back to Glatton, expecting to learn that operations had been notified that Cliff had made a safe landing. Operations had heard nothing, but at that time there was still little concern.

It was two hours after Robbie had returned to Glatton that we learned Cliff had crashed into a grove of trees near Oxford and that all nine aboard had been killed.

I had always admired and respected Cliff, but now that I had been flying with him being the pilot, I had gotten to know him even better and felt closer to him. Sharing the same not-too-common first name, **Clifford**, also seemed to give us an added kinship. I jokingly told Cliff if he would drop the **"on"** from his last name, I could claim him as a descendant of the General Hendricks for whom my hometown was named.

Two from the Robertson crew have now been killed — Rinehart on his third mission, and Hendrickson on his 20th. Strange; both Indiana Hoosiers and both with the same, fatalistic attitude. Both often confessed they doubted they would complete a tour of missions. Cliff was tall, dark, and truly handsome. He had a striking resemblance to the famous movie star, Clark Gable. He even had the same groomed Gable mustache. Clark Gable was a B-17 pilot, too, stationed only a few miles from Glatton. Mankin and Carbery said when they went on pass with Cliff, he was often mistaken for Gable, and Cliff enjoyed every minute of it, especially the attention from women.

What a sad ending to one great person, Lt. Cliff Hendrickson, from Jasper, Indiana. It was also the end to a capable and well-trained crew that didn't fly even a single combat mission.

Now what? Who knows? Without the number-one person, the pilot, I am sure the crew will be disbanded and we will be orphaned again, flying individually as needed, with little chance to be assigned to a crew. For me? Had I not checked out as a radio operator but had stayed as a gunner, I would be much more in demand as a fill-in, since I was qualified to fly in four gunnery positions: the tail, the waist, the chin, and the ball turret. Now with the radio operator classification, I was not likely to fly often.

What does the future hold for me? I had no idea and there was little I could do to control my destiny.

What would be, would be!

June 1998
What We Know Now About
the Cliff Hendrickson Crash

Fifty-four years after the saga of the ill-fated Cliff Hendrickson crew that ended with the crash landing and Cliff's death, the details of that accident were uncovered in the military records' archives, thanks to the combined efforts of the 457th Bomb Group (BG) British historian, Bernie Baines, and Craig Harris, a dedicated member of the 457th BG Association and secretary of the 8th Air Force Historical Society.

The report shows that the accident occurred at 17:45 on December 23, 1944, two miles north of Great Rollerton and not near Oxford as we had been told. I have not located Great Rollerton on the maps I have. The accident investigation concluded the crew became lost, and while attempting an instrument letdown, the aircraft flew into the ground causing complete destruction to aircraft #41–38812 and fatally injuring eight of the nine crew members. One of the crew had major injuries but survived the crash. Initially, we had been told all had been killed. The accident report concluded the accident was caused by a combination of weather conditions and pilot error. The weather at the time of the accident: visibility 2,000 yards in haze, clouds 3/10 at 1,500 feet, 10/10 at 2,000 feet with light variable winds.

Those killed were:
Hendrickson, Clifford–Pilot (0-812261)
Graves, Walter–Copilot (0-825619)
Kilmer, Joseph L. (T-129699)
Williams, David E. (T-129575)
Bruer, George H. (14058137)
Riedel, Robert (35061926)
Hawley, George B. (37625229)
Fitzgerald, Edmund T. (31366494)

The one survivor was **Clifford Heinrich**. Many, many times during these past fifty plus years I have thought about that accident and how, for whatever reason, fate stepped in and took me off that aircraft and mission sometime during the night of December 19, 1944. Now I wonder, had I been on that aircraft, would the one survivor have been Clifford Digre? Probably not!

After V-E Day May 8, 1945, and before I left England, I visited Cliff Hendrickson's grave at Cambridge. At that time I knew none of the names of those who had been killed with him, but I assumed they, too, were all buried at Cambridge. I wonder if that one survivor, Clifford Heinrich, might be still living. If he were, it would be interesting to talk to him. That would truly be the ending to this story.

Cliff Hendrickson, copilot. Killed December 23, 1944. Home: Indiana.

January 1 to January 9, 1945
Flak Leave at Southport

Prior to the war, Southport (located near Liverpool and Manchester) was one of England's prime resort cities with a number of luxury hotels. During the war the best of the hotels were operated by the American Red Cross for R&R (rest and relaxation) for stressed-out 8th Air Force flying personnel.

Cliff Hendrickson's death was traumatic to all of us, and Robbie requested that all of his original crew be granted a well-deserved "flak leave."

Bernie, Sid, John, and I spent our week here doing whatever we pleased: a lot of sack time, horse-drawn carriage rides, rides in the amusement park, roller skating, and horseback riding that included a female instructor for John Brown who had never ridden a horse—a fun-filled, relaxing week and just what we needed.

For whatever reason, Korny and The Head decided not to go with us to Southport, but they still had the week off from flying combat.

Southport is by far the nicest city I had visited in England. I wanted to return there someday as a civilian (and I did in 1998 on a trip with my wife, Bernice).

January 1-9, 1945
Flak Leave (R&R)—Southport, England

Bernie on horseback.

Me on horseback, Southport, England.

Sid and Bernie.

The four horsemen: Me, John, Sid, and Bernie.

118

January 1-9, 1945
Flak Leave (R&R)—Southport, England
A Fun-filled Week at a Luxury Hotel

Sid, Bernie, and John about to take a carriage ride—Southport, England.

John and me.

Me, ready for a carriage ride.

January 10, 1945
Rattlesnake Daddy Will Fly No More

We returned from a fun-filled relaxing week in Southport; now it was back to the reality of combat.

On today's mission Lt. Fred Gauss flew aircraft #44-6088, *Rattlesnake Daddy*. Near the target, the aircraft experienced engine problems. The pilot feathered engines #1 and #3 and then #4 burst into flames. The crew safely bailed out, but Lt. Gauss was killed when his parachute failed to open. The aircraft was destroyed when it crashed in Belgium.

Strange isn't it? The engine problems Lt. Gauss had were identical to the problems our crew had with *Rattlesnake Daddy* on October 5, 1944 when we made the forced landing in Antwerp. The big, big difference—with two engines out and one in flames—we had made a safe landing.

Rattlesnake Daddy was truly a jinx to our crew. We flew this aircraft on six missions and on all six something bad happened. On our second mission, Carbery was hit by flak. On our third mission, Rinehart was killed. On our seventh mission, Mankin was hit by flak. On our eighth, sixty men from our group were reported killed or missing, including five from our barracks. On mission number nine, Bernie Stutman lost power to his heated suit and suffered frostbite that years after the war resulted in having both of his legs amputated. On our tenth mission, October 5, 1944, the last time we flew the aircraft, we had made the forced landing in Antwerp.

It seems #44-6088, *Rattlesnake Daddy*, was destined to end its flying days in Belgium.

Aircraft Serial #43-37828
Remember Me? Georgia Peach

Being escorted back to England by a P-38 after major damage to the vertical stabilizer. (Photograph courtesy of Bernie Baines.)

As much as *Rattlesnake Daddy* was our jinx aircraft, *Remember Me? Georgia Peach* was our favorite. We flew this plane on seven missions and most were "milk runs;" no-problem missions. *Remember Me?* was flown on 86 missions by 41 different crews and after the war returned safely to the USA.

The Charles Barrier crew flew this aircraft on ten missions; our William T. Robertson crew's seven missions were the second most. I am sure aircraft #43-37828 was the favorite of many of the 41 crews that flew missions on *Remember Me? Georgia Peach*.

January 10 to February 23, 1944

These forty-plus days were not my favorite in England. I felt like an orphan, and I was. I no longer had the identity of belonging to any crew. On November 29 I had flown my nineteenth mission and now, two and a half months later, I still had only nineteen missions, while members of Robbie's crew and my other buddies were flying regularly and nearing the end of their tours. Had I not checked out as a radio operator to fly with Cliff Hendrickson, I would still have a gunner classification and would have been flying on a regular basis. As a gunner, I could have flown in four different gunnery positions: tail, waist, chin, and ball turret, but since there is only one radio operator on a crew, it was a matter of supply and demand. I must admit I had mixed feelings. On one hand, I wasn't going on missions to complete my tour and go home, but on the other hand, I wasn't flying combat missions—no flak, no fighters!

I briefly considered asking to be reclassified as a gunner, but then thought just maybe, if I did that, I might lose my T/Sgt rank and the extra money that goes with it, so I decided to leave well enough alone.

What did I do during these days? I flew on several practice missions, flying for other operators wanting time off. I went on passes to some of my favorite places—York, Leeds, and Skipton, all in northern England where fewer Yanks went. I visited buddies at different bases—Doug Mann, Bill Biggie, and Bob Suing. I visited the graves of Rinehart and Hendrickson at the Cambridge Cemetery. On days that I was at the base, I would usually go down to the runways to wait for crews returning from missions. Then when weather permitted, Sid and I would ride our bikes to Sawtry and to our favorite pub, The Oddfellows Arms.

January 22, 1945

The 178th mission for the 457th Bomb Group—Air Commander Major Spencer; Lead Pilot Robbie Robertson.

Top row, left to right: 1) The Head, Louie Dahle, 2) Szydlowski, 4) Robbie.
Bottom row: 1) Bernie Stutman. The others I cannot identify. (Photo courtesy of the base photo lab.)

Robbie flew a total of eight missions as the lead pilot. Both Robbie and Bernie Stutman finished their tour on February 25, 1945, on a rough mission to Munich. Reports said that flak was intense and accurate with 26 bombers sustaining damage.

February 9, 1945

On this date, the Don Sellon crew crash-landed at the base after returning from their mission to Lutzkendorf. Luckily, none of the crew was injured. Ironically, this was the crew I flew with February 23, 1945. Tommy Thompson flew for the pilot, Don Sellon. I flew for the radio operator, James Bass.

The Don Sellon crew walking away from a crash landing at the base. (Photo courtesy of the base photo lab.)

Mission: 20 (Twenty)
Mission Date: February 23, 1945
Mission Length: Nine hours, thirty minutes
To: Ellingen, Germany
Target: Railroad yards and autobahn
Results Reported: Good
Plane: Unnamed, #44-6970

Mission Highlights

At last, my first combat mission since November 29, almost three months ago. My anxieties were almost like they had been on my first mission and for good reason—another unforgettable experience.

I was awakened less than an hour before takeoff. The orderly room clerk who woke me said, "This is your day, Digre—you're flying with a crew from the 748th; their radio operator suddenly got sick." He added, "You won't have time for breakfast, so get dressed, grab some candy, and get over to the orderly room and I'll have a Jeep ready." I hustled and within minutes was at the orderly room and in the Jeep, and away we went—a stop at the radio shack, then on to the equipment room for a heated suit, a chute, and a flak jacket. Then on to the flight line where there was already the drone of engine starts. Fear then started to set in. This was to be my first mission in three months, my first mission without Robbie in charge, my first mission as radio operator—all of these firsts with a pilot and a crew I knew nothing about. I admit I was a bit scared!

The Jeep pulled up to a shining new B-17, Serial #44-6970. I learned later this was only the third mission for this plane, which was still unnamed.

Entering the waist door I was greeted by three gunners—seemed like nice guys, but still strangers. I settled into the radio room, turning on and checking the equipment. I called the pilot on the intercom telling him I was aboard, giving him my name, and reporting all was okay and ready to go in the radio room. He acknowledged my call with a rather cocky voice saying his name was Lt. Tommy Thompson, that this was to be his eighth mission, boastfully stating, "And I have already had four crash landings." I replied straightforwardly, "Well, sir, this will be my 20th mission, and I am not looking for the excitement of a crash landing."

Unsettled weather delayed takeoff and assembly but didn't scrub the mission. The long flight to the target, Ellingen, not far from Germany's eastern border, was uneventful with no flak or fighters. Approaching the target area we found it completely cloud covered, so the entire formation dropped down to 12,000 feet where we had complete visibility of the railroad yards and the autobahn in the city center which was the target of our box. Our hits were right on. We could actually see the bombs striking. To me it appeared as if this small village may have been completely wiped out. It was not a good feeling knowing many innocent civilians were likely injured or killed.

The flak, although moderate, was very accurate, and our plane was hit but no injuries to crew members. After "bombs away" the flak attack ended, too, and still no fighter attack, so it seemed we could term this a routine mission. Just after crossing the border into France, when we were starting to relax, the pilot came on the intercom. "We must have taken a flak hit in the gas tanks. We are running low on gas; we'll never make it back to England." Since we were now in friendly occupied territory, I thought for sure we would be looking for a landing strip as Robbie did when we made the forced landing in Antwerp on my tenth mission back on October 5, but no, this was not Tommy Thompson's style. His command, "Prepare for a belly landing" meant we were to salvo all non-essential equipment. Since we were in friendly territory and somewhat out of the danger of a fighter attack, we were to salvo ammunitions, guns, flak suits, and the most important, we were to drop the ball turret. When it was necessary to jettison the ball turret, the ball gunner was in charge with assistance from the waist and tail gunners.

While the gunners were busy throwing out non-essential equipment and preparing to drop the ball turret, Tommy was surveying the area to find the best site for a belly landing. From the window in my radio room I had a good view of the area he was looking over. He chose a freshly plowed field in which, as we circled, I could see a farmer plowing with a single-bottom plow pulled by a team of horses. When Tommy said this was to be the spot, I must say at least I thought he was making a good decision.

Since I had flown seventeen missions as a ball turret gunner, I had a strange fondness for the ball, feeling this was the safest spot on the aircraft, even though the opinion was not shared by most gunners. During gunnery school training, when I knew I would be a ball turret gunner, I was super conscious about knowing every nut, bolt, and screw, including every detail involved if and when it might be necessary to jettison the ball.

The procedure consisted of three steps:

First   Remove 4 bolts from the azimuth (horizontal) gear case.

Second Remove 4 safety hangers from the gear ring.

Third   Remove the 12 major bolts attaching the ball and the support column to the I-beam/bulk head. The ball will then fall free.

The radio room is directly ahead of the ball turret. When the gunners reported to Tommy that they were having trouble dropping the ball, I opened the door to see if I could help. All three were hammering on the ball with guns and even kicking and jumping on the ball; fortunately for them, it didn't release. In the excitement they had overlooked step 1 — remove 4 small bolts from the azimuth gear case. When I pointed this out, they removed these four small bolts — bingo, the ball fell free. We reported to Tommy that the ball had been dropped and we were all in the radio room and prepared for the belly landing. Tommy came back, "Good, I'll make one more pass and then bring it in." On the final pass when we were only a couple hundred feet over the freshly plowed field, I took one last look out of my window to see the team of horses run away with the plow tumbling behind. The roar of the four engines on the B-17 bearing down on them was just not an everyday occurrence.

As the five of us in the radio room were bracing ourselves and anticipating the pending belly landing, the only sounds were those of the drones of engines and the whistling of air rushing in the large hole where the ball turret had been. Not one of us said a word — absolutely zero conversation.

I'm sure the other four guys were having the same thoughts I had — what will happen when we make contact with the ground? Will the plane explode? Will it burst into flames? Will it flip over? Just what? We did not know and the moments just before touch down were anxious. But I surprised myself — sure I was a bit scared, but not nearly as much as I thought I should have been.

A moment before the impact, the drone of four engines stopped. Then when we hit, it seemed as if the whole plowed field was pouring in through the large cavity where the ball turret had been. Next we heard the sounds of the fuselage twisting and stressing as it plowed its own furrow down the field, a final hard jar, and then a strange quietness. We had stopped. I then realized I had just been a part of a textbook belly landing. I said a prayer of thanks, and thanks for the skills of a cocky pilot—Tommy Thompson—who had just success-fully chalked up his fifth crash landing. Even though we had now landed, we were still concerned that the plane could explode or burst into flames, so within a minute we had all evacuated the plane and run to what we thought would be a safe distance away.

Suddenly, out of nowhere, a French farmer carrying a pitchfork came running up apparently speaking French, which none of us could understand. I don't know if this was the farmer I had seen plowing with the run-away team, but it must have been. Soon others came run-ning across the field to the plane. Some went directly into the plane carrying away their souvenirs and treasures. They took parachutes, Mae West life jackets, and even the clock from the cockpit.

Even as the plane was being looted and men, women, and children were running away with their prizes, one of the crew members pulled out a camera. Tommy lined us up in front of the almost new belly-landed B-17, placing himself in his fifty-mission crush cap front and center, of course. What a showman. By now the farmer with the pitch fork felt he was a member of this crew, so he joined right in on the picture-taking, standing next to me.

A young boy speaking pretty good English came and offered to take us to a home for food and help. I assume this was his parent's home. It didn't take us long to decide to go with him. I was absolutely starved. Other than a candy bar, I had not eaten for nearly twenty-four hours.

The first thing I tried to ask for was a tall, cold glass of water—but no water. Just wine and more wine, with bread, cheese, and a few slices of meat. Either the wine was very strong or it was laced to keep us from flirting with the farmer's two cute daughters. Before I knew it, I was sound asleep on a couch with another crew member, dozing peacefully until we were awakened and taken by truck to a nearby American fighter base.

The next morning after a good breakfast, we were assigned a beat-up, battle-weary B-17 to fly back to our base. Tommy was not a Robbie and I knew it, but we did make it back. Although I was not impressed with Tommy as a pilot, his crew members were real nice guys.

One of the crew members brought me a picture. It would be a real keepsake.

What an experience!

A belly landing near Laon, France. Back row, left to right: Anthony O'Brien, navigator; Pierre Ribaut, French farmer; myself, radio operator; and Dan Nose, flight engineer. Front row: Murray Jett, copilot; Tommy Thompson, pilot; Bennie Johnson, ball turret gunner; Ralph Kenyon, bombardier.

Footnote: The San Antonio 457th Bomb Group reunion, October 15-19, 1993, was the first reunion for us. On our first night at the Menger Hotel, Bernice and I were visiting with Don Sellon whom I had never met before. When I learned Don was from the 748th, I inquired about Tommy Thompson and told Don about the mission and the belly landing. Don's reply was, "You know what? Except for Tommy Thompson, that was my crew you flew with and some are here at this reunion." The next morning I met Bennie Johnson and Dan Nose, who had been on that mission, and James Bass, radio operator, whom I had replaced on that mission. For all these years I have been wondering about these guys, and then to meet them—what a surprise! What a reunion.

For years I had looked at this picture and wondered who was the crew that I flew with that day. They had looked at the picture and wondered who was the radio operator. And now I had met them! We spent the reunion talking, and we developed a close relationship that continues to this day. I even learned that my sleeping mate at the farmer's house was Bennie Johnson.

February 25, 1945

Robbie and Bernie Stutman finished their tours today—Lucky Joes—the marshalling yards at Munich.

Mission Number: 21 (Twenty-one)
Mission Date: March 1, 1945
Mission Length: Eight hours, thirty minutes
To: Goppingen, Germany
Target: Marshalling yards
Results: Unknown
Plane: ?, #072

Mission Highlights

The orderly room clerk rousting me out this morning was the same one on duty February 23, my last mission, and knew all about the belly-landing experience with Tommy. When he woke me saying, "Digre, you're flying with a crew from the 748th again. If you're lucky, it could be with Tommy Thompson." With such a prospect, it didn't take me long to be wide awake.

When I reported to the orderly room, I learned I wouldn't be flying with Tommy but with a Lt. Ben McChesney.

The assembly and the flight to Goppingen were very long, but uneventful—very light flak, and no fighters. McChesney was a very good pilot—almost a Robbie. I wouldn't mind flying with this crew again, but little chance; the radio operator just had a bad cold today.

March 2, 1945

Today the 457th flew its 200th mission. The first mission flown for this group was on February 21, 1944.

March 5, 1945

Today Louie Dahle—The Head—flew his 30th mission, finishing his tour.

March 24, 1945

The 216th mission for the 457th Bomb Group Air Commander Lt. Col. William F. Smith, Pilot Lt. Fisher.

This was the last mission for my very good buddy "Sid" Szydlowski (2nd from left in front row). Sid had the honor of flying his last mission with the popular deputy group commander Lt. Col. William F. Smith. Lt. Col Smith is on Sid's left. (Photo courtesy of the base photo lab.)

Footnote: Lt. Col. William F. Smith was with the 457th since the group came to England. He was an excellent combat crew pilot and flew a tour of missions before he became a deputy group commander. He was the lead pilot on several 457th missions including the group's last mission on April 20, 1945.

After the war the majority of the personnel from the 457th Bomb Group, including Lt. Col. Smith, were assigned to the army airfield in Sioux Falls, SD. Lt. Col. Smith's home was in Boston, and in the later part of July 1945, he flew a B-25, a medium bomber, from Sioux Falls to Boston for his first furlough since returning to the USA. On July 28, 1945, he was to return to Sioux Falls after picking up two passengers at the Newark airport. As he approached New York, he was suddenly caught in a storm of wind, rain, and fog with poor visibility. The reports said that over New York City he became lost or disoriented, crashing his B-25 into the 79th floor of the Empire State Building. In addition to his life, the lives of his two passengers and eleven office workers were also lost in this accident. More details on this accident are on the next page.

Ironic isn't it? This seasoned pilot had survived many combat missions in Europe only to be killed in a freak weather-related accident back in the States.

B-25 Bomber Crashes Into Empire State Building

Above: New York fireman search the wreckage in offices Nos. 7915 and 7916 on the 79th Floor of the Empire State Building. The offices were occupied at the time by a Catholic organisation rent free (Associated Press).

Above: What the brochure does not show — the impact position of the 457th Bomb Group B-25 Mitchell.

The 457th Group had only been in the States a short while when on Saturday, July 28, Lieutenant Colonel William F. Smith lost his way while flying a B-25 Mitchell bomber from Bedford, Massachusetts to Sioux Falls Army Air Base via Newark Airport. Emerging from low cloud at about 900ft, the 457th pilot found himself among the skyscrapers of downtown Manhattan. The aircraft crashed headlong into the 79th floor level of the Empire State Building killing Lieutenant Colonel Smith, two servicemen 'hitch-hikers'

and eleven office workers. The B-25 exploded on impact spraying burning fuel into West 34th Street below, one of the engines completely passing through the building and out the other side! On September 28, 1977, the New York publishers of a new book on the crash (The Sky is Falling), Grosset & Dunlop, presented a plaque which can now be seen on the 86th floor, 'in grateful appreciation to those men and women of the Empire State Building who unselfishly gave their assistance in the crash'.

Left: An Associated Press photo of the impact hole left by the bomber in the northern face of the 1,250-foot building (the height of the skyscraper without TV mast which was added in 1950-51). The damaged offices are now occupied by Askai Chemical Industries of America (Room 7915) and American Yarn Sales Corpn. Inc. (Room 7916). Right: Our own Paul Booker risked a little more than his reputation to take this comparison from the 81st floor in October 1977.

From the 457th Bomb Group newsletter. (Photo courtesy of the base photo lab.)

April 1, 1945—Easter Sunday

This morning Astor, Barnes, Cardwell, and I went to the church service at the Conington Church here on the base—a different service than we have at home—no high-style Easter bonnets you might expect to see at home. More than half of those attending were made up of personnel from this base. We had a service at our base chapel, too, but this was something different. I am glad we went.

In the afternoon, Sid and I flew a practice mission. As we were returning to our base, the crosswinds were terrific, and we were diverted to the 306th Bomb Group at Bedford where we stayed overnight. We went to the NCO Club for a couple beers, and there I met a friend from gunnery school—a fellow Minnesotan from St. Paul, Bill Greenberg. Of course we compared mission notes. His group had flown many of the same missions we had. Three more missions and he will complete his tour.

April 2, 1945

When we returned to the base today, both Sid and I had notices on the bulletin board:
- Stanley P. Szydlowski—shipping orders to the USA— leaving here on April 11.
- Clifford B. Digre, 37561701, was officially promoted from S/Sgt to T/Sgt—means another stripe and more money.

April 4, 1945

John Brown flew his last mission today. The mission he flew on April 2 was recalled so he didn't get credit for it.

April 6, 1945

Today I was transferred to the 750th Bomb Squadron. Apparently there were fewer spare radio operators there. I'd be there on paper only. I was sure I would be at Hut #20 most of the time.

> **Mission Number: 22 (Twenty-two)**
> **Mission Date: April 8, 1945**
> **Mission Length: Seven hours**
> **To: Halberstadt, Germany**
> **Target: Warehouses and railroad Station**
> **Results: Good**
> **Plane: ?, #535**

Mission Highlights

Today I flew with Lt. James R. Latamer of the 750th Bomb Group—a very good crew that included two Minnesota Swedes. The targets were the railroad station and surrounding warehouses. Bombing was visual, and our bombs were right on. After "bombs away," we circled the city, and it appeared as if it was entirely on fire. There was absolutely no sign of resistance, no flak, and although there was a report of fighters in the area, our group saw none. This was a true milk run when there were no signs of flak or fighters. One had to believe the German Luftwaffe was virtually nonexistent and the war was nearing the end.

> **Mission Number: 23 (Twenty-three)**
> **Mission Date: April 9, 1945**
> **Mission Length: Eight hours, forty minutes**
> **To: Munich, Germany**
> **Target: Jet Air Field**
> **Results: Good**
> **Plane: ?, #881**

Mission Highlights

Wow! Flying two days in a row. I hoped it would keep up with six more milk runs like yesterday's and today's.

Today I flew with Lt. Harlan Buettner and Lt. George Grau (copilot). This was his last mission and also the last mission for the copilot and waist gunner. We bombed a jet aircraft field near Munich—direct hits, very successful, very light flak, and no sign of fighters. Have we wiped out the Luftwaffe? We must have—when we could bomb airfields and still see no sign of a fighter attack.

135

Frank and Rose Warren,
Owners of The Oddfellows Arms Pub

Within days after arriving in England, Sid and I discovered this small, cozy pub (public house) that was off the beaten track in the quaint village of Sawtry. We soon became friends with this delightful couple.

The English pubs are truly an institution—a part of the British way of life. After their evening meal, the men went there to socialize, play darts, play cards, and spin their yarns. Sure, they served beer, wine, and spirits, but seldom did we see anyone intoxicated. If someone did "indulge" too much, as the British would say, it was usually a rowdy American. I truly liked the British people. I felt I was a guest in their country; I fully accepted their customs, their food, and traditions, and I got along just fine. Not all Americans felt as I did. Some were constantly negative and critical of the British ways. Those guys were the losers. A few nights before Sid shipped out for the states we were invited to the Warren's for dinner.

Footnote: I returned to England and our base in 1966 and 1971. Both times my wife, Bernice, and I visited the Warrens and got a warm welcome.

The Oddfellows Arms, our favorite pub, indicated by the sign at the left side of the image. (Photo courtesy of Bernie Banes.)

In my diary I had made several mentions of The Oddfellows Arms (on the left in the above image), our favorite pub, and the delightful owners, Frank and Rose Warren. The pub was located on Church Street in the quaint little village of Sawtry, a short three-mile bike ride from the base and our Hut #20.

On Drinking Beer

The reader must wonder if drinking beer was our primary entertainment. Sure, drinking beer was as common as heavy smoking, but I never saw anyone drink while on duty. Being intoxicated was frowned upon, especially on our base. I remember Robbie asking us about our drinking habits when he interviewed us at Plant Park. Our crew was very disciplined in that regard, and we were all dedicated to the safety of one another—we all had too much at stake.

"Going out for a beer" was an expression—an invitation to check out what was going on at the NCO Club or at our favorite pub. Sometimes it was just because we wanted to go visit with Frank and Rose at The Oddfellows.

Yes, we all enjoyed a beer, but it was never a priority.

April 10, 1945

I did not fly today and I was glad for that. After the last two missions when we saw no sign of enemy fighters, we thought perhaps the Luftwaffe had been completely destroyed—but not so! Today the 457th was hit by the new ME-292 jets. The group lead plane piloted by Lt. Melvin Fox, with Lt. Col. Rod Francis flying as air commander, was shot down and exploded. The Fox crew came to the 457th the day we flew our first mission, September 9, 1944. I knew all the fellows on this crew—a real swell bunch they were.

Also shot down today was the plane piloted by Tommy Thompson, the hot shot I flew my 20th belly landing mission with. The crew flying with Tommy was not the same crew I flew with on February 23 but was a crew whose pilot was sick that day. When Tommy's plane was hit, it went into a dive and burst into flames. A wing blew off and then exploded. Reports tonight say it is unlikely there were any survivors. Today's target was an ordinance depot near Berlin. Results reported as good.

Here is the picture of Tommy Thompson's plane with one wing blown off.

Note: Unbelievably, Tommy Thompson survived this one, too! He had parachuted out of the plane and landed deep in German territory where he had an episode of confrontation with a Gestapo officer; he surrendered and became a P.O.W. for the rest of the war. Tommy later returned to the base and returned home with the group.

April 11, 1945

Today was a day I had been dreading for weeks. On this morning, Sid shipped out for a replacement depot. After a few days of more processing, physicals, and the like, he would be boarding a troop ship for home.

A few days after we had met at Plant Park last May, our friendship started to develop, and today we both said we were each other's best friend. There was absolutely nothing we would not do for each other. This had been so very important to both of us as we had faced death on missions together.

Since Hendricks, a predominantly Norwegian Lutheran town, had little to do with the Polish Catholics from Ivanhoe, just twelve miles away except for our very competitive basketball and football games, we had very little social contact with the Polish from Ivanhoe.

So when I left Hendricks on May 10, 1945, nearly two years before, I, the 100% Norwegian Lutheran would not have believed that my best friend in the military was to be a 100% Polish Roman Catholic.

Sid wanted to say goodbye to Frank and Rose Warren, so we spent the last night at The Oddfellows Arms where we promised each other we would get together in the States as soon as we both got out of the service.

Sid's parting words were, "Don't be surprised, C. B., if I go out to Hendricks to meet your folks before you get home." No! I wouldn't because Sid kept every promise he made!

Our goodbyes last night were emotional.

Mission Number: 24 (Twenty-four)
Mission Date: April 14, 1945
Mission Length: Eight hours, thirty minutes
To: Royan, France (mouth of Girande River)
Target: Gun emplacements
Results: Reported poor
Plane: ?, #855

Mission Highlights

Today I flew with the Lt. John Starnes crew—another very good crew. Starnes was on his second tour. We were awakened before 0400 hours for a takeoff scheduled for 0530 hours when the skies were still dark, dark! This was a milk run in the truest form—no enemy resistance. The target was gun emplacements, one of the few German pockets still remaining in France. Bombing was from a relatively low altitude—10,000 to 16,000 feet. This was my third Oak Leaf Cluster Mission. An air medal was given to each crew member after the first six missions. For every six missions flown, each crew member was given an oak leaf to attach to the bars.

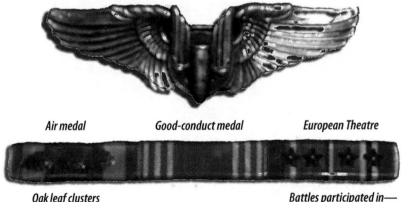

| Air medal | Good-conduct medal | European Theatre |

| Oak leaf clusters | Battles participated in— |
Northern France, Rhineland, Ardennes, Central Europe

The first bar on the left is called the air medal that I was awarded after flying six missions. The oak clusters on the left are small pins that represent six missions each. The middle bar is the good-conduct medal. The final bar is the European Theatre. On this bar are four stars that represent the battles that I participated in—for example, the Battle of the Ardennes. Above are the "gunnery wings." Notice the bullet surrounded by wings.

Military Jacket

This is my Air Corps dress uniform. On the upper sleeve on each sleeve is my rank. In this case, I was a technical sergeant (T/SGT). On the left sleeve, above the rank, is the emblem of the 8th Air Force. On the right sleeve toward the bottom is my radio operator patch. The lapel has the symbol US (United States). The left lapel indicated the branch of the service—in this case Air Corps. Above the left pocket are the gunnery wings and ribbons described above with oak leaf clusters.

April 15, 1945

Today Art Astor and Julie Kornblatt both finished their tours on an easy milk run. They bombed the same target we bombed yesterday, one of the few German gun emplacements remaining in France. On November 29, 1944, I had completed nineteen missions; on that date Art Astor had flown only **one** mission. Now he has completed his tour while I have flown only twenty-four missions—just five missions since November 29.

Both Art and Julie are flying as gunners and that's the difference. Had I stayed as a gunner instead of checking out as a radio operator, I would have finished long ago, maybe. Again it makes me wonder if I did the right thing, but who knows what might have been.

April 16 was Art's birthday, so finishing his tour on this day was an ideal present for him.

April 20, 1945

Little did I know on April 14, just six days before when I flew a mission to Royan, France, that indeed I had flown my final combat mission. My tour of combat was now over. Thank God I had made it!

Today's mission was to Seddin, Germany—the target-marshalling yards. Absolutely no enemy fighters and no anti-aircraft guns. It appeared this horrible war would soon be ending.

Today's mission was the 236th and the final mission for the 457th Bomb Group.

Got a letter from my mother today saying that Don Fjeseth, one of my good friends and high school classmate, had been reported missing in action. My hopes and prayers were that he was okay. Donnie, too, had flown as a gunner in England with the 8th Air Force.

From our small town of Hendricks there had been three of us flying with the 8th; Perwin Knutson, Donnie Fjeseth, and I. It was reported that Perwin was a P.O.W.; now Donnie was M.I.A.—not the best of odds. So far I was the lucky one.

April 21 to 23, 1945

Brown was scheduled to ship out for home on the twenty-third. Kornblatt finished his tour on the fifteenth and would be leaving soon. That means I will be the only one from our crew still here—a depressing thought, so I decided to take a day pass to London to lift my spirits.

Even though I went alone, I had a great time. At the Red Cross Club I met fellows I had gone through gunnery school with so I had no problem finding friends to do things with. I met Dick Wiercioch of Chicago, with whom I had gone through both radio and gunnery school. One afternoon he and I went to the Stage Door Canteen together. Dick had been there before, but it was new to me. It was a lively place with a big band on a rotating stage in the center of a huge dance floor. It was packed with GIs from the USA, England, Russia, and even some Norwegians!

Anna Neagle, a popular British actress and a real beauty, was there signing autographs, so I had her sign my short snorter. A short snorter is a popular fad among flight crew members. It is a collection of currency bills from the countries a flyboy has flown over, taped end to end. Mine started with the USA dollar followed by the Islandic kroner, the English pound, the French and Belgium francs, and, of course, the German mark. I was proud of my collection—all nice, new bills. I had to purchase only the mark; the rest I had acquired from each country. It had been a fun collection, and on these bills I had the autographs of all our crew members, friends I had met here in England, friends from Antwerp, from France, and, of course, USA friends, too. My short snorter would be a real keepsake.

My two days in London were fun-filled and a great diversion for me. By the time I returned to the base, Brown had already shipped out, but Korny and Art were still here. That helps!

The War Is Over!

May 8, 1945—A Tour of the Ruhr

This date, May 8, 1945, will go down in history as V-E Day—Victory in Europe.

We were told yesterday that the official announcement would be made today on BBC, so when Prime Minister Churchill made his speech, it was almost anticlimactic but still welcomed.

That afternoon Catholics and Protestants held joint thanksgiving services at the base chapel. Tomorrow there would be a big parade in Peterborough and a thanksgiving service at the beautiful Peterborough Cathedral that I planned to attend. Today I was on a very special flight back to Germany.

The combat crews could not have been successful had it not been for the ground personnel referred to as the "ground crews"—the mechanics who kept our planes flying, the armament specialists loading the bombs and caring for the guns, the parachute riggers who packed our chutes, the mess hall staff who fed us, medical people tending our health, the clerical people, and on and on. If ever there was a team effort, this was it. After every mission these same people showed their concern for our mission and us. They would ask, "How was it? How does it look? Was the mission a success?"—questions showing they felt a part of the big picture. These people had a stake in our efforts, so today we took all the ground crews that wanted to go on **a tour of the Ruhr**.

Many of our missions had been to Cologne and the industrial Ruhr Valley. Not only did the ground crews have their eyes opened and were filled with amazement, but so did I.

We flew over the area at a relatively low altitude, and without the concern for flak or fighters, we got a good look at the mile after mile of complete devastation the bombing had inflicted—hardly a single bridge over the Rhine River was standing. We flew over the city of Cologne, and to me one thing stood out. On all sides of the famous Cologne cathedral everything was leveled, yet the cathedral appeared to be untouched. To me that was truly a miracle.

The ground crews, as well as those of us who had flown combat, were all in awe as we viewed the total destruction. Except for the drone of the engines, there was a strange quietness in the plane. No one expressed jubilation over the apparent success of bombing.

I was glad I had been privileged to have this experience with our great ground crews.

I flew with a make-up crew; I didn't even get the name of the pilot from the 750th Bomb Squadron.

When we returned to the base, parties had already started at the clubs. I went back to my hut, changed clothes, ate at the mess hall, and then rode my bike to Sawtry to spend the evening with my friends Frank and Rose Warren at The Oddfellows Arms. It was busy, but not rowdy—just a fun night with bitters, milds, darts, and piano sing along—a happy, festive atmosphere.

The most noticeable sign that the war was over were **lights** and more lights, street and house lights with shades open—all over lights and fireworks.

This was a **big day** in history.

The Photo Lab

After my crew and my other flight crew friends from Hut #20 had gone back to the States, I made friends with some of the ground personnel, MPs, mechanics, and spent a lot of time at the photo lab.

These were the photographers and photo technicians who took and developed the pictures taken on the base. It was also their responsibility to develop the pictures taken from the aircraft during the bomb runs on clear days. It was these pictures that often showed the success or failure of the missions.

After V-E Day the photo lab guys were cleaning house, and they offered me the pick of the hundreds of leftover photos. I took my share!

The photo lab gave me many pictures of target strikes. All were unidentified; I have no idea where they were taken. The following two were just a few of the many I had.

A very battered airfield somewhere in Germany. (Photo courtesy of the photo lab.)

A smoking target somewhere along a river—could be the Rhine. A lonely B-24, The Liberator, another heavy bomber in the 8th Air Force. (Photo courtesy of the photo lab.)

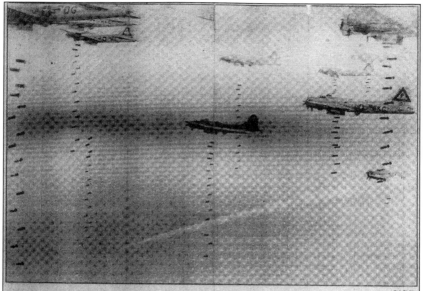

S&S file

A formation of B-17 Flying Fortresses from the 8th Air Force drops bombs on railroad lines in the area around Dresden, Germany, in April 1945. Some Allied pilots who attacked Germany during World War II have become friends with German pilots who defended it.

Bombs Away!

The clipping above shows the 384th Bomb Group (Triangle P) dropping their bombs on the city of Dresden, Germany. When the lead bombardier of a formation gives the command, "Bombs away," the lead drops his bombs; within seconds, the others in the formation will "toggle on" or release their bombs. If the lead plane of that formation misses a target, they all miss the target.

Nearing the end of the war in April of 1945, the city of Dresden was bombed several times by night by the British Air Force and by day by the American 8th Air Force.

In 1972, my daughter Kathleen taught school in Germany and one of her associates, Frau Barbel Nixdorf, had taken shelter during the constant bombardment in the basement of their home in Dresden, Germany. She described her experience as "pure hell;" she has suffered effects from the bombing her whole life.

May 14, 1945—Returning French P.O.W.s

Today I had another great experience flying again with a make-up crew as radio operator.

The mission for the 457th today was to Linz, Austria, where we picked up a load of French P.O.W.s and returned them to a base near Paris. Our B-17s didn't offer many comforts, but P.O.W.s could care less. Somehow they had obtained a generous supply of French cognac and were in a party mood as they climbed aboard. We were treated as their liberators; they offered to share with us their cognac and gave us the traditional kiss on both cheeks, which I would have enjoyed had they been from the French Nurse Corps. Most had been P.O.W.s for four years and more.

The round trip flight was about eleven hours—a full day.

Returning Home

May 28, 1945—Back to the States—And Then?

Since May 8, the day the war ended, rumors have been running rampant as to what was ahead for the 457th. Many were convinced we would be sent directly to the Pacific Theatre, but I for one believed we would first go back to the States for new assignments, and that is exactly what we would be doing.

Today official word had come down that starting within a few days crews would start flying back to the States. Word had it that crews that had only recently arrived here and had flown only a few missions would be the first to leave—getting back for reassignment to the Pacific. Next would be the combat crews that had flown several missions but were still together, then flying personnel who were not assigned to a crew, such as myself, would fly back with a crew as a passenger. Finally, the ground crews and all other necessary personnel (cooks, military police, etc.) would stay until the base closed; they would be going back by ships.

Immediately I decided I would prefer to stay as long as possible. I also reasoned that I might never again visit England, so I would like to see as much of the countryside as possible.

June 2, 1945—The Exodus Begins

Today the first of the crews started their flight back to the States. Sure, it looked inviting to be back home in a matter of hours, but I had made a decision, and it was the right one.

I went to both the base and squadron headquarters asking for permission to stay until the base closed. Jokingly I said, "I would be glad to be the one to turn off the lights." Since most guys were just itching to get a flight home, I was told I could no doubt stay until the end. I would be doing limited duties such as tending the orderly room, answering phone calls, and performing miscellaneous office duties.

June 3 to June 17, 1945—A Time for Goodbyes

During this time I did do limited office duties at the squadron office but also had time to go up to the Skipton/York area to say goodbye to friends I had up there. I made a day trip to the Cambridge Cemetery to visit the graves of Rinehart and Hendrickson. Almost on a daily basis I visited Frank and Rose Warren in Sawtry. Even though I traveled alone, I enjoyed it.

June 17, 1945—It's Time to Leave

When I arrived here ten months ago, I started dreaming of the day my name would be on the shipping orders to go home. Well, today June 17, my name was there. I am to leave on June 19—a train ride to South Hampton and sail from there on June 21.

Sure, it would be nice to be home, but I was not excited about leaving. I liked the British people; I had made many good friends. Some of my buddies called me a "Limey Lover," a term that has a negative connotation, but that didn't bother me a bit. I would soon have to say "Cheerio" to jolly old England, and I would be sad.

A Time for Goodbyes

It was hard to say goodbye to my British friends, but the most emotional farewell was on or about June 15, 1945, when I made my last trip to the Cambridge Military Cemetery to visit the graves of our two crew members.

Grave of Cliff Hendrickson.

Grave of Earl Rinehart.

June 21 to June 27, 1945
Sailing for Home Aboard the General W. P. Richardson

We sailed out of Southampton in the afternoon of the 21st, destination Boston, USA.

Shortly after leaving Southampton, my name and several others was called on the ship's intercom to report to such and such a place at such and such a time for a meeting. At this meeting we were told that we were responsible to assign the duties such as cleaning latrines, sweeping and mopping the floors, and general housekeeping duties to the sixty to seventy men in our bay areas. When I checked the roster of the men in my area, I discovered most were from the infantry, a rough and tough group. These men did not have a great deal of respect for my Air Corps T/Sgt rank; for them rank was hard to come by—most were privates and corporals. They were vocal and resented taking orders from an Air Corps T/Sgt. The Air Corps group I had been with from the 457th soon recognized my problem and quickly volunteered to take their turns at the duties; soon I had set up a schedule for the entire six sailing days. After the first day, and seeing how these jobs were not too menial for those of us from the Air Corps, a few of the infantry troops asked if they could help, too, so we had the cleanest area on the entire ship, and they all seemed to take pride in that. I was chosen to be in charge of this duty not because I had the experience, but rather because I was the highest-ranking non-commissioned officer in the alphabetical sequence in this bay. It was a good experience as a study in human relations, and a real lesson in life's school.

The *SS General Richardson* was a large troop ship although not nearly the size of the *Ile De France* or the *Queen Elizabeth*. We were well fed and the chow lines were not long. We were comfortable in our *spotlessly* clean Infantry/Air Corps Bay. I had heard horrible reports from those who had come over on the *Ile De France* about the food quality and long chow lines. Again, I think I was lucky to sail home on the *General Richardson*.

We have been told the ocean was unusually calm, but one morning while we were in chapel, it became wild. Guys who did not have a hold on a post or a rail actually fell down. Several did become ill, but I wasn't bothered at all. After our housekeeping duties and between the two big meals, time was spent reading and playing a lot of cards.

Most played poker but that was not for this novice. There were some masterful card sharks aboard.

At mid morning on June 27 we sighted land—**the good old USA**. The ship's horns sounded, cheers went up, and a lot of men shed tears. It was an emotional experience.

By mid afternoon we were walking down the gangplank at Boston Harbor with a crowd of people cheering, bands playing, fireworks, and welcome-home banners everywhere. It gave me goose bumps.

I was proud to be an American and glad to be home!

June 27 to June 29, 1945
Camp Miles Standish Near Boston, MA

Shortly after arrival at Boston Harbor, we were escorted to trucks and an hour or so ride to Camp Miles Standish Military Base. Here we were again greeted with fanfare, not usual for military bases—a hero's welcome. We were assigned to comfortable bunks in spotless barracks. We were told we had time to shower and freshen up before a **big dinner**. Showers we did need because facilities on the ship were not great!

Next came the dinner, not elegant, served in a typical GI mess hall, but the food was outstanding. The largest T-bone steaks ever, served hot, and if we wanted a second or third, just holler—potatoes, vegetables, rolls, and the dinner topped off with mounds of ice cream—a real welcome-home dinner. The waiters and KP help were all German P.O.W.s, some with minor disabilities, slight limps, missing fingers and the like. All were very pleasant and seemed happy to be waiting on us.

After dinner, I found a phone booth just outside the mess hall and decided to call home to let them know I was back in the States. Mother and Pearl didn't have a phone, so I called Clara and Carvell. I loaded up on coins, called the operator, and gave her the phone number. She said I could deposit the coins after I had finished my call. Clara and Carvell were, of course, happy I was back safe, and we talked for about ten minutes about when I would arrive in Hendricks, etc. When I had finished talking, I signaled the operator and asked for the charges. Her reply? "I heard a bit of your conversation soldier;

welcome home; this call is on me." A pleasant surprise! Since I was in Massachusetts, I thought I should call my buddy Sid in Ludlow, and sure enough, he was home. What fun it was to hear his voice again. I told him I would be in Hendricks about the 4th of July. His parting remarks, "We'll see, I just might go out there."

The next morning started the typical military processing. First another welcome-home speech, a complete physical, a movie on the symptoms of combat fatigue, what was next for us—the whole day spent with the physicals, films, speeches, etc. Now I knew I was still in the military.

The following morning, June 29, another meeting was held. We were told our shipping orders would be ready to pick up at 1300, and we would then be free to leave for our furloughs.

Waiting for shipping orders was an anxious time. I knew we would be getting furloughs, but I did not know what base I would be assigned to after the furlough. Before we left England, we learned that the crews that had flown back had all been assigned to the Air Corps Base at Sioux Falls, SD. Word had also came back that the facilities at the base were way overtaxed with the influx of over 20,000 troops within just a few days. Some described the conditions as utter *chaos*. So had I flown home early, I, too, would have been in that mess. Sioux Falls is less than one hundred miles from Hendricks, so in some respects, assignment to Sioux Falls would have been nice, but I reasoned I might be spending the rest of my life on the prairie of southwestern Minnesota in the Sioux Falls area. Since before entering the service I had worked at Consolidated Aircraft in San Diego and just loved it, my hope was that assignment would be to southern California.

At 1300 I got my shipping orders and guess what? It read, "After your delay en route, on July 29, 1945, you are to report to the Santa Anna Air Corps Base, Santa Anna, California." **Ideal**! This base is billed as the country club of air bases.

Again—**I lucked out!**

June 29 thru July 24, 1945

Nearly a Month of Furlough Time
June 29 to July 2, 1945

The train ride from Boston to Minneapolis was long, hot, and uncomfortable, but even so, I still enjoy traveling by train. I had a layover in Chicago and tried to contact The Head, Louie Dahle, but no luck. From Chicago I called Minneapolis, Geneva 0093, Gurine and Mert's, to let them know I was en route. When I got to Minneapolis, I had no problem getting the Chicago-Penn streetcar to 26th and Chicago and Columbus Avenue, my second home. As usual, I got a hearty welcome, and Gurine had a bedroom ready for me.

It had been one year since I had been home, and I remember well how much Colleen and Gary had changed; both were and always will be special—Colleen (a novelty) our first niece, and Gary the first nephew, the most lovable with his wet diapers and all.

I'm shown here with my nephew Gary Ellis and niece Colleen Ellis in front of Moron Manor near my Columbus Avenue home.

July 3 and 4, 1945

I spent two days in Minneapolis. On July 4th, Bob Schumacker and Andy Antolick, with whom I had worked at Ohio Chemical Company in Minneapolis, got together for a night on the town.

July 5, 1945

I took the evening bus to Marshall where mother, Pearl, and Carvell met me—a happy homecoming!

The next morning I had to go to see "my little girl," Carol, now seven months old. She was as cute as the pictures Clara had sent to me in England. There were times and places when I chose to play the role of a happily married man with a wife and a baby back in the States. On those occasions, I would pull out Carol's picture and say, "This is my little girl."

The picture of Carol that I carried.

A picture of me holding Carol when I was home on furlough.

Hendricks servicemen were now returning home almost on a daily basis—some already discharged, others like me, just on furlough. Two who recently came home were Perwin Knutson and Donnie Fjeseth. Both had been gunners in the 8th Air Force and both had been shot down and had been P.O.W.s. Art and Gina Uteseth invited Perwin, Donnie, and me to a welcome-home dinner at their home. Of course, the three of us who had all been in the 8th Air Force just had to trade stories about our missions. It turned out we had all three been on some of the same missions. **A fun night**.

Saturday Evening, July 7, 1945, Shall Forever Be a Special Memory...

During this furlough on Saturday, July 7, 1945, at approximately 9 p.m., I met for the first time the love of my life, Elvina Bernice Hoversten. Two years, one month and one day later we were married.

Summer Saturday nights were special in Hendricks. Farmers came to town to shop, chew Copenhagen and spit and visit, mostly in Norwegian. The entire length of Main Street, all two blocks, had cars parked with mostly the "Kjerringes" (the wives) looking at the goings on. Basically, there were those who came to see, and the others to be seen.

Saturday night was truly a social event. On this Saturday, the weather was beautiful and Main Street, to a large extent due to the number of servicemen home whom people had not seen for years, was particularly crowded and spirited.

I, too, was part of the scene on Main Street, visiting with friends. At the most popular spot on Main Street in front of Andy's Café, by the popcorn stand (which Andy would bring out only on nice Saturday nights), people stopped to chat for a few minutes and then move on. Betty Ann Erickson, a life-long friend, stopped by to say " hi" and to tell me she was now in nurse's training and the Nurse Cadet Program. If the war continued, she would be inducted into the military upon graduation. Then Betty introduced me to her girlfriend, also in nurse's training and the Nurse Cadet Program. Her friend immediately caught my eye. She was short and cute with sparkling expressive eyes and a natural, captivating smile. My immediate thoughts were, "I'd like to get to know her tonight," but quickly gave up on the idea knowing I couldn't separate the two, and it would be impossible to quickly find a date for Betty. Betty was a nice gal, but as far as I knew seldom dated in Hendricks. Perhaps a couple reasons were she was the daughter of our conservative Norwegian Lutheran pastor, and she was tall, over six feet. I knew it would take just the right person for Betty; I knew of no such one in Hendricks. The next day we were having a family picnic at C & C's (Clara and Carvell's) cottage at the Lake Park, when I again saw Betty and her "cute as a bug's ear" friend. Had I been out of the service, I know I would have found a way to date her. My thoughts were perhaps we'll meet again.

Footnote 1: Just two years, one month, and one day after I met Betty's cute friend, Elvina Bernice Hoversten, we were married in Hendricks, and Betty was the maid of honor. My dear Bernice, I swear to you this is exactly my memory of July 7 and 8, 1945. As a good Lutheran, I declare unto you **this is most certainly true.**

Footnote 2: Not long after we were married, we found who we thought was just the right person for Betty Ann; one of my classmates at National Radio School, a handsome, 6'2"-tall, 100% Norwegian who spoke that language fluently. Soon there was another wedding in Hendricks (Bernice and I were attendants) when Betty Ann Erickson became Mrs. Joe Krobel.

July 15, 1945

My dear friend Szydlowski came from Massachusetts to Hendricks to spend the rest of my furlough time with me. What a great reunion we had.

My buddy Sid called from Minneapolis saying he would be out on the evening bus. When I told Pearl, she beamed. You see, as he had promised when he left England, Sid had gone out to Hendricks in May and spent a week. He and Pearl had become good friends.

What fun it was to see and be with Sid again. We went to dances in Toronto and at the Bohemian Hall. We fished on Lake Hendricks using Carvell's big, heavy wooden boat. I remember Carvell jokingly telling us we had to wash his car for using his boat. We did it, too!

Sid was impressed with all the walleyes we caught. I remember Mother frying up big platters, and we had a fish dinner in our back yard. Sid had never eaten walleyes before and just loved the way Mother pan-fried them.

Sid just loved it in Hendricks and made a big hit with my family. Pearl particularly enjoyed their evening walks to Lake Park.

On July 24, Sid and I took the bus back to Minneapolis, spent two days with Gurine and Mert, and an evening with friends of mine whom Sid had met when we were at McDill Field in Tampa, Florida.

July 26, 1945, Sid boarded the train back for Massachusetts and I a train bound for California. Although it was a long uneventful ride, I enjoyed it. To me, riding the rails is always exciting.

Footnote: Sid came back to Hendricks again in early August 1947 when he was the best man at our wedding on August 8, 1947.

California Here I Come...

When we were going through processing at Camp Miles Standish, I requested that my next assignment would be on the West Coast, but **never, never** did I expect to luck out and be assigned to the "country club" of Army Air bases. Six weeks of luxury living with zero duties.

Memories of Santa Anna Air Base
July 29 to September 4, 1945

This base was even nicer than I had expected. It was a permanent Air Corps Base that had existed before the war—tree-lined streets, two-story barracks, cheerful mess halls, and an NCO Club. It was even nicer than McDill Field, Florida.

The first few days were spent having physical and psychological exams. I even had a session with a psychiatrist. Apparently, I had endured the stress of combat quite well since I had just the one session.

Most all of us here were veterans of combat, most from the ETO (European Theater of Operation). We were treated royally. The mess hall was open twenty-four hours a day. If I had been on pass and came back to the base at three a.m. and hungry—no problem—go to the mess hall and order up. "I want a steak, French fries, and a malted milk shake." Pure luxury! We never had duties; occasionally we were required to watch military films, listen to lectures and the like; just a few things to keep us occupied.

When nothing was on schedule, we were free to use our class "A" passes to go to Los Angeles, San Diego, or wherever in the area. On my first pass I went to San Diego where I had worked at Consolidated Aircraft in 1942. I still had many friends there, and they welcomed me. One family invited me to their home for dinner and then drove me back to the base.

Not one single friend or even an acquaintance from the 457th was at Santa Anna. Most had been sent to Sioux Falls. I met a real nice fellow Minnesotan, Sylvan Bauer, from Anoka and teamed up with him. We went on passes together, most often to Los Angeles. I remember well the night he and I went to the Brown Derby in Hollywood; the headlining entertainment that night was Les Brown and his "Band of Renown" featuring Doris Day as vocalist singing *Sentimental Journey*. That was a great evening.

All this free time and going to places like the Brown Derby was hard on the pocketbook, so I took a part-time job as a bartender at the Officers' Club. With a wage and tips, it really helped my cash flow. One night while on duty, up to the bar came two guys from Hendricks—Lowell (Big Poop) Midtaune and Lloyd (Buddy) Hexum. What a surprise! After the club closed at midnight, the three of us went to a nearby amusement park. We rode a few rides, hustled cute gals, and had a picture taken (next page). After a few beers, we had the bright idea to send it on to our hometown paper, *The Hendricks Pioneer*. Fortunately, no one followed up on that. We did have a fun night!

August 1945—Santa Anna—Santa Monica, California

On a trip to Los Angeles, I got in touch with and spent an evening with a good buddy from Hut #20, Art Astor. I remember that being a fun get-together. On yet another visit to Los Angeles, I met another friend, William "Bill" Biggie whom I first met at gunnery school. From gunnery school, we were together until we arrived in England. Bill was not in our bomb group, but I did visit him at his base in England. Bill had a knack for getting into trouble, never anything serious, but he said he was always at the wrong place at the wrong time. Just before leaving for overseas, he was busted from sergeant to private for a brawl he said he had nothing to do with. I spent a night with Bill at his parents' very nice home in Glendale; his parents were very hospitable. That evening Bill and I visited some of his haunts and cruised Glendale in his convertible—a really fun day and night.

Left to right: Lowell "Big Poop" Midtaune, Lloyd "Buddy" Hexum, and me, Clifford "Cooky" Digre. We had our picture taken at the amusement park photo studio: "Santa Monica Jail."

Note: When I was growing up, most guys had nicknames. Big Poop's brother, Arnold, was known as "Little Poop." My own nickname ("Cooky") came from my next-door neighbor, Donnie Knutson. When we were perhaps three or four years old, he could not say Clifford so, when he came to our door, he asked for "Cooky" to come out and play. Nicknames in Hendricks could be a story unto themselves.

Life at the Santa Anna Air Base was luxury living for a service man, but after many visits to Los Angeles, San Diego, and the beaches, I began to look forward to moving on.

Dropping the "A" bombs on Hiroshima and Nagasaki quickly ended the war in the Pacific. Japan surrendered on August 15, 1945; the official papers of surrender were signed on September 2, 1945.

Talk of upcoming discharges soon became the topic of the day. Preparing us for the discharges soon to come, notices went up on the bulletin boards advising us that we could request to be transferred to bases near our homes. My choices were either Truax Field, Madison, Wisconsin, or the Air Base at Sioux Falls, South Dakota. I had heard that things were still a mess at Sioux Falls, so I elected to be transferred to Truax Field.

On September 11, 1945, I boarded a train in Los Angeles, arriving in Madison, Wisconsin, on September 14, 1945.

Memories of Truax Field
September 14 to October 7, 1945

During the military buildup and throughout the war in Europe, Truax Field was one of the three radio operator and mechanics schools for the Air Corps. I had many friends who had attended this school, and although Truax was a great base, now the radio school had closed; the base was primarily a processing center. Some of the veterans were there to be processed for reassignment, but the majority were awaiting discharge. Most all were transients.

Since I had been stationed at Truax for less than a month, the base held no special attachment to me. To a large extent, it was a big let down after the luxury of Santa Anna Air Base. The best part of being at Truax was the closeness to Minneapolis, only 300 miles.

During my short stay there, I did make two trips to Minneapolis. Even though the distance to Minneapolis was only 300 miles, train connections were not good. There were no direct trains, and I always had to make one transfer.

On one occasion, I decided to try hitchhiking, and that was a memory that really stands out. Here's the story:

On a Friday afternoon at about 1400 hours, I posted myself on US Highway 12 not far from the base, the main route from Chicago to

Minneapolis. There were perhaps a dozen of us out there hitchhiking west. My chances of getting a ride did not look good, but within a few minutes, a car pulled up to me. The driver asked where I was going, and when I said Minneapolis, he said, "Well, I can give you a ride a few miles down the road, if you like." I reasoned that a few miles would take me away from this cluster of other fellows, so I said "Great!" When he said a few miles, I thought perhaps twenty or thirty miles or so, but soon we had gone one hundred miles and still going west on US 12, all the time visiting. He seemed interested in my combat flying experiences, so we kept talking and time went fast. Soon we had gone two hundred miles and were still looking into the sun. As we were crossing the St. Croix River at the Wisconsin-Minnesota border, I just had to say, "This is a lot more ride than the few miles I expected." He explained, "Whenever I pick up a hitchhiker, I always say I can give you a ride for a few miles." This, he said, gives him an out. "If the person makes me nervous, or if I am bored with his company, I just say, 'This is as far as I am going.'" He added, "You have been good company, and yes, I am going to Minneapolis." He told me he was temporarily working in Chicago. His family lived in Wayzata and he made this trip every weekend. He dropped me off right at the door at Columbus Avenue at Gurine and Mert's, my second home—another experience!

Another memory, but not a good one, happened on the night of October 6, 1945, the night before my discharge. The barracks at Truax were not what they had been at Santa Anna. Here we had a clothes locker without a lock and a footlocker without a lock. Every night here, I had slept with my billfold under my pillow, but on this last night, I was careless. I had left my billfold in my trousers hung up in the closet in an unlocked locker. During that night, someone came through the barracks and snatched ten billfolds out of the unlocked lockers, including mine.

The loss of $10 in cash was hard to take, but my biggest loss was my Short Snorter bills (See April 21-23, 1945). A Short Snorter Collection of Bills was a tradition of the flight members of the Air Corps. The first bill started with an American dollar. Each serviceman would collect an equivalent dollar bill from each country that we had been in. So for example, I had a German mark, Belgian franc, Icelandic kroner, and English pound. All of these bills were taped together with

Scotch tape, and we carried this treasured memento in our wallets. The longer the snorter, the more impressive. I had at least seven or eight of these. I had had this collection since training in Florida, combat in Europe, back to the States, and now to lose it on my last night in the service just made me sick. All in the barracks who had been robbed went in mass to the MPs, but all to no avail. Later I wrote an article that was published in the base paper appealing for the return of my "Short Snorter"—no luck. By noon on October 7, 1945, I had gone through a brief discharge ceremony, received my travel pay of $14.10 and one hundred dollars of my three hundred dollars mustering-out pay, my discharge papers, and I was on my way to Minneapolis as a civilian—Mr. Clifford B. Digre.

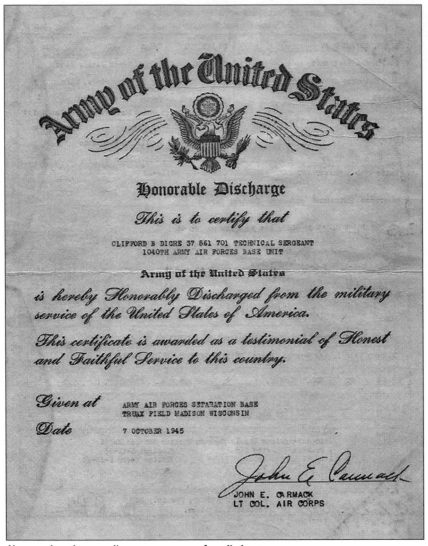

Above and on the preceding page are some of my discharge papers.

What Happened To The Crew?

These memories would not be complete without telling what happened after the war to each of our crew members, starting with the number-one person:

Pilot "Robbie" Robertson...

Robbie had been in the Army Air Corps before Pearl Harbor so we knew he intended to make the military a career. Robbie had distinguished himself in England when he became a 457th Bomb Group lead pilot. He continued to receive honors and promotions in the Air Force. Robbie retired with the rank of Lt. Colonel, dividing his time between his home in Florida where his daughter, Grace, lived and at his villa in Spain.

Returning to the USA after completing his missions, Robbie became an avid golfer and a good one. That doesn't surprise me since the Robbie I knew was a perfectionist doing everything well.

See my meeting Robbie in 2003 at the end of this chapter.

Bombardier Charles "C.W." Carbery...

Charlie returned to his roots in New York City. Within days after his discharge, he was back at various positions with a jewelry-manufacturing firm he had worked at before he enlisted in the Army Air Corps.

He soon met Betty, a lovely American Airline flight attendant, and they were married on April 17, 1948. Shortly after their marriage, C. W. or "Buddy," a nickname we knew nothing about, decided to strike out on his own and start a wholesale jewelry business. He chose Kansas as his home base and has lived there ever since.

Charlie and Betty have three children. Their son, Craig, born in 1949, lives in Kansas; their daughter, Mimi, the musician, born in 1951, lives in New Orleans; and the youngest of the family, Suzanne, born in 1956, lives in Washington, D.C.

When he retired, Charlie spent his days reading *Businessmen's Daily*, *The Wall Street Journal*, and tracking his many good investments.

Charlie passed away on July 22, 2005.

Navigator Elmer "Luke" Mankin...

After his discharge, Elmer returned to his home in Alexandria, Virginia. He completed his college education and his entire working career was in various management positions with Washington, D.C., utilities.

After retirement, Elmer and his second wife, Marguerite, made their home in Gransonville, Maryland, a Baltimore suburb.

A few years after retirement Elmer had a severe stroke that left him partially paralyzed with difficulty speaking. This was followed by a series of small strokes. Elmer passed away in the fall of 1997.

Radio Operator Gunner Bernard "Bernie" Stutman...

Bernie the entrepreneur returned to Philadelphia and his food business interests he had even during his time in the service.

After the war, my diary records helped Bernie establish a claim with the Veterans' Administration that he had suffered frostbite on our ninth mission on September 30, 1944.

In the fall of 1972, Bernice and I had dinner with Bernie and his charming wife, Marge, in Philadelphia. At that time I learned he had had one leg amputated. In 1990 I received a letter from his son Randall saying Bernie had passed away after a long illness caused by the frostbite that had taken both legs and one hand. Randall lives in Berwyn, PA. Since then I have met Randall Stutman in 2007, his wife, Linda, and son Benjamin at his ranch in southern Utah, The Shooting Star Ranch. We spent an entire weekend reminiscing about his father, Bernie, and the crew.

Tail Gunner John Brown...

John also returned to New York City after his discharge. I know nothing about his family or activities. After the military I learned through a tracer that he had died in the early 1950s.

Engineer Gunner Louie "The Head" Dahle...

After his discharge, The Head did not immediately return to his Chicago roots. He traveled the country, mostly the West, and even attended college in Wyoming. After a while, he decided to return to Chicago and settle down a bit. I don't think he really did settle down until he met Helen, the love of his life, now one of our dear friends.

After their marriage, Helen and Louie lived on the north side of Chicago before moving to the northern suburbs. The Head found his niche in construction and built himself a beautiful house in Lake Bluff, Illinois. Here they raised their three daughters—Denise, Desiree, and Dominique.

After retirement, The Head and Helen moved to beautiful Montana where they still reside.

Our good friend Art Astor...

Art was not a member of our crew but he had lived in our Hut #20 since the day he came to the base. When his crew was shot down on September 28, 1944, Art was then orphaned, and we made him an honorary member of the Robbie Robertson crew.

After the war, Art returned to his California home and continued in the entertainment business he loved.

Art owns and has interests in several radio stations all over southern California. He also has a collection of valuable antique automobiles and a museum that houses the automobiles and radios and televisions from times past. A mutual acquaintance has told me Art's radio businesses are very successful and that he "isn't hurting." Art and his lovely wife, Toni, live in an upscale southern California community.

Waist Gunner Julie "Korny" Kornblatt...

Korny returned to his New York City roots. The very day he came home he renewed a friendship with Judy, a girl he had known for only two weeks before going overseas. The friendship quickly became hot romance and Judy and Julie were husband and wife within two weeks of his return.

They moved fast. Next they were off for Washington, D.C., where Korny attended and graduated from law school. He took a job with the federal government before returning to New York City where he continued his legal work in a combination state/county/city agency where he worked until retiring in Arizona. Their daughter Janet, an attorney, and son-in-law Sam Benjamin, a physician, reside in Scottsdale, Arizona. Julie and Judy's two sons, Steven and Ira, and their families live in New York City.

Korny and I left England in 1945, and we next met at a 457th reunion in Reno in 1995, fifty years later. It was at that reunion that I first met his very sharp wife, Judy. Since then we have enjoyed many fun days together in Arizona where my wife, Bernice, and I have spent time as Minnesota snowbirds.

Armament Gunner Stanley "Sid" Szydlowski...

We all seemed to return to our roots and Sid was no exception, returning to the central Massachusetts area. Not finding a job to his liking, Sid became bored and restless. He went to Boston and joined the Maritime Service. Sid made two trips around the world including a stop at Reykjavik, Iceland, where we had stopped on our flight from the USA to England.

Sid and I were special buddies—the 100% Polish and the 100% Norwegian. When Sid was the best man at our wedding in August 1947, and met my 100% Norwegian wife, he took my lead, went back home to the Polish community he had lived in since childhood, and found his love, "Tillie," 100% Polish. Tillie is another of our favorite people. Sid and Tillie have a son, Michael, and a daughter, Sandy.

Sid spent most of his working years with the chemical firm giant, The Monsanto Company, and then enjoyed his retirement in the beautiful rambler home he helped build on a large wooded lot in central Massachusetts.

Since the war, for the past fifty+ years on every Christmas morning, Sid has called me without fail. On Christmas morning 2004 I didn't get my Christmas morning call, and I knew something was wrong. The next day, his son, Michael, called us to say Sid had died from a stroke on December 26, 2004.

Myself—Clifford "CB" Digre...

After the war I had three ordinary jobs before I met and married the love of my life, Elvina Bernice Hoversten, a nurse. We were married in 1947. The details of this will follow.

I decided I needed more education. The Army Signal Corps school at Camp Kohler had given me a great background in radio operations and mechanics, so this was the field I chose. While in school I became interested in loudspeakers and now, fifty-plus-years later, we still have a family-owned speaker manufacturing business called MISCO (Minneapolis Speaker Company). My son Dan is the general manager of MISCO. Dan is married to Luz Paz; their daughter is Cali Berit.

My daughter Carrie is the company bookkeeper and is married to Chad Murphy; their children are Jordan and Joshua. My older daughter, Kathleen, is a neurologist/neuro-ophthalmologist at the University of Utah in Salt Lake City. She is married to Dr. Michael Varner, a highly regarded obstetrician/gynecologist; their children are Johanna and Gita. My son Rolland, a dentist in Hendricks, Minnesota, is married to Janet. They have two sons, Peder and Neal, and two daughters — Amy Cech, married to D. Stepan, and Ann Cech whose husband is Jeremy Aho; their children are Kaleb, Landon, and Karlee.

Bernice and I are semi-retired and find time to enjoy our lake cottage, time with our four children, their spouses, and our nine grandchildren.

I know for certain this story is not without errors, but I believe it is mostly correct from the best of my memory and the information and letters I have received from crew members and their families.

Some Visits After the War . . .

Since WWII, I have had contact with every crew member or their families with the exception of John Brown, who passed away shortly after the war, and our copilot Cliff Hendrickson's family. Cliff's hometown was Jasper, Indiana. Returning from Florida one spring, we spent four hours in Jasper trying to locate someone in his family. I learned that his parents were deceased and that his only sibling, a sister, had left the Jasper area and her whereabouts were unknown.

There is a very impressive plaque in the Jasper City Center listing all the area servicemen killed in the war. There listed is:

Lt. Cliff Hendrickson
Killed December 23, 1944

From Jasper we drove up to Romney, Indiana, Earl Rinehart's hometown. We stopped at a small cafe and visited with the local people there. We soon learned that the Rineharts were a very prominent family and that Earl, "Tucker," as he is known there, was highly respected. We were directed to the local cemetery where Earl is buried. I also visited with Earl and Ruth's daughter "Sissy," born on September 30, 1944, just eighteen days after Earl was killed. Meeting and visiting with Sissy was emotional for both of us. She is an outstanding young lady. Earl, you would have been proud of her.

I have had contacts and personal visits from several of the Rineharts, Earl's sister Alma and her husband, Myron Miller, and their two children.

I have had many phone calls and personal visits from Earl's conservative, quiet, reserved brother Parker Rinehart, a retired Army Major Sergeant. There was never a dull moment when Parker was around. What a guy! He's as proud as can be of his new grandson named "Tucker," Earl's nickname.

In Florida, I visited with Robbie's daughter, Grace, on two occasions. Both times Robbie was at his villa in Spain. The first time we were together we spent two hours visiting over dinner. On our second meeting she gave Bernice and me, and our daughter Kathleen and her family a behind-the-scenes tour of Epcot Center where she works. Grace is a very bright lady. We could tell as she gave us the tour that she is highly respected by her fellow employees and the staff she manages.

Meeting Robbie 58 Years Later
March 15 and 16, 2003

Finally I had located and arranged a get together with our elusive pilot, William T. Robbie Robertson. It had been 58 years since I last saw him in England.

Bernice and I were with Kathleen, Michael, their daughter Gita and her friend, Katie, vacationing at a condo near Disney World in Orlando. We invited Robbie and his daughter, Grace, to dinner. We had all met Grace before when she gave us a personal first-class tour of Disney World where she worked as a very knowledgeable horticulturist, perhaps the best on Disney's staff. Would I recognize him? Would he still be the self-assured, very definite, a bit cocky person I remembered? Robbie was a commissioned officer and I was a non-com so we socialized very little. But Robbie always treated his entire crew the same, reminding us all that we were a team and all were officers, some commissioned and some non-commissioned. He was somewhat a loner—usually going on passes to London alone.

When he pulled up and parked in front of the condo, I immediately felt good. Why? Because he was driving a Chevy El Camino, the same color, same model and style as my practical and conservative brother-in-law Carvell drove. Yes, Robbie was the same person I knew, practical, conservative, self-assured, and still had the, "I'm in charge" attitude. His appearance had changed so very little. He was the same Robbie his crew had respected.

After handshakes, a slight embrace, and a few pictures taken by Michael, it was time for introductions. My family was anxious to meet this special person I had talked and bragged about for years. From the time Robbie came, it was non-stop talking and visiting. Grace came directly from her work an hour or so later, so it was then dinner time. Bernice had made lasagna, and it was served with good wine, compliments of Robbie. **A great afternoon and evening!**

The next day Kathleen, Michael, Gita, and Katie flew back to Salt Lake City so Bernice and I checked into a motel in Orlando. That afternoon Robbie and Grace joined us, and while Bernice and Grace visited, Robbie and I discussed my book of memories I had sent to him. He said he read it cover to cover and he was very complimentary. We discussed several of our missions and experiences and we even disagreed on some happenings. But the one thing we did agree on was that our tenth mission, the forced landing in Antwerp, was the highlight mission. From the cockpit he had a different view than Stutman, Sid, Brown, and I had from the waist and radio room.

The following is a summary of our discussion:

The Turnaround and Forced Landing in Antwerp . . .

When we made the turnaround heading for England alone, we were fortunate there was solid overcast beneath us into which we could enter the forced decent. This would offer us some protection from German fighters. We entered the overcast at 15,000 feet and at 10,000 feet Robbie ordered armament gunner Szydlowski to replace the pins in the bombs so they would not detonate when we dropped them. We knew wc would have to drop the bombs to reduce our weight and enable us to possibly fly back to England. As we had no idea where the front lines were, we did not want to drop live bombs on perhaps our friendly troops or cities. We broke out of the overcast at 7,000 feet and the weather was clear. Robbie alerted the crew to a possible crash landing and asked them to watch out for any body of water where we could safely drop our bombs.

Finally at 500 feet we passed a small field as we were flying toward a city that turned out to be Antwerp, Belgium, which Carbery had correctly guessed. On the other side of the city was a body of water into which we dropped our bombs.

Note: Antwerp had been liberated just three days before. The good people of Antwerp later told us that when our plane flew over the city with our bomb bay doors open, they could actually see the bombs and thought for certain they were to be bombed.

Crossing Antwerp, we flew over the water, an estuary of the North Sea, and safely dropped our bomb load. At that very moment we found ourselves with a fighter on each wing tip. They were a couple of English "Typhoon" fighters.

Unable to communicate to indicate that we were friendly, Robbie ordered, "Drop landing gear." Seeing this, the fighters left us and we retracted the gear. This cost us 200 feet, and we found ourselves at 300 feet.

We headed back for the small airfield trying to regain some altitude. Robbie alerted the crew that if the field was friendly, we would attempt a landing. If it wasn't, we would fly as long as we could (toward England) and if we could no longer keep the aircraft flying, Robbie would order the crew to either bail out or he would elect to do a belly landing.

Crossing back over that small airfield Robbie noted there were English "Spitfires" taking off. There was no mistaking that, so we knew we had a friendly airstrip.

We passed the end of the runway onto which we should be landing (into the wind). We kept having trouble with #4 engine that we had shut down and now it started to smoke. It became imperative; we had to land or bail out. We could not take the chance to keep flying in order to come around again and land into the wind. Flying around to the right of the runway we could see "Spitfires" taking off. Robbie ordered our engineer, Dahle, to fire flare, "Red-Red." The ground fired "Red-Red" right back to tell us we could not land. As we turned around again into the approach to land, Robbie ordered Dahle to fire another "Red-Red." "Lower the landing gear," was the next order. We approached the runway flying into the "Spitfires" that were taking off. They veered off and then no more "Spitfires" were taking off.

The "Spitfires" were taking off to attack the German troops no more than three or four miles from the city of Antwerp. We undoubtedly flew right over the German troops on our approach to land.

It was a good landing! We stopped at the very end of the runway. No. 4 engine had stopped smoking so we had no more worry about an explosion, but we were soon aware of eight or ten English military men in front of our aircraft with rifles at fire ready! We explained to the officer in charge who we were and why we were forced to land. At that time the English base commander, a captain (equal in rank to an Air Corps colonel) drove up and dismissed the English officer and the eight or ten military that were standing guard over us. Before the English captain left, he wrote (on a half sheet of paper) a commendation citing Robbie for a job well done in saving the crew and aircraft.

From the captain we learned the Canadian First Army had captured the field just three days before.

On the Antwerp Jail. . .

Bernie Stutman went down to the Century Hotel and asked Robbie to check out the enlisted men's facilities at the city jail. He lost no time in going to the English sergeant in "charge of billets." As he was explaining to the sergeant that all the crew members were officers, an English officer came and asked, "What's the problem?" Robbie replied, "No problem officer, this sergeant is to be commended for the manner in which he is taking care of our crew." With that the officer walked away. The sergeant thanked Robbie and with that our entire crew billeted at the Century Hotel for the next nine days.

On Flying Back to England . . .

On the ninth day in Antwerp, Robbie received a telephone call from Brussels. They had a repaired B-17 aircraft and asked if our crew would be ready to fly it back to England. His answer was simply "Yes, send us a truck!" The next morning we were up at 0700 hours. We had breakfast at the hotel and at 0900 an Army truck picked us up at the hotel entrance for the 50-mile ride back to Brussels. Soon we were flying that war-weary B-17 back to England.

By coincidence that base was "Polebrook" near "Glatton," our own base. Robbie called Glatton, identified our crew and told them we were flying a repaired B-17 from Brussels to Polebrook and would they send a truck over to bring us home. The answer, "The truck is on its way." He then contacted Polebrook and told them we were returning one of their aircraft and would they clear us in. By the time we landed and turned the aircraft to Polebrook our truck had arrived. We were soon on our way returning to our home base Glatton. Robbie and I agreed that this, our tenth mission, was without a doubt the most dramatic of all missions flown by our crew.

We Remembered and Reminisced About John Wilson . . .

The sixteen-year-old English air cadet rode his bike from his home in Peterborough to our base just as often as he could. Many times he told me it would be, "pouring rain but that didn't stop me."

John logged flying time as a passenger with several crews on training flights, but was particularly fond of flying with the Robbie Robertson crew. He was proud to tell us that "Robbie even let me sit in **his** seat." John respectfully referred to Robbie as the "Great Character" and Elmer Mankin he called "The Rebel." After the war, I saw and visited with John at several state-side reunions and spent time with him when I last visited our base in England in 1999. He wrote to me often and primarily, I think, to see if I have had word about his hero, Robbie. John passed away on October 19, 2001. His obituary is from the Nov.-Dec. 2001, *457th Association Newsletter*:

"We were saddened to learn of the death of John Wilson, one of our long-time English historians, on October 19, 2001. John Walker telephoned to inform us of the death, and report that he and the other historians would represent the 457th at the funeral service.

Wilson's association with the Bomb Group goes back to our days at Glatton when, as a teenage member of the Air Training Corps, he was able to log flight time as a passenger on training flights.

John was a FOTE member and had been quite active in the earlier days of our organization attending a number of stateside reunions as a guest of several of our members.

John Wilson, an English air cadet

The contributions of our English historians are greatly appreciated and vital to the success of our organization."

Robbie and I ended our afternoon of remembering and reminiscing about a couple of lighter events.

Duets Sid and I Sang on the Aircraft's Intercom . . .

Szydlowski, the 100% Pollack, and I, the 100% Norwegian, became close friends, spending most of our off-duty time and leaves together. We both spoke a bit of our parents' language. Sid taught me some Polish words and I, in turn, taught Sid some Norwegian. Sid taught me to sing a Polish song, the name I can't remember, and I taught Sid the song *Nar jeg var en Gute* (*When I was a Boy*). Neither of the songs would have been appropriate for church Sunday Schools.

When we had memorized the two songs, we decided we would sing to the crew over the intercom, Sid from the waist and I from the ball turret. We chose to sing them one day when the plane was bouncing around from the burst of flak, over which we had no defense. The crew found it funny, so from then on every time the flak became intense, Hendrickson gave the command "OK, Sid and Cliff, give us that Polish-Norwegian serenade." We would burst into song and it did lighten the moment.

The Cockpit Fire . . .

Robbie reminded me of this event that could have been serious but turned out to be really humorous. Neither one of us could remember the mission number nor was it important, but we both remember the incident. I only heard about it while Robbie saw it unfold from start to finish.

Nearly all combat crew members were heavy smokers and for the most part our crew was no exception. We were allowed to smoke and most of us were chain smokers. As we started to climb to altitude we knew we could not smoke after we put on our masks and went on oxygen, usually around 10,000 feet. Our copilot, Cliff Hendrickson, was as heavy a smoker as any of us and he, too, smoked as many cigarettes as he could before going on oxygen.

On this particular mission, Cliff had already plugged in his oxygen mask when he decided to have just one more cigarette. Louie Dahle thinks we may have been close to 15,000 feet when Cliff decided he needed another fix. With oxygen flowing, he held his mask a short distance from his face and lit up. Instantly the oxygen ignited his mask and according to Dahle, it threw a flame two feet long. Cliff started to bang the mask against the control panel attempting to put the fire out, while Dahle went for the fire extinguisher planning to use it on Cliff and the mask. Before Dahle could activate the extinguisher, Robbie had the fire out and everything was under control. Dahle asked Robbie, "How did you do that?" Robbie replied, "Very simple, Dahle. I reached down and unplugged his hose. Eliminate the oxygen and flow, and you have no more fire!"

Cliff was not seriously burned although his eyebrows were nearly singed off. The most damage to Cliff was the temporary devastation to his ego and pride with the loss of his perfectly groomed "Clark Gable" mustache. I was told he took a lot of razzing when he showed up at the bar of the Officers Club. Dahle said Cliff's oxygen mask was ruined but fortunately Dahle carried spare masks, headsets, parachutes, and the like. Combat was always scary but fortunately we found ways to lighten things up.

The two get-togethers Robbie and I had reminiscing about tour experiences were very special and hopefully we will meet again either in Orlando or Minneapolis.

As I have been writing this, I am even more convinced that our crew was outstanding; I am proud to say: "I was a member of the original Wm. T. Robbie Robertson crew."

March 15, 2003. Finally, Robbie (right) & I meet after 58 years!

CHAPTER 3

Into Life:
The Two Years After the Military and Beyond

October 1945 thru December 1947

The first week as a civilian I decided to stay in Minneapolis and start sorting out my options for the future. Of course I stayed at my second home on Columbus Avenue with Gurine, Mert, Colleen, and Gary. They again welcomed me as part of their family, treating me royally as usual. I shall forever be grateful to them.

My second home was with my sister Gurine and her husband, Merton Ellis, and their children, Colleen and Gary. They always welcomed me.

For twenty-eight months, twenty-five days, and twenty-nine minutes the military had been making my decisions. The military decided *what* I would do, *when* I would do it, *where* I would do it, *what* I would wear, *where* I would wear it, *when* I would wear it, *what* I would eat, *where* I would eat, *when* I would eat, *when* I would go to bed, *when* I would get up—just on and on; the military made my decisions. Now to start making my own decisions again was one of the first adjustments I had to cope with. The military had made life quite simple; after we were discharged, they offered many incentives to reenlist. There were times I actually had fleeting thoughts of **reenlisting**.

On one of the first days back, I visited the personnel office at Heidbrink, where I had worked before entering the service. *If* I wanted to return to work there, would I be rehired? They assured me I would, and if I came back within six months of my discharge, I would receive a $200 bonus and wage increases that had been given during the time I had been in the service. Heidbrink had been a great place to work, and just knowing I would have a good job waiting for me was a feeling of security.

On one of the first evenings at home, Gurine, Mert, Colleen, Gary, and I went over to Selby Avenue in St. Paul to visit Gerhard and Alice and my new nephew Peter who had been born while I was in the service. We had a nice evening visiting, and it wasn't long before the conversation focused on *my* plans for the future. I told them of the opportunities at Heidbrink and that I also planned to again visit St. Cloud State University to consider picking up the plans I had before entering the service to get a teaching degree and fulfill my ambition to become a high school football/basketball coach. My dear brother Gerhard, with the interest and concerns of a father, strongly endorsed the college idea but suggested that since the GI Bill would be paying all the tuition as well as a living stipend, that I could go to any college I chose. Gerhard encouraged me to consider Augsburg. I started thinking, "Why not Augsburg?" It's right here in Minneapolis where I live and I am very well acquainted with the campus. The year before going into the service, I had a special friend at Augsburg whom I had visited many, many times.

The very next day I went down again to visit the campus, thinking that perhaps being out of high school four years I would feel old and out of place, but walking around campus and seeing the new crop of students and the returning vets on the GI Bill, at age 22 I knew I would not be known as the "Pops" around campus.

After the visit, I did get excited about the idea of going to college, but I still needed time to think things through. But now I had made my first concrete decision. If college were the route I chose, it would be Augsburg.

Now with two options to consider, working at Heidbrink or college at Augsburg, I made another decision. It was time to go out to Hendricks to be with Mother, Pearl, Clara, and Carvell. I also wanted to see if there were any possible job opportunities in Hendricks.

I took the bus to Marshall where I was met by Mother, Pearl, Clara, Carvell, and little Carol, then nine months old—another **warm welcome home**.

To find out what was happening in Hendricks I needed only to visit Andy's Café on Main Street. Here I met my friends, already home drinking coffee and swapping war stories. Albert and Esther Anderson, the cafe owners, knew every detail about every serviceman. They knew where we had been stationed and what we had done. They knew who was home, who was coming home, when they would be coming home—just everything about all the local servicemen. Esther, in particular, was interested in gossip and knew who was dating whom and if she didn't approve of whom a person was dating, **she would let you know**. Esther was one of a kind.

Andy's Café had been owned by my parents between 1914 and 1920 and was known then as the P. O. Digre Confectionery. It was at that time and still is today the most popular gathering spot in Hendricks.

Besides swapping war stories, another hot topic of discussion over coffee at Andy's was **what are your plans for the future**? This was a primary concern for all of us. Our high school class of 1941 was very typical. Most of us had been in the military. We had been unusually lucky. Donnie Fjeseth had been a P.O.W. but returned safely. None from our class had been killed or seriously injured. After the war, we were all faced with the same concerns: **Now what do we do**?

Orrin Aune—Planned to use his Navy machinist training and work for the Thompson Implement Company in Hendricks.

Arnie Johnson—Planned to join his father's farm machinery business in Hendricks.

Donald Fjeseth—Planned to attend the University of Minnesota Engineering School.

Bob Morseth—Planned to attend the University of Minnesota School of Pharmacy.

Darwin Holian—Planned to attend the University of Minnesota School of Medicine.

Lowayne Dorn—Planned to take over his father's farm.

"Donnie"Knutson—Not a classmate, but my very good friend, joined his father at the Mobil Oil station in Hendricks.

Yes, we all eventually found our niches in civilian life and enjoyed successful careers.

I am proud of the **men** and **women** of our generation. All of us had come through the depression and the trials and hardships of World War II. We were a hard-working, loyal, dedicated, and conscientious group.

One of the first things I heard about while drinking coffee at Andy's was the 52-20 Club. Most of my friends now home belonged; they insisted I should join, too. What was the 52-20 Club? Well, the government had a program for veterans who declared they could not find suitable employment. The government would pay twenty dollars a week for up to fifty-two weeks or until we found suitable employment. Even though they were employed, many collected the money for the entire fifty-two weeks. To collect the twenty dollars required car pooling to the courthouse in Ivanhoe on Tuesdays. After getting the money, the next stop was the Ivanhoe Liquor Store to buy cheap Pete Hagen booze. Now we were fortified while playing pool at Pete Tiller's pool hall and until we went to the Blue Moon in Marshall on Friday night. Then on Sunday, we had a choice of dances at either the Show Boat in Lake Benton or Bohemian Hall between Hendricks and Canby. The next Tuesday the cycle started again—to Ivanhoe, collect $20, to the liquor store, etc., etc.

I soon decided the 52-20 Club was not for me, and after collecting a total of $40 for two weeks, I knew that even though I loved my home and Hendricks, there was no future for me there, so I boarded a bus and went back to Minneapolis to Gurine and Mert's on Columbus Avenue. For nearly a year, the east bedroom there was my home.

Back to Minneapolis...

Within a week, I had collected a $200 bonus and was back at work at the Heidbrink Company at 2633 4th Avenue South. The company personnel director, Vince McConville, offered me the choice of working on any of the three shifts—the day shift from 7 a.m. to 3 p.m., the swing shift from 3 p.m. to 11 p.m., or the night shift (also called the graveyard shift) from 11 p.m. to 7 a.m. Since I never liked being an early riser, although in the military I had to be, I chose the swing shift.

The day shift foreman was Wally Sontag. I had worked for Wally and liked him, but I had a closer relationship with the swing shift foreman, "Doc," and so that also influenced my decision to work the 3 p.m. to 11 p.m. hours.

The day I reported back to work, Doc said I could come back as a machine operator, or since the tool room/tool crib manager had just retired, I could have his job. It didn't take me long to decide I wanted the tool room manager position. Before going into the service, I had been a machine operator, and although I liked it, doing the same repeated operations hour after hour became a bit boring. I had always envied the person in charge of the tool room. He was constantly doing something different. The machine operators came to the tool crib with a job routine sheet. I then issued the tooling necessary to do that job. When the operator completed the job, he returned the tools to me. It was my responsibility to examine the tools making certain they were all there and in good condition. If they were, I returned the tooling to stock. If they needed repair, I sent the tools to the maintenance department before putting them back into stock. Although I did not repair the tools or operate all the machines, I did have knowledge of every job in the plant. I learned about tools, jigs, and fixtures. I had an understanding about the operations of every machine—the kick press, punch press, drill press, lathes, screw machines, milling machines, hand tools—all equipment used in many manufacturing operations. The training I got here was so very essential when I started our business—a big lesson in "Life's School."

My social life during this time included several friends but no special girlfriends. Andy Antolik and Bob Schumacker had worked with me at Heidbrink before we went into the military, returning to work a couple of weeks after I did. Both elected to work the swing shift, so the three of us on occasion would go out after work. We usually went to the then-popular Danny's at 15th and Chicago Avenue. Bob and I did occasionally get together, but we never developed a close friendship.

Often I did things with my cousins, Joe and Vernon "Buddy" Mathison. At that time both lived at the Wartburg Hospice on 7th Street near Portland Avenue. Buddy and I were the youngest of the 30 Mathison cousins; we had had a close friendship since childhood, but during the time we, Joe and I, worked at Heidbrink, I was with Joe more than with Buddy.

Milee Larson, a friend from Hendricks, lived with his aunt only a block from Gurine and Mert's, so Milee and I did things together.

I found a new friend, Don Peterson, who worked part time at Mac's Standard Station at 26th and Chicago Avenue across the street from Gurine and Mert's and one of my hangouts. Don also lived in the area, and he and I became good friends and were together a lot. I introduced Don to Bonnie Foss who lived with two other girls from Canby at a girls' room and boarding house on 26th Street between Columbus and Park Avenues. There must have been fifteen or more girls living there. One of the highlights of the day for the guys working and hanging out at Mac's station was watching all **the girls go by**—cute nineteen- to twenty-year olds getting off the streetcars strutting their stuff as they paraded to their boarding house where they lived according to the rules of their strict housemother. Don Peterson and Bonnie Foss were married in 1948, and at about the same time, the boarding house was sold and became the Thompson Brothers Mortuary, which it is to this day.

The girls' boarding house was very near my Columbus Avenue second home. We would watch the girls who lived there.

I have many memories of the time I was living on Columbus Avenue and working at Heidbrink. A couple of these I will remember forever. One was with Milee Larson. On a late November Sunday afternoon Milee and I set out to visit two former Hendricks teachers, Dorothy and Wendell "Wink" Benson, who lived on Thomas Avenue. We boarded the Chicago-Penn streetcar at 26th Street going **north** thru downtown to the end of the line at 43rd and Penn Avenue **North**. The next two hours we spent walking up and down Thomas trying to find 4929. The number was elusive because there is no such number on Thomas Avenue North. Finally it occurred to us—the Bensons lived on Thomas Avenue **South**—just 100 blocks from where we were. How could I forget this? Our present home on Vincent Avenue is only a few blocks from Thomas Avenue South, and over the years we often visited with these friends Wendell and Dorothy. If you knew Benson, you knew the champion at razzing and giving the needle. My dear Swedish friend would often razz me, asking if Norwegians knew up from down since they didn't know north from south!

Another Lasting Memory was with my Newfound Friend, Don Peterson...

Don had a big four-door car, a 1938 Buick, I believe. My wheels at that time were the Minneapolis streetcars. When Don would ask me to double with him, I never refused.

On this night it was Don, Bonnie, me, and one of Bonnie's Canby friends. After driving around for a while, it was the usual—**parking** at what was Don's favorite spot. I knew we were parking by a lake but just where I had no idea! We hadn't parked long before Don suggested, "Why don't you guys take a walk." So we did, a short fifty feet or so to the shore of the lake. We had just started to enjoy the city lights reflecting on the water when we heard and saw Don's car drive away. Here I was, twenty-two years old, a world traveler, a veteran of aircraft combat, and yet I had a few minutes of anxiety. Where was I? Was this Don's idea of a joke? Would he come back? I thought he would, but what if he didn't? Where are the streetcar lines? I knew the area around 26th and Chicago and I knew Lake Street, but this area was completely foreign to me. They did come back in about fifteen minutes; yes, Don thought it was funny because he knew Cliff had no idea where he was. That night it was not funny, and I told him so. But the next day when we met at Mac's, we both laughed about it.

In the daylight, Don drove me back to his favorite parking spot. It was next to tennis courts on the west side of Lake Harriet. Even in the daylight this area seemed like a long way from 26th and Chicago, and with the curved and dead end streets, I still felt disoriented.

Why will I always have this memory? Because nearly every day for years I have driven by this exact spot in the confusing area that I have learned to love because it is only five blocks from my Vincent Avenue home.

With friends like Don Peterson, Milee Larson, Bob Schumacker, Buddy and Joe, there was always something going on. Yes, I dated, but there was no special girl in my life. I just knew I had not yet met **the right one**.

Heidbrink where I was working was a closed union shop. That meant all production workers were compelled to belong to the Machinists Union. Like many others, I paid monthly union dues, but I was not active in the union affairs. In February 1946, the Union/Heidbrink contract was up for renewal. My coworker and friend, Andy Antolik, was active in union politics; he encouraged Bob Schumaker and me to attend a union rally where the new contract was to be discussed. Since I had never attended previous union meetings, I had no idea of what to expect, but I soon found out. It was a fist-pounding, loud, and emotional meeting. It reminded me of church tent meetings I had attended in Hendricks. Instead of an evangelist preaching about the evils of sin, however, here the leaders were shouting how we were being mistreated and underpaid while the management was making the money. I couldn't believe the anger displayed. It was really an eye opener for me. I thought the company was super; we were all treated very fairly, and I assure you this union meeting did not change my mind. The union's contract demand convinced the parent company, Ohio Chemical, to leave Minneapolis and the local union and combine the Heidbrink division with another Ohio Chemical plant in Madison, Wisconsin.

When I had been discharged from the service, I had been stationed at Truax Field in Madison, and I thought then that Madison was a nice city. My foreman, Doc, encouraged me to move with the company, but although I liked my work and the company, I could see little future there for me, so I elected not to move. Heidbrink moved in early June of 1946, and before looking for other work, I decided to again spend some time at home.

Within a few days after returning to Hendricks, while visiting with Carvell's dad, A. P. Johnson, he told me he had an old car stored in a garage, and although it hadn't been driven for years, it had been in running condition when he put it into storage. It was a 1929 Pontiac four-door sedan with 29,000 actual miles. I remembered the car well; old Lisho Ramlo, a farmer north of town, would drive it down Main Street with the motor roaring, never shifting it out of second gear. I did a bit of dickering with A. P. before I paid him $200. Jay Danielson towed the car to his garage and soon had the motor in good running condition, but he cautioned that after being in storage that long the tires would give me trouble, and although he shopped around, he could not locate this odd size. Lack of those new tires proved to be quite a problem.

My 1929 Lisho Ramlo Pontiac packed and ready to leave for a fun-filled week of fishing in northern Minnesota with, from left to right, Orville Ronning, Lowayne Dorn, and Donnie Knutson. I'm on the right.

But in spite of the tire concerns, I was anxious to take my new car on a trip. I promoted a fishing trip to the Detroit Lakes area with Lowayne Dorn, Orville Ronning, and my very good friend Donnie Knutson. We had discussed doing this when the four of us made our trips to Ivanhoe to collect our twenty dollars a week as members of the 52-20 Club. I convinced the three that now was the time to do it.

With my car packed with fishing gear, groceries, a few cans of beer, and most important, tire repair supplies courtesy of the Knutson Service Station, we set out bright and early. We had traveled all of twelve miles before we had our first flat tire. For the next week, we had a whale of a time hanging out in Detroit Lakes, fishing on Lake Melissa, and fixing no less than eight flat tires. Had it not been for Donnie's service station skills, we would not have made it past Ivanhoe. Since Donnie took care of all the tire repairs, he was excused from cooking, cleaning fish, and KP duties. We had a fun-filled week.

Time for a beer break after Donnie had repaired one of the many flat tires.

It was summer now, and I was really enjoying my time in Hendricks with my many friends, going to dances at Bohemian Hall, the Show Boat, and the Blue Moon. But I again realized opportunities in Hendricks were limited, so when Buddy Mathison called to tell me of a position available at Western Electric, I drove my Pontiac back to Minneapolis with only one flat and again settled into my quarters at Gurine and Mert's.

Deciding on a Career...
Buddy and I were both hired by Western Electric, and after a three-week training program on installing and wiring telephone switch-boards, Buddy was assigned to the Pillsbury Company in Minneapolis, and I was assigned to work for the telephone company in downtown St. Paul.

I liked the work at Western Electric and the variety offered each day such as being involved from start to finish with the wiring and telephone installation of a new St. Paul exchange, the "Capital Exchange." The experience here was again valuable for what was to be my future business. Here I learned new techniques in running wires, troubleshooting, and locating bad wiring and solder connections with the latest in meters and circuit testers.

The education I had had at Camp Kohler helped with my work here; I started to think more about finding employment using the skills and experience I had as a radio operator/mechanic in both the Signal Corps and Air Corps.

Through a St. Paul acquaintance—Mr. Russell—I was introduced to Mr. Driscoll, the personnel director of a small, upstart airline called **Northwest Orient**. Northwest's employment office was at a small storefront building on University Avenue in St. Paul. Mr. Driscoll spent a lot of time with me telling me what a bright future an employee of Northwest Orient would have. My Signal Corps training was a good base, but Northwest required their radio operators/mechanics to be graduates from an accredited electronics school and to have passed the test for a first-class operator's license. "Get that," he said "and I can almost assure you employment." I also made applications to KSTP and WCCO Radio. They had the same requirements—graduate from an accredited electronics school and hold a first-class license. Both KSTP and WCCO said employment opportunities would be excellent with the new medium—**television**—just around the corner. With the positive encouragement of Northwest Airlines, WCCO, and KSTP, I made up my mind. This was the career I wanted. All three of the personnel directors had mentioned the Coyne School of Electronics in Chicago, a premier school, but they also said two local schools, Northwest Electronics in St. Paul and National Radio School in Minneapolis, were good accredited schools. I immediately contacted and requested literature from the three schools.

About the time I had made the decision to make a career in electronics, out of the clear blue I got a call from my brother-in-law Carvell in Hendricks who ran his dad's A. P. Johnson General Merchandise Store in Hendricks. Carvell said his brother Walter, now out of the military, had planned to come back to Hendricks and work with him in their family-owned store, but had changed his mind and was going to work for the Veterans' Administration in Missouri. Carvell said he desperately needed help and asked if I would consider coming back to Hendricks and working with him. I told him of my plans to go on to an electronics school, but that I had not yet decided which school I would be attending or when I would be enrolling. My plans were to stay at Western Electric until I made that decision. He encouraged me to give his store a try until I had made the decision. I slept on his proposal and decided, **"Why not?"** It would be fun to be home while gathering information on the schools I had written to.

That **"why not"** decision was one of the best decisions I ever made. I resigned my job at Western Electric the last part of August 1946, and started working for Carvell the early part of September.

Returning to Hendricks...

I called it "Carv's Store" although the official store name was A. P. Johnson General Merchandise. I had been in the store many, many times, occasionally as a customer, but more often just to visit with Carvell or his dad, A. P., but not until I became a clerk in the store did I realize just how much merchandise he carried. With the exception of fresh meats, he had a complete grocery department. He carried quality merchandise throughout the store: shoes, boots and rubbers, overalls, towels, linens, blankets, and men's and women's ready-to-wear clothing. During the winter months, he often had a tub of lutefisk out in front of the store. This was truly the small town general merchandise store, started in 1903 by Carvell's father, A. P., known as one of the sharpest and richest businessmen in the Hendricks area. My father, P. O. Digre, had the P. O. Digre Confectionery from 1914 to 1920, a few doors north of A. P.'s store. I was told that A. P. and P. O. were good friends, so our families go back a long time together.

The months I spent working for Carvell were another important experience and training I would need in my business. From Carvell I learned a lot—purchasing, inventory control, and reconciling packing slips and invoices. He was very exacting about details and carefully went over every unit and extension price on invoices. If he found even a 10-cent error on an invoice, he would debit the supplier back.

On Wednesday and Saturday nights, we were open when the farmers came to town to shop and visit with one another. On those nights, we were always busy. I would be busy putting up a grocery order a farmer had given me on a handwritten slip of paper when someone else would want me to fit a pair of shoes on them, and then I next might be carrying a fifty-pound bag of flour to a car parked a block away. It was on these busy nights I learned a lot about human relations. I might be putting up a grocery order for my favorite customers, like Louis Welte or Joe Milton, and at the same time, I might be patiently waiting on Julia Eggen trying to decide on the color of a $.25 hand towel she thought she might buy sometime in the future. Pleasing and accommodating customers is essential in every type of business. I did it well at Carvell's; I learned from those experiences.

It was now nearly a year since I had been discharged from the military and had spent a couple of weeks in Hendricks as a member of the 52-20 Club. Things had changed a lot since then. Most vets had now gone away to college or trade schools; others had gone off to the cities to find employment. Those who were in Hendricks were working on their family farms or businesses, planning to make Hendricks their permanent home. During this year, some had married and most of the others had steady girlfriends and marriage plans.

My high school classmate Arnie Johnson was working in his father's implement business and was dating and engaged to Gladys Johnson. Donnie Knutson worked with his father at the Mobil oil station. Donnie and I were neighbors and friends since childhood; he had given me the nickname, "Cooky." We often got together for coffee at Andy's Café and chatted about old times. Donnie was constantly encouraging me to settle down here, but I would tell him I couldn't see much future for me in Hendricks. Even though Donnie and I got together often for coffee at Andy's, we **never** got together socially in the evening because he had his steady girlfriend, Arlene Hogie, a nurse at the Hendricks Hospital. Donnie and Arlene never missed a night together when she wasn't working.

Donnie seldom came into Carvell's store to visit with me, so when he did come in one afternoon, I knew he had something in mind, and he did. "Cooky, how about going out on a date with Arlene and me? There is a new nurse working at the hospital, and Arlene thinks you two would hit it off." He added, "All I know is that Arlene says she is short, cute, nice, and her name is Bernice." It didn't take me long to again say, "**Why not?**" There were only two girls in town I had even considered taking out, so it would be interesting to meet someone new and go out with Donnie and his girlfriend, Arlene.

I had been on blind dates before, and since the girls were usually losers, I wasn't expecting much this time either. But when I met Bernice, I immediately realized this was not the run-of-the-mill blind date. Arlene had said she was short, nice, and cute. Yes, she was short, but not too short; just right I thought. Arlene could have said she was very nice and very cute. The first things that physically attracted me were her smile, her eyes, and her Rita Hayworth legs. I did not immediately recognize her as the same cute Bernice I had met more than a year earlier on July 7, 1945, in front of Andy's Café when she was staying with Betty Erickson in Hendricks.

Dancing at the Show Boat in Lake Benton was not the memorable part of our first date. This girl immediately intrigued me. She was so genuine and completely different from the many frivolous girls I had dated. At the end of the evening, I knew that I very much wanted to see her again, and that first date was the beginning of our courtship.

Memories of Our Ten-month Courtship—and Some Unwelcome Competition...

After our first date we were together pretty regularly, so when she called me at Carvell's store to tell me her brother Garfield was home from college and was coming to take her home for the evening, I didn't think too much about it **until** that evening when I was walking home from work and I saw a 1938 Ford coming from the hospital towards Main Street. In the back seat was a couple, and the woman looked an awful lot like my new friend, Bernice.

I had not met her family yet, but she had told me her parents had a 1938 Ford. But if her brother was coming to drive her to the farm, why would she be sitting in the back seat with a man while the driver was sitting alone? Was it just a coincidence that someone who looked like Bernice was in a 1938 Ford I had never seen before? Well, the next morning at Andy's Café, Esther, the town's "information" lady, had the word out. Cooky Digre's new girlfriend had been seen in the back seat of a 1938 Ford with an unidentified man, and Virginia Thompson from Hendricks was sitting close to a blonde-haired man, a stranger to the Hendricks area. Given the facts straight from Esther's knowledgeable mouth, Bernice leveled with me. Garfield had dated Virginia before, and Bernice was with a fellow from Ghent she was dating when we met.

Now had our dear "Lady of Information" not let me and the whole town know about this evening of intrigue, would Bernice have told me? I think she would have. I admitted to Bernice that I was hurt, and, yes, jealous, because I really cared for her. A few days later, she told me she had sent her friend from Ghent a "Dear John Letter."

Now we had been dating for about two months, and Bernice had, of course, met my mother, my sisters Pearl and Clara, Carvell, and baby daughter, Carol, who all lived in Hendricks. But of all the members of Bernice's large family, I had only met Bernice's brother-in-law Bernard Amundson, who came in to Carvell's store, did a bit of shopping, but whose main mission, I'm sure, was to check on Bernice's new boyfriend. Being a grocery store clerk in Hendricks I am sure did not impress Bernard, so I can only assume his reports to Bernice's sister, Clara, were not at all glowing.

It's Time to Meet Bernice's Family...

Bernice had a few days off from work and decided to spend time with her parents. Yes, this time her brother did come to honestly take her to their farm home ten miles southwest of Marshall.

Our plan was that I would come to the farm on Saturday afternoon to pick her up, and at the same time, I would meet her parents and whoever from her family of twelve brothers and sisters might be at home. Bernice had given me a bit of a profile of her brothers and sisters, but she thought only Emanuel would be home when I came. Emanuel, she cautioned just might test me with a bit of an initiation.

It was a clear crisp afternoon, ideal for Big Ten football, and I was listening to a Minnesota football game as I was driving, but the football game was secondary and I was a bit apprehensive. As I pulled into the yard and parked near the east porch, Bernice came out to meet me and that helped. As we walked up to the house, Bernice took my hand as if to give me courage, so I guessed that Emanuel was home. As we stepped onto the porch, I had my first memory of the Hoversten farm — the aroma of freshly baked bread, a smell I have loved since my childhood.

Bernice's mother opened the kitchen door and gave me a warm welcome (so far, I was comfortable). Stepping into the kitchen, I saw a mound of bread loaves on the large kitchen table. Across the table, sitting on a bench and looking out the south windows sat Emanuel puttying the windows. As he continued to apply the putty and without even looking at me, he greeted me with, "Hi, Cook" and then started right in with the initiation. "I heard a good story yesterday about a couple on their honeymoon and…" The story was funny and it deserved my acknowledgment, but I could see Bernice's mother with a frown on her face as she switched a towel and took bread out of the oven. **I was between a rock and a hard place**. Emanuel knew it and loved it because this was exactly what he had planned, no doubt before I drove into the yard. Emanuel and I had a warm handshake and greetings, and I acknowledged his story with something like, "That's a good one; I've got to remember it," and then I quickly turned my attention to Bernice's mother.

I remember well every detail of that afternoon because it was important to me. I wanted to make a good impression. I told Bernice's mother that since my early childhood I had loved the aroma of fresh-baked bread. I said that now my mother doesn't bake bread, but when all five of the children were at home, it seemed she baked bread every week. I remember as a small child when I came home from school and stepped into the back shanty/porch, the smell of fresh-baked bread gave the whole house a cozier atmosphere and a feeling of well being, and any concerns I had seemed to disappear. Now, coming to Bernice's home for the first time and reliving that childhood memory seemed to be a good omen.

Bernice's father wasn't in the house when I first arrived. Perhaps a half hour or so later he came walking up from the barn. I had been told he was very stern and demanded discipline, and that all the children had experienced a whipping from him when, for example, they didn't pick the cobs or windfall apples when he had told them to. But this now seemed hard for me to believe because the Elias I met on this day seemed so subdued and laid back—a very gentle person, and I felt comfortable with him immediately.

We didn't stay for supper, but before Bernice and I left I had several slices of fresh baked bread with homemade jelly—good!

Less than a month later, I was back to the farm again to pick up Bernice after she had spent a few days at home. Once again there was another Hoversten testing and initiation experience. This time it wasn't Emanuel; it was double trouble—the twins, Kermit and Vincent— were home for Christmas break from Augsburg College, geared up and prepared to give Bernice's new friend a royal razzing.

Bernice later told me that before I came she had asked them to change their overalls that had a patch or two, but instead they found overalls loaded with patches. I didn't notice how they were dressed, but it didn't take me long to realize that I would be dealing with two kids who were exceptionally sharp and witty and fresh out of four whole months of college. During my time in the military, I had met and dealt with every type of individual you could imagine. I had learned how to size them up, so I quickly realized that these two would be a real challenge, and no way would I try to match wits with them.

It was in the dining room/parlor that I first met the twins where they sat on the sofa so angelic and benign looking. They stood up from the sofa and in unison and started in, saying, "Here, Bernice, you and Cook can sit here on the sofa and hold hands. You can kiss if you want to. We won't bother you. We'll be real quiet on the other side of the room."

They went on and on for a few minutes, but it seemed like hours. Ever since, Kermit and Vincent have been special to me, and I have always had the utmost respect for them, but for those minutes on a Saturday afternoon in December of 1946, the two of them were incorrigible.

I weathered that Hoversten harassing, too, and soon we were discussing their college life, The Young Republican Club they had joined, and my sister-in-law's brother, Allen Bunny Norby, a classmate and a good friend of Kermit and Vincent.

For Christmas that year, I gave Bernice cosmetics from Siverson's drug store and a Cannon blanket from Carvell's store. I gave her the blanket with two purposes in mind: first, I wanted her parents to see me as a down-to-earth, practical person; second, I wanted Bernice to start thinking that we might be sharing that blanket in bed in the near future. My first purpose was successful. When she opened the blanket gift on Christmas Eve, her father was impressed by such a practical gift. As far as my second purpose, I think Bernice got the message that **yes**, I was serious about our relationship.

During the winter of 1946-1947, I had to get into the spirit and swing of small-town living again. After the excitement of the military service, and the additional excitement of both living in Minneapolis for the past year, it took a bit of adjusting to a quieter pace of life. Hendricks had a good basketball team that year, so going to games both home and away was a fun thing to do. We went to many ball games with Donnie and Arlene. Besides going to basketball games that winter, we played a lot of cards. I remember one fun night when Pearl, Bernice, and I went to a Rook Party, a card game popular in Hendricks, at my cousin Gyda Pederson's farm. Food was always an important part of such parties and going to Gyda's was always a special treat.

Many, many nights that winter, we trudged through the snowdrifts to Clara and Carvell's little house in the far northwestern section of town, barging in uninvited with our same greeting every time, "You lucky people, we are going to keep you up to play a few rounds of Whist, and hope you make us lunch."

They always welcomed us. After a few rounds (Clara and Bernice against Carvell and me), we would have the same lunch—coffee, and Goteborg sandwiches, and sometimes cake, before we trudged through the snowdrifts to the nurses' home on the far east side of town.

That winter we also spent many evenings at my mother's home where Bernice helped me organize a photo album. She had a neat writing style, printing with white ink under each of my many pictures. I know she didn't particularly enjoy printing the names **Barbara** and **Helen**, but she did it, making me appreciate and love her that much more.

Double Dating...

Since I didn't have a car at that time, we double dated quite often. We always enjoyed going out with Donnie and Arlene, the couple who had introduced us. When my cousin Joe came to Hendricks he often dated Avis, another nurse at the hospital. One day Avis and Bernice packed a nice picnic supper, and we **rowed** (no motor) nonstop in Carvell's big, heavy, wooden boat across Lake Hendricks to a park on the South Dakota side. It was a beautiful, calm spring day, and on the way over we had no problems, but it was getting dark before we started back, and about halfway across the lake a heavy wind came up. We had no life jackets and neither girl could swim a stroke. I am not fast to admit to making mistakes, but this was just plain stupid.

We double dated often with Carl Oliver (C. O.) Thompson and his girlfriend, Lillian Leuning (Lil). C. O. was one of the two doctors at the hospital, known by most everyone in town as just plain C. O. When we double dated with C. O. and Lil, we knew we would have what I called a "C. O. Experience." Something funny had to happen, like rescuing and giving shelter to a tiny shivering chicken on a cold April evening or attempting to plow a furrow on a gravel road with a low-hung sports car in the dead of night. What fun and unforgettable times we had with C. O. and Lil.

Our friendship with C. O. and Lil did not end when we got married. They, too, married shortly after our wedding, and we would often visit them at their big, beautiful house on Lake Hendricks. When they came to Minneapolis/St. Paul, they sometimes stayed at our humble, but cozy, attic apartment on Selby Avenue. We can never go to Hendricks without thinking of C. O. and Lil. Why? Because our son Rolland and his wife, Janet, bought that beautiful house on the lake when C. O. and Lil retired and moved to Arkansas.

By spring I knew without a doubt, to quote a phrase from an old, old love song, I had found "The girl of my dreams." Cooky Digre was never known to be bashful around pretty girls. Yes, I had dated a few before Bernice, both in the USA and Europe, but I knew for sure that she was the one for me, and I hoped she felt the same. She had the qualities no other girl I had dated had; physically she was attractive to me—a beautiful face, a nice figure, Rita Hayworth legs, sparkling eyes, and all with a captivating smile. But more important than her physical attributes, she was the most intelligent, caring, considerate, and genuine girl I had ever known.

Besides her physical and personality attributes that attracted me, we had a lot in common—both 100% Norwegian, both with a parent who had immigrated from Norway, both from the Lutheran Free Church, and although we lived 30 miles apart, the same pastor served both congregations, which meant similar Sunday school, Bible school, and Luther League experiences. And perhaps of most importance was our shared commitment to family values.

Wedding Plans...

On May 23rd, her father's birthday, I gave her a huge 1/5 carat diamond. To make the evening special, our good friend, Otto Sorenson, the band director in Hendricks, insisted we use his brand new Buick that evening. He told us to go wherever we pleased. I remember him saying, "Go to Minneapolis if you like. I don't need the car for several days." Since this was Bernice's father's birthday, we decided to go to the farm so that her parents would be the first to know.

The months of May and June were filled with the romance, but by early July, we set the wedding date—August 8. Then the romance took a bit of a back seat as the reality of the commitments we would make started to set in.

I remember well the day we drove over to Ivanhoe to get our marriage license. As we walked down the courthouse steps, neither of us said a word. We got in the car and started back to Hendricks. Still both of us were silent. Finally, I pulled off County Road #17 on to the corner of the township road 6 miles east of Hendricks. It was perhaps fifteen minutes since we had left the courthouse and neither of us had said a word. I remember saying, "Okay, Bernice, let's talk," and we did for perhaps another thirty minutes. We both expressed that, yes, this is a big, big step in our lives and did we know for sure this was what we wanted. We obviously concluded that it was. But at that time we were both pondering the same concern: marriage is a big, big step with no turning back. The commitment is forever. My concern was: how would I be accepted in this family of 12, all exceptional students, all driven to excel?

My family had already accepted Bernice. When we told my mother of our engagement, she shed tears, embarrassed Bernice, and said she was the answer to her prayers. Mother adored her from day one. My three sisters—Gurine, Clara, and Pearl—were delighted and proud that she was to be their sister-in-law. For Pearl, it was a big relief— she had feared I would end up with a girl I had dated a few times in Minneapolis. Pearl's fears were unfounded, and I told her so; I had absolutely no interest in that woman as a life mate. My brother, Gerhard, and his wife, Alice, lived in St. Paul and had not yet met Bernice, but I knew they, too, would quickly see just how special she was.

By this time, besides her parents, I had met her siblings Clara and Bernard, Emmanuel and Frieda, Christine and Roy, Garfield, Esther, Kermit, and Vincent. I had yet to meet Chester, Clarence and Marguerite, Joseph and Gertrude, and the highly respected senior member, Knut and his wife, Hazel. I had survived some initial harassing, but how did they feel about me? Bernard expressed his concern that if I continued to be a clerk in Carvell's store, Bernice would need to continue to work. Christine and Roy made me feel comfortable from our first meeting, and I felt I had their approval. Chester was married to Phyllis Johnson from Hendricks, an outstanding student one year ahead of me in school. I wondered just what was Phyllis's impression of Cooky Digre. I am sure she was asked and she could not say that I was the scholarly type. Phyllis knew me instead as somewhat of a free spirit, participating in all sports, class plays, concert bands, swing bands, and the like.

By my own choice, a few days before high school graduation I chose to skip school with a few other seniors. After a private severe reprimanding by Supt. Theo. Hinderacker, he concluded by saying, "**Clifford**, I have known you your entire life. I have had you in several classes, and I want you to know that had you pursued the academics in school with the same ambition as you have had for extracurricular activities, you would have been a straight "A" student like your sister, Clara." Perhaps Supt. Hinderacker was right, but it didn't matter to me because I was and still am convinced that I had received an excellent high school education. I had enjoyed and learned a lot from the activities in which I participated. Besides that, I had continued my education in life's school.

The thirty-minute interlude Bernice and I spent discussing our concerns certainly didn't dispel them, but I believe that we showed each other we would be dedicated to the commitment of marriage. I also think it showed we would both be willing to discuss problems and concerns.

From then on, it was full steam ahead with plans for the wedding. Bernice's first concern was where to have the ceremony. With the size of her immediate family, my family and relatives living in the area, the hospital staff, and our many friends to invite, we knew it would be a big wedding. When she added the numbers, she concluded her home church of Hemnes could not accommodate a wedding of that size, and besides at that time Hemnes did not have a basement for a reception. To add to her concerns, her mother was having knee problems and was on crutches, so she would be limited in helping with the reception. Consequently, Bernice made the decision to have the wedding at Calvary Lutheran Church in Hendricks that was served by Rev. M. A. Erickson, who was also the pastor at Bernice's home church, Hemnes.

When Bernice had decided to have the wedding at Calvary, she reserved the church for August 8, but she reminded me repeatedly, "There will be no wedding until you ask my father for my hand in marriage." At first I thought she was kidding, but in her determined and definite style, she convinced me she was not. Bernard had asked for Clara, and Roy for Christine, so without her father's blessing there would not be a wedding.

About two weeks before the wedding date, there was a surprise shower for Bernice at the church. I knew of the shower and decided this would be the time to talk to her father. I waited in front of the church until her parents and Esther came. At that time, most of the bridal showers were for the women only, so I decided to give Mr. Hoversten a "sight-seeing tour" of Hendricks. After driving around the town for a half hour or so, I parked the car by the lake near Horse Shoe Bend where Bernice and I had spent many hours holding hands. While her father and I were walking along the lakeshore, I came up with the courage and what I felt were the right words. We stopped walking, and I looked him directly in the eyes, and this is exactly what I said, "Mr. Hoversten, may I assume you have no objection to our marriage? I love Bernice very much." A slight pause followed before I heard his familiar chuckle and then his reply, "I have been wondering when you would be asking." Then he put his hand on my shoulder and added, "I am proud to give you my blessing." We had a firm handshake (no hugging) and I said a sincere, "Thank you."

From the first time I met Bernice's parents, I always addressed them as Mr. and Mrs. Hoversten. They were outstanding, and I had the utmost respect for both of them. We drove back to the church and I gave Bernice the good word that we had her father's blessing. I helped pack gifts into her parent's car. I was relieved and "**Fait Accompli**"—mission accomplished.

From that evening on, every spare moment Bernice was taking care of wedding details. Nurses from the hospital quickly volunteered to help serve at the reception, decorate the church, arrange flowers, and on and on. Hendricks had no photographer so our dear friend Dr. C. O. Thompson offered to take pictures. My sister Clara was the church organist, so that was taken care of. Bernice asked Eda Hinsverk to sing, and although Eda did a great job singing Edvard Grieg's, "Jeg Elsker Dej" (I Love You), Bernice regretted that she had not also asked Bernice Kolden, then Garfield's girlfriend, to sing, but she had no idea if she would come from Portland, Oregon. Bernice Kolden had a tremendous voice, and with training, she would have had the ability to be an opera singer.

For her maid of honor she chose her good friend, Betty Ann, Rev. M. A. Erickson's daughter. The bridesmaids were her sister Esther Marie and my sister Pearl. I chose my very good friend from my Air Corps days, Stanley P. Szydlowski, known as just plain "Sid" to be my best man. Donald Knutson, a friend from childhood, and the person who got Bernice and me together on the blind date, was one of the groomsmen together with Bernice's brother, Garfield.

Our Wedding...

On the morning of our wedding day all the details had been taken care of, and everything was under control except my stomach. I woke up with cramps and diarrhea. Carrie Johnson, Carvell's mother, stopped by to see how things were going. When she heard of my problems, she scooted home and was soon back with a half-full bottle of blackberry brandy and ordered, "Take a shot of this and your stomach will settle right down." She was quick to add, "I take this for medicinal purposes only." I don't know about the "medicinal purposes only," but I do know she was right on; the blackberry brandy did the trick.

August 8, 1947, has always been an important date in our lives, but it is also in the weather record books. August 8, 1947, was the hottest August 8 on record in Minnesota. At mid afternoon, the thermometer in front of Andy's Café read 105 degrees—**that is hot**!

On our wedding day Sid seemed nervous and uptight. He paced the floor, walked downtown several times, and was smoking more cigarettes than usual. I asked if something was bothering him. He said that at the rehearsal he got the impression that the pastor was somewhat cool to him, and he thought it was because he was a Roman Catholic and that he should not be part of this conservative Lutheran wedding. I reminded Sid that he and I had been through hell and high water together; I wanted him as my best man. I told him that I had told Rev. Erickson that Sid was a Catholic and the pastor didn't seem to have a problem with that. I added, "It probably bothers Rev. Erickson more that you are **Polish**." With that, we both laughed and Sid was his old self.

A short time before the ceremony was to begin, Sid and I were in a small room just to the side of the altar. While sister Clara was playing prelude music and Garfield and Donnie were ushering people into the nearly full church, I started thinking, "You know Cliff, if you want out of this, you can be out of here and on a bus that leaves in a half hour." Of course, I didn't want out—what I was really saying was when I stepped in front of that altar and before the congregation said, "I do," I would be making a lifelong commitment. That was a decision and commitment that I have **never ever** regretted.

Although the temperature in the church had to be over 100 degrees, and we were all dripping with sweat, the ceremony went without a hitch. Everyone was complimenting Bernice on the most beautiful wedding ever. The receiving line seemed to be endless and finally I met Knut and Hazel, Clarence and Marguerite, and Chester. I now had met all of Bernice's brothers and sisters except Joseph. At that time, the Hoversten numbers overwhelmed me.

The wedding party consisted of Bernice's brother Garfield, my friend Donnie Knutson, my best man Sid Szydlowski, me, Bernice, the maid of honor Bette Anne Erickson, my sister Pearl, and Bernice's sister Esther.

I had few memories of the reception in the church basement except that it was beastly hot and jammed with people. Most everyone we had invited came, and that made us both happy. I remember we stayed and visited with family and friends until most had left and Bernice felt comfortable leaving. For me I suppose I would have left after we had said our, "**I wills**."

Bernice changed from her wedding gown at Betty Ann's home just a few doors from the church. Her gown was beautiful, custom designed, and made for this beautiful bride. We picked up our suitcases and went up to Carvell's to get the 1929 Model A Ford Coupe he had loaned to us for a short trip. We had assumed it would be safe locked up in Carvell's garage, but after driving only a few blocks, **wow**, what a stink! Some local pranksters had smeared Limburger cheese on the engine manifold and when that cheese gets hot, it stinks. And I knew that stink would be with us for our entire trip; whenever we would put in gas, people would know we were newlyweds. Putting Limburger cheese on the manifold was a common and harmless prank or trick in the rural areas. But the odor of Limburger cheese became the least of our problems. We had only driven for a couple of miles when the radiator started to boil and steam, so it was back to town where we had the cooling system drained, flushed out, and we were back on the road, with no more car problems.

Envisioning a nightcap and a bit of dancing on our wedding night, I had made reservations at the plush Lowry Hotel in downtown St. Paul, but the car trouble delayed us by hours, forcing us to stay at a second-rate hotel right on Highway 19 in the center of Redwood Falls, a small, hot room without air conditioning and with the bath across the hall; at nearly midnight, and in 1947, there were no Holiday Inns just down the road!

This was the Redwood Falls Hotel where we spent our first night. It was very *hot*.

The next day we drove to St. Paul and stopped to meet Frank and Vic Sylvester, owners of the upstairs apartment I had rented on Selby Avenue. After seeing Frank and Vic and seeing the apartment, we drove up to Big Lake where we got a small-but-clean cabin on the lake. From there we traveled to Duluth where we stayed in a bed and breakfast, then across the state to Lake Melissa near Detroit Lakes and another small 1947-style cabin with a stove and refrigerator. Fishing was great there. We caught a big basket of sunfish and crappies. After pondering a decision for ten seconds, we threw them back. Honeymoons were not meant to be spent cleaning fish. From there, it was back to Minneapolis where we spent a night at Columbus Avenue, alone for the evening with Gurine and Mert still on vacation. From Minneapolis we drove down to Rochester for one night there, and then to the Hoversten farm.

A few days after we returned from our honeymoon, Grandma Hoversten, with help from Christine, hosted a nice reception dinner for my family—Mother, Pearl, Gurine and Mert, Colleen and Gary, Clara, Carvell, and Carol. I remember it was a nice, fun-filled day playing horseshoes and getting acquainted. It meant a lot to me—not only were they accepting me but also my family. This had been one of my concerns.

By the first of September we were settled in our small, cozy, furnished apartment on Selby Avenue in St. Paul. The owners, Frank and Vic Sylvester and their three children, Kathleen "Cappy," Jim, and Bill, lived downstairs. When my brother, Gerhard, arranged for us to rent this apartment, he did us a big favor. First apartments were hard to find, and the price was a real bargain, $45 a month including all utilities except telephone. Frank and Vic were so good to us, treating us like family. I could write pages about our relationship with the Sylvesters. Frank and Vic were just plain, good, solid people with three interesting children.

Career Choices...

My roles in the military affected my career choice. I had decided to attend National Radio School in Minneapolis, but the next class did not start until after January 1, so until then I needed a job. I was twenty-four and Bernice twenty-three—both young and full of ambition. Within a week of settling in at Selby Avenue, we were out surveying the possibilities. Nurses were in high demand so Bernice had no problem finding employment. She first worked at Western Electric Company in downtown St. Paul doing industrial nursing—taking care of minor accidents with bandages and band aids, giving out aspirins to women with menstrual problems—a variety of nursing duties. When they required her to work nights, I objected. Bernice then got a job at Bethesda Hospital in St. Paul. Wendell Benson's uncle, the superintendent of the hospital, hired her immediately. Soon she got an unexpected call from her alma mater, Deaconess Hospital in Minneapolis, offering her the perfect job, *days only and no weekends*. She worked at the Deaconess until shortly before Kathleen was born.

Our cozy apartment was upstairs in this house.

I, too, found good employment at Montgomery Ward, within walking distance from home. I worked in the catalog division doing furniture repairing and packing. I started full time, and after school started, I worked part time. I set my own hours and was allowed to work as many hours as I chose. This was absolutely the perfect part-time job for a student.

Although we had very little money, the years we lived on Selby were happy ones. We entertained a lot at our small, cozy apartment with some of our dearest life-long friends like Sally and Ken Benson. Bernice worked with Sally Daun at the Deaconess and they became friends. She invited them to visit us. I'll never forget the first time I met Sally and her boyfriend, Ken Benson. I was out in the front of our apartment when they pulled up. Wow!! Ken was driving a brand-new 1948 tan Chevrolet with a smart windshield visor. Man-o-man was that car something. It was a far cry from the 1929 model-A Ford we had at that time. Sally and Ken married a few months later, and we have enjoyed their close friendship these 60 years later.

Two of our other close friends whom we enjoyed coming to see were my Army buddy Don Fernlund and his wife, Vita. One weekend with them really stands out. We went with Don and Vita to Cross Lake, Minnesota, and stayed at his parent's home. The four of us shared a large bedroom with two double beds. When we were in the military together you could always count on the *Minnesota Swede*, Don Fernlund to entertain us with jokes and stories. After we had gone to bed he started in—laugh, laugh, laugh. I think it was nearly morning and almost time to get up when Don either ran out of funny stories or fell asleep. I remember the whole weekend was fun-filled, spending very few of our precious dollars, which neither Don nor I had many of.

St. Paul's Lutheran Church—the first church of our married life.

We became somewhat active, particularly in the Couples' Club at St. Paul's Lutheran Church at Marshall and Chatsworth. We loved our dear pastor and friend, Carl Sunwall. We joined the church within a short time after our marriage, and we were scolded for doing so. Our dear pastor, M. A. Erickson, who had married us, thought it was disgraceful that Bernice and I, both 100% Norwegian and members of the Norwegian Lutheran Free Church, would associate and join the Augustana Synod Church. Rev. Erickson clearly let us know the people of that church are **Swedes**.

A Light Goes On...

In early January I started classes at National Radio School, and from the very first day of class I loved it; I knew I had made another right decision. I made many new friends among the students, but the best new friend was an instructor, Roald E. Dybvig (Rollie), my friend and tutor for his entire life.

Before we were married, Bernice had purchased a small radio at the Coast-to-Coast store in Hendricks. After playing for only a few minutes, the sound became horribly distorted. She returned the radio to the dealer. Tubes and condensers were replaced, but to no avail. It was still distorted. Bernice gave up and concluded she had purchased a lemon.

Had it not been for the defective loudspeaker in this radio, it is unlikely MISCO would be in existence today.

When I was attending National Radio School, I brought the radio in to an instructor, Tom Tolefson, in charge of the radio repair class. A quick listen to the distorted sound and Tom concluded, "It's simple—it's a speaker with a rubbing voice coil." He added, "Your choice is a new speaker for $4.50 or have this speaker reconed for $1.50." My choice was simple—the $3.00 price difference was a lot of money in 1948.

At that time there was only one speaker reconing company in the entire state, and he was so busy it took weeks to have speakers repaired. After waiting for six weeks and the speaker had not returned to the school, I went over to the reconing shop located at Oxford and Selby Avenue in St. Paul, not far from our home, to inquire about my speaker. The owner admitted he had lost the speaker. I even searched for it in his messy shop, but no luck—so my only choice was to pay the $4.50 for a new speaker.

My frustration led to a "light going on." He needed competition. "I am going into the speaker reconing business in Minneapolis." Thus was born the idea of Minneapolis Speaker Reconing Company. Reconing is the complete rebuilding of loudspeakers.

I discussed my idea with my good friend and tutor, Rollie. He too agreed that the service and quality from the St. Paul Company was bad and added that he would be interested in being a partner in the new venture, but said he would continue being an instructor at National Radio School.

January 1, 1949, we had Minneapolis Speaker Reconing Company up and running with all of the woes of a start-up company—sorely undercapitalized—working long hours without enough profits to pay my salary. Bernice continued nursing until our first child, Kathleen, was born in 1950. By then I was drawing a portion of my $200-a- month salary. It was at that time that Rollie offered to sell us his interest in the company, so Bernice and I became sole owners.

By 1953 television was the popular medium, and fewer radio speakers were being reconed. We then aggressively pursued reconing speakers for the drive-in theatres. This proved to be a good decision, and we were soon the largest reconing service in the country.

Reconing Leads to Manufacturing...
One of our reconing customers was Wright, Inc., owned by Douglas Wright, located at 2233 University Avenue in St. Paul.

Doug Wright and Donald DeCoster founded Wright/DeCoster manufacturing loudspeakers in the mid 1930s. When Mr. DeCoster died in 1939 at the young age of 44, the Wright/DeCoster Company was dissolved. Doug Wright, however, continued in the speaker business, and for sometime Doug was associated with Joe Zimmerman as the Wright Zimmerman Company, manufacturing speakers for the Setchell Carlson Radios and TVs. Doug later formed his own company — simply Wright, Inc. It was then that I became acquainted with him.

In 1956 Doug purchased speakers from several manufacturers, labeled the product Wright, Inc., and sold to some customers who previously purchased from Wright /DeCoster. In making a delivery to Doug's office, he remarked that for all of the speakers we had reconed for him, he had never had a reject. At that time one of his most popular speakers was an 8-inch model that he was selling to sound dealers. He was receiving considerable complaints both on the sound quality and mechanical failures, and asked if we would design and manufacture an 8-inch speaker with the quality of our reconed speakers. Again knowing that there was this *need*, we began our design. We chose the components that would give the response he wanted, and with our experience working out the durability of drive-in speakers, we knew we would overcome his mechanical problems also.

After supplying Wright, Inc., with samples, Doug ran his own tests, and also sent samples out to a few select customers. He reported that the samples were terrific and placed an initial order for 200 pieces. We realized an order for only 200 pieces of the various components we required would not be very exciting to our vendors, but we found that they were all cooperative to help us get a start. Shortly after receiving the 200 speakers, Doug reported back that the response to our product was terrific. He then placed a new order for 500 speakers. Again we experienced complete cooperation from our vendors and within a few weeks after we delivered the order for 500 pieces, Doug reordered, this time, 1,000 speakers. Wow, were we excited, but just as we started to assemble the order for 1,000, his secretary called to tell us that Mr. Wright had passed away and they were canceling all orders and closing the offices. Suddenly our excitement turned to a near panic.

Now *we* had a big **need**. We had to pay debts to several vendors for the 1,000 components. Neither Mr. Wright nor his office told us who their customers were. We had only *one choice*—sell the 1,000 speakers ourselves. We made calls on local parts jobbers and sound contractors. Since they knew nothing about our product, most initially ordered only six or twelve pieces just to help us out, and they felt sorry for poor Cliff. Soon repeat orders and more calls and we had sold the 1,000 8-inch speakers. We also started adding different sizes— 5x7" and 6x9" speakers for automobiles and 12" speakers for Hi-Fi. We now knew we were in the manufacturing business to stay. We were no longer only a speaker reconing business; we were a speaker manufacturing business. We changed our name from, Minneapolis Speaker Reconing Company to Minneapolis Speaker Company. From here we coined and registered the trade name, MISCO.

On a sales call to a parts distributor of Stark Electronics, the purchasing agent asked me: "Cliff, what are you, another 'Me too'?" His comment plagued me. Even though I knew we had a superior product, our product was visually no different from the other speakers on the market at that time except for the gold color of the dichromate plating of our baskets. All manufacturers used black cones, gray felt dust caps, and gray-white gaskets. Except for a manufacturer's label and stamp, all had similar appearance. The *need* was for a product with a distinct appearance difference. (One of my lessons at this time was: respond to the *need*.)

Since the cone of the speaker is the most prominent component, we concentrated on the cone for identification of our product. After considerable research and discussion with our suppliers, we decided to go with a red, molded cone. The red color had exactly the eye appeal we were looking for. With the gold-colored basket, red cone, black gasket and dust cap, our product had a distinctive appearance without sacrificing quality. We had overcome the "Me too" image. It soon became obvious our established product identity was important and we registered "Red Line" as a product trade name, and became the first manufacturer to have a full line with colored cones.

Soon after other manufacturers followed suit and there were blue, green, and yellow cones. MISCO was the first to have colored cones. MISCO was the first speaker company with a complete line of speakers from 3-inch to 15-inch with colored cones. We were no longer a "Me too" speaker company.

MISCO has made several industry innovations and we have three U.S. patents; these have become industry standards throughout the world.

Our Buildings...

In 1949, we started at a run-down store-type building at 2401 Cedar Avenue with approximately 600 square feet of usable space. This site is now part of the Little Earth American Indian housing complex in Minneapolis.

When the building was sold in 1951, we relocated across the street to 2312 Cedar Avenue. We rented space from Ralph Burt, a barber. Again we had only 600 square feet upstairs and downstairs. But Ralph, a great person, built on another 500 feet to accommodate our needs.

As our business continued to grow we needed even more space, and in 1956 we purchased a building at 3804-06 Grand Avenue; in October of 1993, we purchased the adjoining buildings at 3800 and 3802 Grand Avenue.

We were on Grand Avenue until 2001 when we purchased the land from the City of Minneapolis and built our present 20,000-square-foot building—a beautiful facility at 2637 32nd Avenue South—only a couple of miles from our original 2401 Cedar Avenue location. I am proud to tell how a long-time acquaintance, Willard Weikle, built our new facility. First, we gave him the plans. Within a few days he gave us a ballpark price. We shook hands and both said, "It's a deal." No contract—just grass-roots trust and honesty.

In 2001, MISCO built a new 20,000-square-foot facility in south Minneapolis.

In 1982, after four successful years of teaching high school choral music in New Ulm, Minnesota, our son Dan came into the business. Step by step he learned the business and today he is completely in charge of all operations and is doing a superb job.

Life's School's Lessons Continue...

In 1956, we had started manufacturing one 8-inch speaker for one customer. Today we manufacture 1,500-plus models for hundreds of customers worldwide. In 1956 there were about 25 American loudspeaker manufacturers. Today there are only one-half dozen or so loudspeaker manufacturers. *We must have done something right!*

There is so much I could write about the years of our marriage and the years we lived on Selby Avenue, 13th Avenue, Park Avenue, and Vincent Avenue, but we will do that when and if Bernice and I write the memories of our life together—and that we should because we have had a good marriage and a blessed life together.

I have been blessed in learning lessons from "Life's School" before the military service, during the military service, and after the military service. I am still learning Life's School's lessons every day.

I'm so proud of my family: Daniel, Kathleen, Bernice, me, Carrie, and Rolland—2008.

Returning to England

Now that the book is completed, I have shared in it the personal journey of my time in the military, the missions I flew, and the tragedy of losing friends. But for thousands of young "flyboys," questions about comrades remain.

Just when Marcia, Kathleen, Rosalie, Carol, and Sue—The Book Team—were all sighing with relief that they had put the book to bed and it was ready for the printer (their personal *Fait Accompli*), I threw them a ringer.

I started thinking that I had not told readers about the reunions I have attended or about my trips back to our base in England (Covington— Glatton). I thought about the people who will read these memoirs. Many will read and digest every word. These readers will wonder what happened to these young twenty-year olds and what they look like 60-plus years later. Thus was born the idea for this Appendix A, and Appendix B.

Memories of my going back to England and to the reunions have given me the realization of just how lucky I was. Sure I had some rough missions, but mine were "milk runs" compared with Bob Christofferson's and Thomas P. Thompson Jr.'s last mission. Had I not spent a full month doing absolutely nothing at Hamer Field before going to gunnery school, I would have been flying combat about a month sooner when missions were much tougher, and Robbie would not have been my pilot. Or another big if—had I not checked out as a radio operator and had chosen to continue as a gunner, the chances are I would have flown 11 more missions and only God knows what my fate might have been. Yes, I was lucky.

Again I remind readers, I am not a Hemmingway, a Steinbeck, or Minnesota's own Sinclair Lewis. I am not an author. Clifford "CB" Digre's life's work was that of a loudspeaker designer and builder, and I proudly admit I was good at that. But I was a keen chronicler of what I experienced during the war, and it is those memories I want to share with you. Thank you for reading them.

Returning to England and Glatton 1966, 1971, and 1998

In 1966 while on a trip to Norway, my wife, Bernice, and I made a side trip to England that included a stop at Glatton, wartime home of the 457th Air Force Bomb Group.

Years later on another trip to Norway in 1971, we repeated this side trip to England and Glatton. Both times it was a trip down memory lane; a few remnants of Quonset huts, familiar streets, and the runway. We also visited my favorite pub, The Oddfellows Arms. The owners, Frank and Rose Warren, were still there, and at that time in good health. They invited us to a nice dinner at their home.

In 1998 Bernice and I made an extensive six-week tour in Europe including several days in Antwerp, Belgium, the location of that forced landing on October 5, 1944. Our daughter Kathleen, her husband Michael, and their two daughters, Johanna and Gita, joined us in England. After we all toured Ireland, we visited Valley, Wales, the place where we had left the B-17 we had ferried over in August of 1944. Then we spent a full day in Southport, site of a flak leave in January of 1945.

Our next stop was Petersborough, where Bernie and Sadie Baines joined us. Bernie gave us a first-class tour of the base. My son-in-law Michael made a video of that tour which shall be a keepsake. After the base tour we had lunch in Sawtry before a visit to the American cemetery at Mattingly. After teatime at the Baines' home, we hosted a dinner at the Bull Hotel for Bernie and Sadie, and John Wilson. Although we had many highlights during our six weeks in Europe, an especially important side trip was another return to Glatton.

I captured some of the highlights of our three trips with the following photos.

(1966) This road leads to the 749th Squadron Area. My Hut #20 was at the very end of this road.

(1966) Remnants of one of our huts.

(1966) The Oddfellows Arms, no longer a pub, is now a private home where Rose and Frank Warren lived.

(1966) The Connington Church steeple. This church was truly a landmark in the center of our base.

(1966) The first memorial to the 457th located in front of the Connington
Church soon decayed.

(1971) Visiting with a Connington resident whom I remembered from
combat days. An hour or so after this picture was taken, we saw the same
man at the Connington Church service. He pumped the organ.

(1971) Frank Warren standing in the bar area where he took orders for bitters and milds and at closing time would say, "Time, gentlemen please—time please."

(1998) Bernie Baines (left) and myself in front of the newly rebuilt memorial to the 457th located next to the Connington Church.

(1998) Bernie and Sadie Baines in front of their house. We had teatime here before going on to the Bull Hotel for dinner.

(1998) Bernie and Sadie's home.

(1998) We hosted a dinner for Sadie and Bernie Baines, and John Wilson, with cocktail time in the lobby of the Bull Hotel before dinner.

(1998) Left side of table, L to R: John Wilson, me, and my wife, Bernice. Right side of the table R to L: my son-in-law Michael Varner, Sadie Baines, Bernie Baines, and my daughter Kathleen.

In 2004 a new memorial was dedicated. This very impressive memorial is seen by thousands of motorists yearly as it stands near what was the main entrance to our base on the Great North Road, Highway A1, one of England's busiest motorways.

The 457th Bomb Group Reunions

How the Association Came to Be

In 1971, Homer Briggs of Bentonville, Arkansas, quite by chance, came upon Ken Rurode of St. Joseph, Missouri, working on his car at a Bentonville service station. It was because of this chance meeting that the two former 749th Squadron "buddies" not only renewed their own friendship, but also decided to form a reunion group of the 457th Bomb Group in the interest of reuniting other "old buddies." After a lapse of nearly 25 years, Mickey Briggs, Homer's wife, began placing ads in veteran's magazines in search of other former 457th Bomb Group members who had served in England during WWII.

Ken Blakebrough supplied many more names, and the first reunion was held in Bentonville, Arkansas. The reunion was co-hosted by the Briggs, Rurodes, and Teagues, and was attended by 39 men and their families to "fight the war all over again." The tradition continues today.

From the first reunion in Bentonville in 1971, Homer and Mickey Briggs were the lifeline of the Bomb Group Reunion until Mickey retired in 1999 and Homer passed away in October of 2001. Without the dedication of Homer and Mickey, the 457th Bomb Group Reunion may not exist today, but the reins of the 457th Bomb Group secretary were picked up by Nancy Toth, daughter of Joe Toth. Nancy started assisting Mickey before she retired, so when she was officially elected the association secretary, she was familiar with all aspects of the position and has done an outstanding job since.

Mickey and Homer Briggs.

The objectives of the association are the preservation of the historical significance of the 457th Bomb Group (H), United States Army Air Corps, and the continuity of the spirit of friendship and camaraderie that first came into being as a result of military service in that organization during World War II.

Nancy Toth, 457th Bomb Group association secretary.

Sites of the 457th Bomb Group Reunions

1971 Bentonville, AR	1993 San Antonio, TX
1973 Topeka, KA	1995 Reno, NV
1976 Bentonville, AR	1997 Savannah, GA
1979 Omaha, NE	1999 Gettysburg, PA
1981 Colorado Springs, CO	2001 Colorado Springs, CO
1983 Houston, TX	2003 Rapid City, SD
1985 Rapid City, SD	2005 Savannah, GA
1987 Burlington, VT	2007 Pensacola, FL
1989 San Diego, CA	2009 Colorado Springs, CO
1991 Gulf Shores, MS	

The San Antonio Reunion—1993

This was the first reunion Bernice and I attended. Before then we felt we were just too busy running our business and paying the high costs of college education for our four children. By 1993 our son Dan was running the business and the other three children had also established their life's careers, so the time was right for Bernice and me to vacation and attend.

One goal I wanted to accomplish at this reunion was to learn about a crew I had flown with on February 23, 1945. The only thing I knew was the pilot's name—Thomas P. Thompson Jr.

On our first night at the Menger Hotel, I was visiting with Don Sellon whom I had never met before. When I learned Don was from the 748th, I inquired about Tommy Thompson and told Don about the mission when we did that incredible belly landing in France. Don's reply was, "You know what? Except for Tommy Thompson, that was my crew you flew with; some of that crew are here at this reunion." The next morning at breakfast I met Bennie Johnson and Dan Nose, who had been on that mission, and James Bass, the radio operator whom I had replaced on that mission. Since the war I have been wondering about these guys; now finally came a chance to meet them. What a surprise! What a reunion! I was already looking forward to 1995—our next reunion.

In addition to the Sellon Crew, we made other new friends:
- Phyllis and George Conover from Williston, North Dakota.
- Norman and Irene Menard from Massachusetts. Norm had flown with Tommy Thompson, "The Great Character," as he described him.

We also met a few friends I had known before:
- From England, John Wilson, a British F.O.T.E. (Friends of the Eighth). I knew John from our combat days in England. He was then a young 15-year-old British Air Cadet who flew with our crew on many practice missions.
- Paul and Rhoda Birchen from Hastings, Minnesota. We got together with Paul and Rhoda and other 457th veterans for a dinner and a Minnesota reunion in Hastings.

We met Homer and Mickey Briggs from Bentonville, Arkansas, in 1973 when we were driving our daughter Kathleen to the University of Arkansas in Fayetteville. Without the efforts of Homer and Mickey, the 457th Reunion may never have been organized.

Much of the time at the San Antonio reunion we spent with our new friends, members of the Don Sellon crew, including a night at "Durty Nelly's," a sing-a-long bar, drinking a few beers and throwing peanut shells on the floor. We entertained them with a couple of Norwegian "Ole and Lena" jokes and they made us honorary members of the Don Sellon crew. We proudly accepted the honor.

I was giving James Bass (right) a bad time. Actually, I was thanking him. If he had not become ill, I would not have met the Sellon crew members.

Bennie Johnson with his wife, Mary Lou. Bennie was the crew's ball turret gunner.

Bernice and I with John Wilson, a F.O.T.E. member, and a friend of Robbie's and our crew.

Phyllis and George Conover, Williston, North Dakota.

Norm and Irene Menard. Norman was on Tommy's original crew.

The Reno Reunion—1995

After Bernice and I had such a great time at the reunion two years ago in San Antonio when we met the Don Sellon crew, I got in touch with members of my Robbie Robertson crew and encouraged them to attend the reunion in Reno. Two of my crew members, and a friend who lived in our hut, made it to Reno, making it a very special event for me.

I had not seen crew member Julius Kornblatt since April 1945— some 50 years ago—so meeting Julie and his wife, Judy, was great. Crew member Louis (Louie) "The Head" Dahle was always in the mood for a good time, and he was in a high-spirited mood here, too. I had been with "The Head" and his jolly wife, Helen, several times since the war; these get-togethers were always upbeat.

Another special friend, Art Astor and his charming wife, Toni, were also at the Reno reunion. Art and his crew lived in our Hut #20, so we became good friends. On September 28, 1944, Art's crew was shot down. All survived, but became P.O.W.s. Because Art had not flown that day, he continued living in Hut #20 and we made him an honorary member of our crew. Having Kornblatt, Dahle, and Art Astor at this reunion was extraordinary.

One day Bernice and I were looking over personal diaries in the reunion memorabilia room and I read one person's account of the September 28th mission. I commented to Bernice that I remembered that mission and the very plane that went down. I told her that I had seen only three fellows bail out before the plane exploded, so I knew that six guys had been killed. Suddenly I got a tap on the shoulder and a fellow said, "I was one of those three." What a surprise and what a story he had to tell! His name was Bob Christofferson, and he and his wife, Grace, hailed from Hibbing, Minnesota. We immediately became friends, and he told us some details about that awful day. Just before he bailed out, his leg was shot off, but he was the only one of the three who had survived. What a story! See the footnote on page 85 for the story.

Although we spent most of our time with Kornblatt, Dahle, and Astor, we did get together with our friends from the Sellon crew for dinner, and we were looking forward to the 1997 reunion in Savannah, Georgia.

Were we ever this young (1945)?

Art Astor   Cliff Digre   Julius Kornblatt   Louis Dahle

Art Astor, me, Julie Kornblatt, and Louis Dahle—1995

Judy and Julie Kornblatt.

The one and only Louie Dahle, "The Head."

Mr. Louis A. Dahle.

Toni and Art Astor.

Grace and Bob Christofferson. What an unbelievable story he told.

James and Erma Bass.

The Savannah Reunion—1997

This time the reunion was held in Savannah, the home of The Mighty 8th Air Force Museum. We can all be so proud that people had the foresight to preserve this bit of history. The museum holds the history of every bomb and fighter group that made up The Mighty Eighth with an unbelievable display of memorabilia and videos of missions. We spent about four hours there; however, I could have spent four days.

Plans are now underway to build a chapel on these grounds. That I want to see!

A visit here is a "must see" for family members of those of us who made up The Mighty Eighth.

Bernice and I have been in Savannah before, but we always enjoy this charming, historic city. Again, we had a great time with Don Sellon's crew members at a dinner at Mrs. Wilkes' Boarding House as well as a memorable evening dinner.

Now we look forward to Gettysburg in 1999.

Me, pictured with my wife, Bernice.

Dan and Jeanne Nose.

Members of the Don Sellon Crew, from left to right: Bennie Johnson, Anthony O'Brien, Bob Tavgney, Don Sellon, Dan Nose, and James Bass.

The Gettysburg Reunion—1999

This was the fourth 457th reunion we had attended. We left Minneapolis at mid afternoon on October 9th on Sun Country Airlines and arrived at Washington Dulles International Airport about 6 p.m., stayed over-night at the Airport Holiday Inn, and the next morning I bargained with a cabbie for the 50-mile trip to Gettysburg. We arrived at the Eisenhower Inn shortly after noon. That afternoon was spent register-ing for upcoming activities and greeting friends we hadn't seen since the Savannah reunion two years ago.

Unfortunately the front desk staff was rude and unaccommodating. They absolutely refused to allow room registration until 4 p.m. The dining room staff was completely unprepared to accommodate the 400 plus who took over the entire facility. Even though the Eisenhower Inn grounds were beautiful and the facilities excellent, our first impres-sions were not the greatest, but as the week went on, things improved and we had a good time. The first evening we had dinner with our friends from the Don Sellon crew.

Reunion Highlights...

...The three-hour bus tour of the Gettysburg battlefields, a bit crowd-ed, but a fun luncheon at the Dobbin House, an old, old Civil War home converted into a pub and café.

...A full-day bus tour to Washington, D.C., seeing all the main D.C. attractions.

...A car tour of the battlefields with our new friends, Rollie and Helen Bolier from Champlin, Minnesota. They had driven to Gettysburg.

...A festive banquet with a big band. At our table seated with Bernice and me were our good friends, Don and Jeanne Sellon, Dan and Jeanne Nose, Mary Addison, and Paul and Rhoda Birchen.

A Chance Meeting Highlight...

On our first combat mission on September 9, 1944, we flew Aircraft #42-32086, named *You'll Never Know*. The plane was good to us with no injuries so we hoped to fly *You'll Never Know* the next day. But no! We were assigned to #44-6088, *Rattlesnake Daddy*. After the mission we learned that *You'll Never Know* was shot up badly and crash-landed. That's all I'd known for these 55 years. I have often wondered about the crew of *You'll Never Know*. Were they all killed? Or what? Well, at Gettysburg I learned all about it.

While waiting to register for rooms on the afternoon we arrived, we had time to visit with many guys. I met Russ Karl from Peru, Illinois, for the first time. Our conversation led to mission highlights such as which were the toughest, etc. Russ said his toughest and scariest was on September 10, 1944. My ears immediately perked up. He said, "They had just dropped their bombs on the target at Baden Baden, Germany, and their plane was hit hard by flak. The pilot came on the intercom and said, 'We can't make it back to England, but I think I may make it to France and try a belly landing, but you guys may choose to bail out.'" Two of the crew chose to bail out, and both were shot and killed by the Germans. The others stayed with the plane and safely belly-landed in France. The plane was #42-32086, *You'll Never Know*. At the reunion I also met Tom Farrell and his friend, Rosalie Franklin. Tom was also on the crew of *You'll Never Know*.

Russ Karl and me. We hit it off after we found our common bond—*You'll Never Know*.

Ella and Russ Karl. New friends we met for the first time.

Rollie and Helen Bolier, Champlin, Minnesota. New friends we toured the battlefields with one afternoon.

Rhoda and Paul Birchen, Hastings, Minnesota. Two special friends.

The Colorado Springs Reunion—2001

In spite of the terrorist attacks of September 11th, our reunion was not called off. It was very well attended and a big success. A visit to the Air Force Academy was cancelled, but all other activities went on as scheduled.

Bernice and I flew to Colorado Springs on a NWA flight at 11:30 a.m. on Saturday, September 22nd. At the airport we met four new 457th friends, Lee and Helen Zimmerman of Jackson, Michigan, and Jim and Ardis Rodel of Eau Claire, Wisconsin. Leon (Lee) was the past president of our 457th Association.

Joe and Jeanne Toth of Pueblo, Colorado, were the official coordinators of the reunion, but their daughter, Nancy, took over most of the responsibilities. Nancy was well organized, and the reunion went like clockwork. This is the fifth reunion we have attended so we have made many friends. We have a particularly close friendship with Dan and Jeanne Nose and other members of the Don Sellon crew. It was with these guys that I crash landed in France on my 20th mission on February 23, 1945.

At this reunion we spent some time with new friends, Lee and Helen Zimmerman. We even went to a Lutheran church with them on Sunday morning.

Another great reunion, and we look forward to the 2003 get together.

Our new friends, Lee and Helen Zimmerman, from Michigan, with Bernice and me.

Jeanette and Frank Hallson, Minneapolis. We live within a few blocks of Jeanne and Frank, a great couple, loyal to the 457th reunions.

From left to right: Me, Craig Harris, Lee Zimmerman, and Dan Nose. Craig Harris was an outstanding person. After retiring from Duke University as an associate professor of radiology, he became active in the 457th B.G. Association as well as in the Eighth Air Force Historical Society, a national organization. He served on the board of directors and became the president of both organizations. Craig passed away August 6, 2007. His death was a big loss to all of us.

The president-elect, Will Fluman. Will Fluman has been another outstanding member of our association. He has served on the board of directors and as president. Not only has Will been an active member, but his daughter Candice and son Will Jr. are also active and contributing members.

The Rapid City Reunion—2003

This was the first reunion we missed since our first in San Antonio. Where were we? Traveling about Europe.

During this time we flew *first class*, thanks to our son-in-law Michael's frequent flyer miles:

Houston to Paris
Paris to Oslo
Oslo to Paris
Paris to Rome
Rome to Paris
Paris to Boston

What a great experience. In addition to the first-class tickets, Kathleen and Michael gave us *first class* care all of the time.

Yes, we hated to miss the reunion, but for a trip like this, it was worth it.

The Savannah Reunion—2005

The theme for this reunion was "Back to Savannah." We had been there for our reunion in 1997. That was great, but this was even more impressive.

We again spent a day at The Mighty Eighth Air Force Museum. This reunion was more meaningful to me since "The Chapel of the Fallen Angels" had been completed. It was adorned with beautiful stained glass windows, one of which was sponsored by our group. These windows will stand as a memorial to those who had served our country in World War II. The memorial service was held in the chapel and honored 60 deceased since our last reunion; two were our crew members—Charlie Carbery and my very dear special friend, Stanley P. Szydlowski.

Bernice and I spent a lot of time with our good friends the Sellons, Dan and Jeanne Nose, Bennie and Mary Lou Johnson, James and Irma Bass, and our good Michigan friends, Lee and Helen Zimmerman.

Bernice and I stayed a day after the reunion and enjoyed touring Savannah on trolley rides. We were already looking forward to the next reunion to be held in Pensacola, Florida, in 2007.

The 8th Air Force Chapel of the Fallen Eagles.

The 457th stained glass window in the chapel.

Memorial Service Honoring Those Deceased Since 2003

> This was a special service for me because
> Charles W. Carbery and Stanley P. Szydlowski were remembered.

**MEMORIAL SERVICE
SAVANNAH 2005
CHAPEL OF
THE FALLEN EAGLES**

Blair Arsenault
Russel Auten
Charles R. Blackwell
Joseph M. Budich, Sr.
L. Bradley Bunker
*Charles W. Carbery
Fred Castle
William Clarkson
Aaron B. Connelly
Edmund G. Coomes
Hamilton Doherty
William J. Dufford
Carl E. Gamblin
Lloyd Gray
Jack Gumm
Vernon H. Hawbaker
Evert R. Heins
Patrick Henry
Edmund W. Hubard

Walter W. Hunt
Charles H. Kaufman
Harry M. Kennedy
William R. Kilpatrick
Hulitt Kirkhart
James Paul LaPaze
Leonard Luchonoke
Santo Maira
Stan Majer
George D. McCurry
Harold L. McDaniel
William J. P. Meng
George Metzger
Augustus L. Moore
George Murphy
William H. Murry
N. Kenneth Nail
William T. Meidhardt
Mark Osborne

Dee Kemp Owsley
Theodore P. Panaretos
Robert T. Payne
Ray Pobgee
Wilbur S. Pursell
Edward J. Reppa
Carl Robbie
Robert L. Schaaf
Julius Smith
Leonard P. Soenke
William H. Steffen
Charles Stewart
Guy C. Sturdevant, Jr.
Raymond A. Syptak
* Stanley P. Szydlowski
Charles R. Ward
William C. Watts
Clyde R. Weid
Leonard E. Wolfer
Robert Wood
Bernard Wrobleski
Stanley Zocks
Irvin Zweibel

The Pensacola Reunion—2007

The 457th Pensacola Reunion, November 1-4, 2007, was again filled with highlights. What was the biggest highlight to me? Our two daughters, Kathleen and Carrie, joined Bernice and me for the festivities. I was so very proud to introduce them to our 457th friends. But along with the thrill of having them with us, we had a couple of disappointments. Our good friends, Don and Jeanne Sellon and Dan and Jeanne Nose had to cancel. Jeanne Nose had broken her arm and Don Sellon picked up a bug just days before the get together. But my very good friend Bennie Johnson from the Sellon crew was there with his daughter Christy and her husband Pete. They drove to Pensacola from their home in Baton Rouge, Louisiana. We missed Bennie's wife, Mary Lou.

Other special friends we always enjoy being with are Lee and Helen Zimmerman from Jackson, Michigan; Russ Karl and his wife, Ella, from Peru, Illinois; Bill Morse and his German wife, Ericka, from Lake Ann, Michigan and a very special person to me, James Bass from Carthage, Tennessee, who was the person responsible for making me an honorary member of the Don Sellon crew. At this reunion, James conducted his last official meeting as the association president. He has done a masterful job as the association president. While visiting with George Grau, the president-elect, we discussed our missions, discovering we had flown our last mission together. George is a dedicated association member and will do a great job as president.

We made new friends again. We sat with Albert Williams and his wife, Shirley, and daughter Cindy Mackool at the luau. Carrie and Cindy sat together on the flight from Memphis to Pensacola but had no conversation as to what and to where they were going so when they again met, they found they had much to visit about. Al had been on Lee Zimmerman's crew and was also a P.O.W. He is now writing a book of his experiences. I look forward to an interesting read.

All reunions have had their surprises, and this was no exception. We met Ed Stevens, a 457th veteran, and his sons Ed Jr. and David. We had never met Ed or Ed Jr. before, but we had met David way back in 1975 when he was married to Miriam, sister of my son-in-law Michael. It was good to see David again. What a surprise!

Now we look forward to the next reunion in Colorado Springs in 2009. What surprises are in store next time? We all make a valiant effort to attend these reunions. As we sort through the personal diaries and faded pictures of the boys we were then and the grown, graying men we have become, no doubt more names will have been added to the "Wall of the Deceased," and more chance encounters will reunite us with friends from those wartime years. Yes, we are all looking forward to the next reunion.

No friendships compare to those forged in war. For we of our bomb group, the war ended, we returned to our hometowns, met and fell in love with "the girls of our dreams," raised families, and worked hard to establish ourselves in careers. And of course the memories of the wartime years were always a part of us. Then through luck and coincidence, we men of the 457th were brought together again, and arranged the reunions that have made whole the continuity of our lives. Stories were told, men met comrades not seen since the war years, and accounts of downed planes and P.O.W. camps were shared.

Old friends—me, left, with Joe Toth.

Bernice and I with Bennie Johnson, his daughter Christy, and son-in-law Pete.

My younger daughter, Carrie, loved combing the beach...

...while my older daughter, Kathleen, was bending Bennie Johnson's ear.

Bill Morse, a crew chief, and his German wife, Ericka. Bill and Ericka attend every reunion.

While visiting with George Grau, I discovered we had flown our last mission together.

With the Ed Stevens family. Top left Ed Jr., with his brother, David.

Albert and Shirley Williams with their daughter Cindy Mackool.

How proud I was, shown here with my daughters, Kathleen and Carrie, and my wife, Bernice, all dressed for the banquet and party held on the last evening of each reunion.

My two lovely daughters, Kathleen and Carrie.

We didn't dance 'til dawn, but...

...we did dance until the music stopped!

The P.O.W.s who attended the reunion.

These are the vets who attended. Our numbers are shrinking.

APPENDIX C
Loading Lists, Track Charts, and Narratives of the Missions

Loading Lists were posted on the evening before each mission. The ship is designated by the last three numbers of the plane's serial number. Each position was listed as well as each serial number of the man flying.

Since I have been reviewing the loading lists, I find many errors in name spellings, serial numbers, etc. For example, the first four digits of my serial number is listed on several lists. Also Clifford V. instead of Clifford B.— nothing too serious.

A **Track Chart** is an official record of each mission. The chart includes a map of the target, key locations, the flight plan, and the I.P. (initial point). The I.P. is the beginning of the bomb run. Once the plane was on the bomb run, there was no deviation from the plan without the permission of the group's air commander. The briefed route is in a darkened line; the actual route is in a lighter line. The track chart also includes a brief narrative of the mission. Photographs from the target are sometimes included. On many of the missions, the lead crew is photographed from the mission.

I have included the loading list and track chart of each of my missions, and the ill-fated Cliff Hendrickson mission in this appendix.

A **retyped narrative** of the mission follows each track chart. The reduced size and lack of contrast on many of the track charts make the narratives of the missions difficult to read. For this reason, we retyped each narrative exactly as it was originally recorded, including misspellings, unusual punctuation, abbreviations, etc., to make the description of each mission more accessible.

A **glossary** of abbreviations and terms, especially those used in the track chart descriptions, is located in Appendix D, page 319.

Loading List—September 9, 1944 • My Mission #1

```
SHIP   086
P      P      ROBERTSON. WILLIAM T.        1st Lt      O-525177
CP     CP     HENDRICKSON. CLIFFORD        2nd Lt      O-812261
N      N      MANKIN. ELMER L              2nd Lt      O-2057973
B      B      CARBERY. CHARLES W.          2nd Lt      O-712271
E      TT     RINEHART. EARL A.            Sgt         15083847
RO     RR     STUTMAN. BERNERD             Sgt         13052839
       BT     DIGRE. CLIFFORD B.           Sgt         3756
       WG     MCDERMOTT. ALEXANDRA         T/Sgt       12064068
       TG     BROWN. JOHN F.               Sgt         12151503


SHIP   154
P      P      BURGESS. OLIVER. G. JR       2nd Lt      O-764870
CP     CP     TEUTSHELL. ALBERT V. JR      2nd Lt      O-767685
N      N      PIKE. LOUIS                  2nd Lt      O-720004
B      B      ELWOOD. JOHN E.              2nd Lt      O-769021
E      TT     MOLESTATORE. ALDO            T/Sgt       33102264
RO     RR     PARSONS. GEORGE A. JR        T/Sgt       31519167
       BT     DURKE. ROBERT J              S/Sgt       32401099
       WG     DOLIAR. HERBERT.             S/Sgt       38509207
       TG     VEVIER. ROLAND               S/Sgt       11088710


SHIP   079
P      P      WHITMAN. HARRY J             2nd Lt      O-761830
CP     CP     GILBERTSON. ALBERT O JR      F/O         T-62919
N      N      PATRICK. HAROLD              2nd Lt      O-718409
B      B      STONER. LEONARD.             2nd Lt      O-772767
E      TT     MELLY. JOSEPH                T/Sgt       11119454
RO     RR     MUNGER. HOWARD.              T/Sgt       17150363
       BT     SITEK. BERNARD               S/Sgt       31284558
       WG     SCHARNHORST. WILLIAM         S/Sgt       37571842
       TG     MCGRIFF. KENNETH             S/Sgt       39704936


SHIP   034
P      P      MCCALL. WILLIAM R. JR        2nd Lt      O-756295
CP     CP     GREGORY. THOMAS L            2nd Lt      O-823592
N      N      LIVINGSTONE. ARTHUR M        2nd Lt      O-712618
B      B      PLAGIANOS. LEON M            2nd Lt      O-708040
E      TT     PERRY. GEORGE W.             S/Sgt       7001463
RO     RR     HAYES. ROBERT J              S/Sgt       20952240
       BT     WILLIS. LINVILLE             Sgt         35872372
       WG     COOKE. GEORGE                S/Sgt       6975178
       TG     BATTISTI. LARIDO             Sgt         16127713


SHIP   088
P      P      HEDRICK. RAY D. JR           1st Lt      O-742715
CP     CP     DUNDAS. BASIL R. JR          2nd Lt      O-770978
N      N      PARKER. JOHN B.              2nd Lt      O-722930
B      B      BENSON. EDWIN B              2nd Lt      O-706671
E      TT     SNYDER. PHILIP H. DIR        S/Sgt       12176625
RO     RR     GRAVELLE. DONALD H           S/Sgt       36597044
       BT     SWEENEY. JOHN J              T/Sgt       11042459
       WG     MCGILLIAN. JOHN F.           Sgt         20250794
       TG     RAY. HARVEY G.               Sgt         33564680
```

Track Chart—September 9, 1944

Mission #119, Mannheim, 9 September, 1944

Although Ludwigshave was briefed for a possible visual primary target today, heavy cloud coverage caused the three 12 a/c boxes dispatched by this group to choose the M/Y at Mannheim as its PFF target. Being the sixth group in the Division formation, we comprised the 94th "C" Wing, all other wings in this force having the same MPI's. The targets assigned to the 2nd and 3rd Divisions were the Mainz M/Y and armament works at Dusseldorf respectively.

Taking off under hazy conditions, Major Watson led the group on the briefed course over England, departing from the coast of Clacton. Entering the enemy coast above Dunkirk, a direct southeast route was followed to approximately 0336E, at which point the formation flew about 18 miles left of course in trail of the Division. At the last turn before the I.P., however, the formation returned to course.

With swelling cumulus increasing to 8/10 near the target, the formation approached the town of Mannheim to bomb by PFF. The group was now flying at 25,000 feet and proceeding on the bomb run. Three or four jet-propelled aircraft skirted the formation from a safe distance, but the fighter support was good and the E/A did not choose to attack. Trouble developed in the PFF equipment of the lead ship however, and the lead was turned over to Lt. Ormsby flying the deputy PFF A/C. The AFCE functioned smoothly on the run and the 500-pound G.P.'s and leaflets were released at about 1050 hours on the smoke markers of the Deputy Wing Leader.

Ten-tenths clouds obscured the pattern area of the bombs, but small breaks in the clouds at bombs away permitted estimation of the bomb hits. The pattern of the strikes appeared in Waldhof, the northern part of the city of Mannheim, about 12,000 feet from the assigned MPI. Since several aircraft salvoed their bombs there was no doubt a concentration of bursts below the pattern covering an industrial area and the railroad bridge across the Industrie Hofen.

After bombs away the group turned right and swung back again to the I.P., the course out coinciding with the briefed course in.

The moderate to intense flak encountered at the target was accurate and of the tracking type. The crews were surprised, however, by unplotted flak at Germersheim on he route back. Although it was quite accurate only 12 guns were reported firing. Enemy activity at this point was noted. Crews reported observing vehicles of an armored force crossing the Rhine eastward at Germersheim as well as a concentration of barges along the river banks.

At 1315 the enemy coast was reached. The Wing began a normal let-down over the channel and returned to base, the last plane landing at 1425 hours. All planes returned safely, only 4 planes receiving major damage and 13 minor.

Loading List—September 10, 1944 • My Mission #2

SHIP 079

P	P	WHITMAN, HARRY J.	2ND LT	0-761230
CP	CP	GILBERTSON, ALBERT O. JR	2ND LT	T-62919
N	N	PATRICK, HAROLD W.	2ND LT	0-718409
B	B	STONER, LEONARD G.	2ND LT	0-772767
E	TT	MELLY, JOSEPH P.	T/SGT	11119434
RO	RR	MUNGER, HOWARD	T/SGT	17150363
	BT	SITEK, BERNARD F.	S/SGT	31284358
	WG	SCHARNHORST, WILLIAM A.	S/SGT	37671842
	TG	McGRIFF, KENNETH E.	S/SGT	39704936

SHIP 948

P	P	FIEDLER, WILLIAM F.	2ND LT	0-761579
CP	CP	ERNEST, FREDRICK	2ND LT	0-693457
N	N	PACE, HERBERT W.	2ND LT	0-717688
B	B	SAGE, EDWARD R.	2ND LT	0-771975
E	TT	ATTAWAY, MICAEL	T/SGT	18116002
RO	RR	STELTZER, GEORGE A.	T/SGT	32042843
	BT	MOONEY, JOSEPH M.	S/SGT	33595287
	TG	STEGEMAN, RUDOLPH E.	S/SGT	12191719
	WG	STEVENS, GERALD D.	S/SGT	35874618

SHIP 161

P	P	McCALL, WILLIAM R. JR	2ND LT	0-756295
CP	CP	GREGORY, THOMAS L.	2ND LT	0-823504
N	N	LIVINGSTONE, ARTHUR M.	2ND LT	0-712618
B	B	GIANNICO, DOMINICK	2ND LT	0-769029
E	TT	PERRY, GEORGE W.	S/SGT	7001463
RO	RR	HAYES, ROBERT J.	S/SGT	20952240
	BT	WILLS, LINVILLE	SGT	35872372
	WG	McDERMOTT, ALEXANDER	T/SGT	12064088
	TG	BATTISTI, LARIDO	SGT	16127713

SHIP 088

P	P	ROBERTSON, WILLIAM T.	2ND LT	0-523177
CP	CP	HENDRICKSON, CLIFFORD	2ND LT	0-812261
N	N	MANKIN, ELMER L.	2ND LT	0-205773
B	B	CARBERY, CHARLES	2ND LT	0-712271
E	TT	RINEHART, EARL A.	SGT	15083847
RO	RR	STUTMAN, BERNARD	SGT	13052839
	BT	DEGRE, CLIFRORD	SGT	3756
	WG	SZKYDLOWSKI, STANLEY P.	SGT	20408024
	TG	BROWN, JOHN F.	SGT	12151503

Track Chart—September 10, 1944

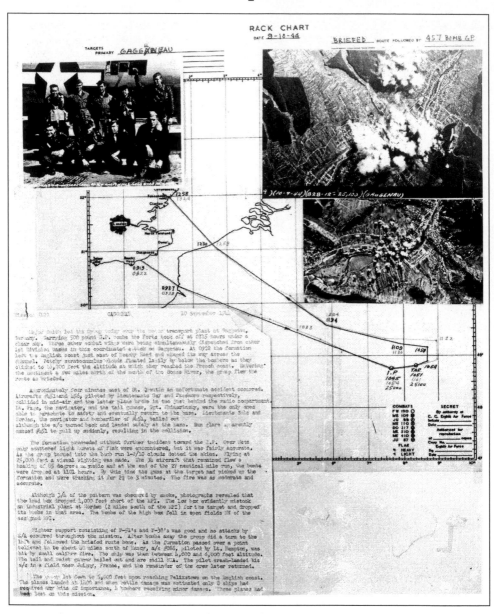

Mission #120, Gaggenau, 10 September, 1944

Major Smith led the Group today over the motor transport plant at Gaggenau, Germany. Carrying 500-pound G.P. bombs the Forts took off at 0715 hours under a clear sky. Three other combat wings were being simultaneously dispatched from other 1st Division bases in this coordinated attack on Gaggenau. At 0922 the formation left the English coast just east of Beachy Head and winged its way across the channel. Patchy stratocumulus clouds floated lazily by below the bombers as they climbed to 16,000 feet the altitude at which they reached the French coast. Entering the continent a few miles north of the mouth of the Somme River, the group flew the route as briefed.

Approximately four minutes east of St. Quentin an unfortunate accident occurred. Aircrafts #451 and 456, piloted by Lieutenants Gay and Passmore respectively, collided in mid-air and the latter plane broke in two just behind the radio compartment. Lt. Page, the navigator, and the tail gunner, Sgt. Chimerinsky, were the only ones able to parachute to safety and eventually return to the base. Lieutenants Sale and Nordan, the navigator and bombardier of #451, bailed out although the a/c turned back and landed safely at the base. Sun glare apparently caused #451 to pull up suddenly, resulting in the collision.

The formation proceeded without further incident toward the I.P. Over Metz only scattered light bursts of flak were encountered, but it was fairly accurate. As the group turned into the bomb run 1-2/10 clouds dotted the skies. Flying at 25,000 feet a visual sighting was made. The 34 aircraft that remained flew a heading of 85 degrees magnetic and at the end of the 27-nautical-mile run; the bombs were dropped at 1101 hours. By this time the guns at the target had picked up the formation and were tracking it for 2½ to 3 minutes. The fire was as moderate and accurate.

Although 3/4 of the pattern was obscured by smoke, photographs revealed that the lead box dropped 1,000 feet short of the MPI. The low box evidently mistook an industrial plant at Horden (2 miles south of the MPI) for the target and dropped its bombs in that area. The bombs of the high box fell in open fields NW of the assigned MPI.

Fighter support consisting of P-51's and P38's was good and no attacks by E/A occurred throughout the mission. After bombs away the group did a turn to the left and followed the briefed route home. As the formation passed over a point believed to be about 40 miles south of Nancy, a/c #086, piloted by Lt. Hampton, was hit by small caliber fire. The ship was then between 4,000 and 6,000 feet altitude. The tail and waist gunner bailed out and are still MIA. The pilot crash-landed his a/c in a field near Joigny, France, and the remainder of the crew later returned.

The crew let down to 5,000 feet upon reaching Felixstowe on the English coast. The planes landed at 1400 and when battle damage was estimated only 8 ships had received any hits of importance, 4 bombers receiving minor damage. Three planes had been lost on this mission.

Loading List—September 12, 1944 • My Mission #3

SHIP 633				
P	P	WILLIAM R. McCALL JR	2ND LT	0756293
CP	CP	THOMAS L. GREGORY	2ND LT	0823504
N	N	ARTHUR M LIVINGSTONE	2ND LT	0712612
B	B	LOUIS F. BRICKMAN	2ND LT	0703565
E	TT	GEORGE W. PERRY	S/SGT	7001463
RO	RR	ROBERT J. HAYES	S/SGT	20952240
	BT	LINVILLE WILLS	SGT	35872572
	WG	ALEXANDER P. McDERMOTT	T/SGT	12064088
	TG	LARIDO A. BATTISTI	SGT	16127713
SHIP 088				
P	P	WILLIAM R. ROBERTSON	1ST LT	0523177
CP	CP	CLIFFORD HENDRICKSON	2ND LT	0812261
N	N	ELMER L. MANKIN	2ND LT	02057973
B	B	THOMAS S. CROWLEY	2ND LT	0771901
E	TT	EARL A. RHINEHART	SGT	15082847
RO	RR	BERNARD STUTMAN	SGT	13052839
	BT	CLIFFORD B. DIGRE	SGT	3756
	WG	STANLEY P. SZYKLOWSKI	SGT	12151503

Track Chart—September 12, 1944

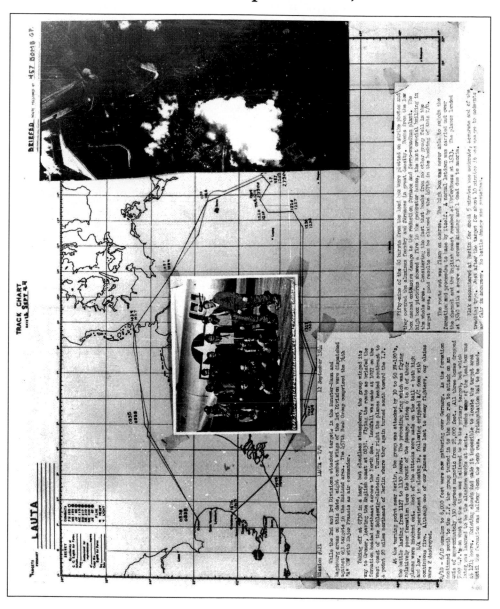

Mission #121, Lauta—T/O, 12 September, 1944

While the 2nd and 3rd Divisions attacked targets in the Munster-Hamm and Magdeburg areas on this date, eight combat wings of the 1st Division were dispatched against oil targets in the Ruhland area. The 457th Bomb Group comprised the 94th "A" CBW with Major Francis as air commander.

Taking off at 0730 in a hazy, but cloudless atmosphere, the group winged its way to Cromer, leaving the English coast at 0838. Flying the route as briefed the formation headed northeast across the North Sea. Landfall was made at 1027 on the west coast of the Schleswig-Holstein. Turning right the planes heading southeast to a point 20 miles northeast of Berlin where they again turned south toward the I.P.

At the turning point near Berlin, the group was attacked by 30 to 50 FW-190's, the battle lasting from 1127 to 1130 hours. The preceding wing which was flying relatively poor formation bore the brunt of the damage, since 6 to 8 of their planes were knocked out. Most of the attacks were made on the tail – both high and low. E/A were persistent in closing in, following crippled A/C down with continuous fire. Although one of our planes was lost to enemy fighters, our claims were 2 destroyed.

4/10 – 6/10 cumulus to 8,000 feet were now gathering over Germany. As the formation continued south to the IP the group turned in to the bomb run to attack on an axis of approximately 330 degrees magnetic from 28,000 feet. All three boxes dropped 500# G.P.'s on what at the time was believed to be the primary target, but which later, was learned to be the aluminum works at Lauta. Bombs away of the lead box was at 1214 hours. Existing clouds had made it impossible to locate the target area until the formation was halfway down the bomb run. Triangulation had to be used.

Fifty-nine of the 80 bursts from the lead box were plotted on strike photos and they covered the aluminum foundry and furnaces in great density. Bombs from the low box caused extensive damage to the reduction furnace and ferro-vanadium plant. The high box pictures showed a fire in the generator house, the most crucial building in the whole area. Considering the fact that bombs from no other group fell in the target area, good results can be claimed by the 457th in the bombing of this T/O.

The route out was flown on course. The high box was never able to rejoin the formation and proceeded to base by itself. A normal letdown was carried out over the channel and the English coast reached at Orfordness at 1513. The planes landed at 1540 with a score of 3 crews missing and 1 dead to anoxia.

Flak encountered at Berlin for about 5 minutes was moderate, accurate and of the tracking type. Just after the target for about 10 minutes it was meager to moderate and fair in accuracy. No battle damage was sustained.

Loading List—September 17, 1944 • My Mission #4

SHIP 948

P	P	WILLIAM T ROBINSON	1st Lt	0523177
CP	CP	CLIFFORD HENDRICKSON	2nd Lt	0812261
N	N	ELMER L MANKIN	2nd Lt	02057973
B	B	HORACE W WHIPPLE	2nd Lt	0557548
E	TT	LOUIS A DAHLE	Sgt	16034867
RO	RR	Bernard Stutman	Sgt	13052839
	BT	Clifford B Tigre	Sgt	5756
	WG	Julius Kornblatt	Sgt	32669450
	TG	John F Brown	Sgt	12151503

SHIP 164

P	P	WILLIAM S FISHER	2nd Lt	0819781
CP	CP	WILLIAM C BONNELL JR	2nd Lt	0714628
N-B	N-B	RUPERT L PHIPPS	2nd Lt	0707437
CHIN		Roland F Vevier	S/Sgt	11008710
E	TT	David M Peterson	S/Sgt	36818325
RO	RR	Herman J Ratica	S/Sgt	13086759
	BT	Stanley P Gillespie	Sgt	37578695
	WG	Alexander P McDermott	T/Sgt	12064068
	TG	Buford B Lawson	Sgt	34684913

SHIP 161

P	P?	WILLIAM F FIEDLER	2nd Lt	0761579
CP	CP	FREDERICK C ERNEST	2nd Lt	0693457
N	N	HERBERT W PACE	2nd Lt	0717688
B	B	EDWARD R SAGE	2nd Lt	0771975
E	TT	Michael E Attaway	T/Sgt	18116002
RO	RR	George A Staltzer	T/Sgt	32042843
	BT	Joseph M Mooney	S/Sgt	33595287
	WG	Rudolph E Stegemann	S/Sgt	12191719
	TG	Gerald D Stevens	S/Sgt	35874618

SHIP 034

P	P	WILLIAM R MCCALL JR	2nd Lt	0755295
CP	CP	THOMAS L GREGORY	2nd Lt	0825504
N	N	ARTHUR M LIVINGSTONE	2nd Lt	0712518
B	B	ROBERT P SMITH	2nd Lt	0717906
E	TT	George W Perry	S/Sgt	7001463
RO	RR	Robert J Hayes	S/Sgt	20952240
	BT	Linville Wills	Sgt	35872372
	WG	Walter L Slate	S/Sgt	12033727
	TG	Karldo A Battisti	Sgt	16127713

Track Chart—September 17, 1944

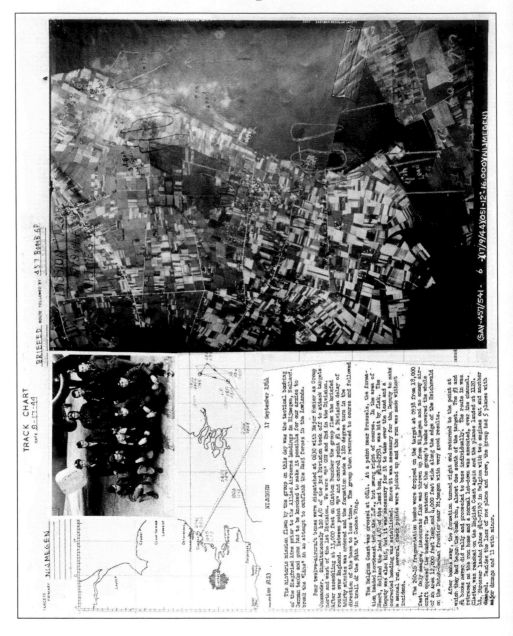

Mission #123, Nijmegen, Holland, 17 September 1944

This historic mission flown by the group on this day was the tactical bombing of the Siegfried Line prior to the Allied Airborne landings in Nijmegen, Holland. German tanks and guns had to be knocked to make it possible for our armies to break the "Line" in an attempt to outflank the Nazi forces in the Lowlands.

Four twelve-aircraft boxes were dispatched at 0630 with Major Hozier as Group Commander. Simultaneously 420 A/C of the 3rd Division took off to attack targets north and west of the 1st Division. We were "B" CBW and 2nd in the Division. After assembling at 13,000 feet on Glatton Buncher the group flew the briefed route over England. Between point "B" and control point #1 a Division delay of thirty minutes was ordered and the formation made a 180 degree turn in the direction of the base to lose time. The group then returned to course and followed in trail of the 94th "A" Combat Wing.

The Belgium Coast was crossed at 0841. At a point near Brussels, the formation headed northeast into the I.P., but swung right of course. In the area of Weert, Holland the lead A/C of the lead box, #42-47951, was hit by flak. The Deputy was also hit, but it was necessary for it to take over the lead and a corrected heading was established. Since it was necessary for the Deputy to make a manual run, several check points were picked up and the run was made without incident.

The 260-lb fragmentation bombs were dropped on the target at 0938 from 18,000 feet. Only meager, inaccurate flak was thrown up from Nijmegen and no enemy aircraft opposed the bombers. The pattern of the group's bombs covered the whole of an area 12,000 feet long and 4,000 feet wide along the edge of the Reichswald on the Dutch-German frontier near Nijmegen with very good results.

After bombs away, the formation turned right and returned to the point at which they had begun the bomb run, almost due south of the target. The #3 and #4 boxes never did rally and proceeded to base individually. The route in was retraced on the run home and a normal let-down was executed, over the channel. Lt. Strosser landed plane #42-97190 in Belgium with two engines out and another damaged. Besides the loss of one plane and crew, the group had 5 planes with major damage and 11 with minor.

Loading List—September 19, 1944 • My Mission #5

```
SUBJECT: Combat Crew Loading List.

SHIP  649
P     P     HURDIS. WILLIAM D.          1st Lt    O-814148
CP    CP    SYPTAK. RAYMOND A.          major     O-409770
N     N     ASTELL. FREDRICK W.         1st Lt    O-698252
N     N     POND. MERTON L              2nd Lt    O-717495
N     N     ANDERSON. GEORGE D.         1st Lt    O-699972
B     B     MILLER. MARK K.             2nd Lt    O-769169
E     TT    MAYO. ELIHUE                T/Sgt     15328206
RO    RH    RICHMOND. DANIEL            T/Sgt     19095141
      WG    JOHNSTON. LAWRENCE          S/Sgt     39520103
CP    TG    MITTWOCH. ELMER.            2nd Lt    O-764737

SHIP  181
P     P     FISHER. WILLIAMS.           2nd Lt    O-819791
CP    CP    BONNELL. WILLIAM C.         2nd Lt    O-714628
N     N     EKBLOM. ROBERT X JR         2nd Lt    O-723328
B     B     PHIPPS. RUPERT L.           2nd Lt    O-707437
E     TT    PETERSON. DAVID             S/Sgt     36818325
RO    RR    FATICA. HERMAN J.           S/Sgt     13086759
      BT    GILLESPIE. STANLEY          Sgt       37578695
      WG    BRANTLEY. CECIL B.          Sgt       34854382
      TG    LAWSON. KENNETH BUFORD B.   SGT       34884013

SHIP  079
P     P     WHITMAN. HARRY J.           1st Lt    O-761230
CP    CP    GILBERTSON. ALBERT O.       F/O       O-62919
N     N     PATRICK. HAROLD W.          2nd Lt    O-718409
B     B     STONER. LEONARD.            2nd Lt    O-772757
E     TT    MELLY. JOSEPH P             T/Sgt     11119454
RO    RR    MUNGER. HOWARD B.           T/Sgt     17150363
      BT    SITEK. BERNARD              S/Sgt     31284358
      WG    SCHARNHORST. WILLIAM A.     S/Sgt     37671842
      TG    MCGRIFF. KENNETH E.         S/Sgt     39704936

SHIP  828
P     P     ROBERTSON. WILLIAM T.       1st Lt    O-523177
CP    CP    HENDRICKSON? CLIFFORD       2nd Lt    O-812251
N     N     MANKIN. ELMER.              2nd Lt    O-205797
B     B     CRAIG. CHARLES W.           2nd Lt    O-749618
E     TT    DAHLE. LOUIS A.             S/Sgt     16034857
RO    RR    STUTMAN. BERNARD.           S/Sgt     13052839
      BT    DIGRE. CLIFFORD B.          Sgt       3756
WG    KE    KORNBLATT. JULIUS           Sgt       32689450
      TG    BROWN. JOHN F.              Sgt       12151503
```

Track Chart—September 19, 1944

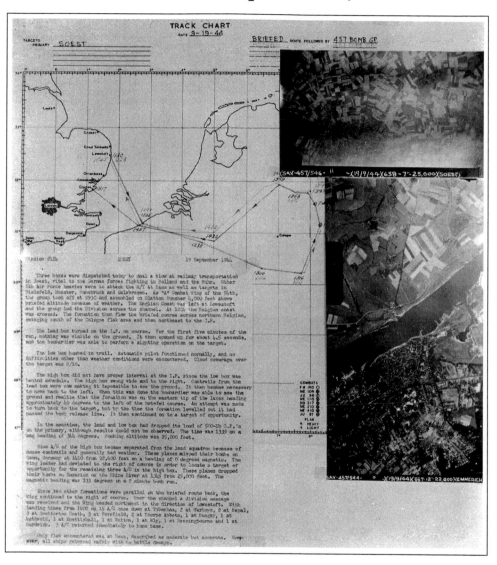

Mission #124, Soest, 19 September, 1944

Three boxes were dispatched today to deal a blow at railway transportation in Soest, vital to the German forces fighting in Holland and the Ruhr. Other 8th Air Force heavies were to attack the M/Y at Hamm as well as targets in Bielefeld, Munster, Osnabruck and Salzbregen. As "A" Combat Wing of the 94th, the group took off at 0930 and assembled on Glatton Buncher 4,000 feet above briefed altitude because of weather. The English Coast was left at Lowestoft and the group led the Division across the channel. At 1204 the Belgium coast was crossed. The formation then flew the briefed course across northern Belgium, swinging south of the Cologne flak area and then northeast to the I.P.

The lead box turned on the I.P. on course. For the first five minutes of the run, nothing was visible on the ground. It then opened up for about 4.5 seconds, and the bombardier was able to perform a sighting operation on the target.

The low box bombed in trail. Automatic pilot functioned normally, and no difficulties other than weather conditions were encountered. Cloud coverage over the target was 8/10.

The high box did not have proper interval at the I.P. since the low box was behind schedule. The high box swung wide and to the right. Contrails from the load box were now making it impossible to see the ground. It then became necessary to move back to the left. When this was done the bombardier was able to see the ground and realize that the formation was on the eastern tip of the lakes heading approximately 40 degrees to the left of the briefed course. An attempt was made to turn back to the target, but by the time the formation leveled out it had passed the bomb release line. It then continued on to a target of opportunity.

In the meantime, the lead and low box had dropped its load of 500-lb G.P.'s on the primary, although results could not be observed. The time was 1339 on a mag heading of 344 degrees. Bombing altitude was 25,000 feet.

Nine A/C of the high box became separated from the lead squadron because of dense contrails and generally bad weather. These planes salvoed their bombs on Hamm, Germany at 1410 from 22,600 feet on a heading of 9 degrees magnetic. The Wing leader had deviated to the right of course in order to locate a target of opportunity for the remaining three A/C in the high box. These planes dropped their bombs on Emmerick on the Rhine River at 1345 from 25,000 feet. The magnetic heading was 233 degrees on a 2-minute bomb run.

Since two other formations were parallel on the briefed route back, the Wing continued to the right of course. Over the channel a division message was received and the Wing headed northwest in the direction of Lowestoft. With landing times from 1600 on 15 A/C came down at Tibenham, 2 at Warboys, 2 at Nepal, 3 at Snetterton Heath, 3 at Fersfield, 2 at Thorpe Abbots, 1 at Bungay, 1 at Methwold, 1 at Knettshall, 1 at Watton, 1 at Ely, 1 at Bassingbourne and 1 at Hardwick. 3 A/C returned immediately to home base. Only flak encountered was at Hamm, described as moderate but accurate. However, all ships returned safely with no battle damage.

Loading List—September 25, 1944 • My Mission #6

SHIP 706				
P	P	WILLIAM C HITCHIN	2nd Lt	0817215
CP	CP	ROBERT C HEID	2nd Lt	0822966
N	N	JAMES J KLEIN	2nd Lt	0718337
B	B	LOUIS F BRICKMAN	2nd Lt	0703555
E	TT	Harley J Ellsworth	T/Sgt	13171217
RO	RR	Hilary A Turley	T/Sgt	39038158
	BT	William C Craig	Sgt	33737286
	WG	Ronald A Weber	Sgt	19151782
	TG	Norman J Thorman	Sgt	36868197
SHIP 540				
P	P	WILLIAM T ROBERTSON	1st Lt	0523177
CP	CP	CLIFFORD HENDRICKSON	2nd Lt	0812261
N	N	ELMER L MANKIN	2nd Lt	02057973
B	B	CHARLES W CARBERY	2nd Lt	0712271
E	TT	Louis A Dahle	Sgt	16034867
RO	RR	Bernard Stutman	Sgt	13052839
	BT	Clifford B Digre	Sgt	3756
	WG	Julius Kornblatt	Sgt	32689450
	WG	Stanley P Szydlowski	Sgt	20108024
	TG	John F Brown	Sgt	12151503
SHIP 828				
P	P	ALLEN D SHEAKLEY	2nd Lt	0823989
CP	CP	BERNARD J YAVOROSKY	2nd Lt	T123215
N	N	LEO B BUNKER	2nd Lt	0717175
B	B	MARSHALL H HOYT	2nd Lt	0757718
E	TT	Edward L Nolan	T/Sgt	16044973
RO	RR	Murrell N Tobian	T/Sgt	16083648
	BT	Richard L Gibbs	S/Sgt	37504229
	WG	Allen A Sharpe	S/Sgt	34109788
	TG	Homer D Reich	S/Sgt	35234090
SHIP 088				
P	P	KEYLON W CLARKE	2nd Lt	0821961
CP	CP	ROBERT N HOWLAND	2nd Lt	0771031
N	N	WALTER SUNDLING	2nd Lt	0723204
B	B	ROBERT P SMITH	2nd Lt	0717906
E	TT	Albert D Griffith	Sgt	36054912
RO	RR	WILLIAM C Dethloff	Sgt	32377433
	BT	David R Dooley	Sgt	38482251
	WG	Reed F Simpson	Sgt	39915784
	TG	Richard H Anderson	Sgt	19145166

Track Chart—September 25, 1944

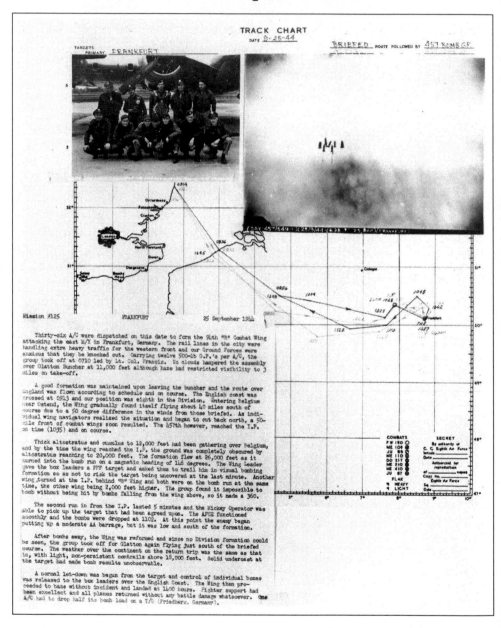

TRACK CHART

DATE 9-25-44

TARGETS PRIMARY FRANKFURT

BRIEFED ROUTE FOLLOWED BY 457 BOMB GP

Mission #125   FRANKFURT   25 September 1944

Thirty-six A/C were dispatched on this date to form the 94th "B" Combat Wing attacking the east M/Y in Frankfurt, Germany. The rail lines in the city were handling extra heavy traffic for the western front and our Ground Forces were anxious that they be knocked out. Carrying twelve 500-lb G.P.'s per A/C, the group took off at 0710 led by Lt. Col. Francis. No clouds hampered the assembly over Glatton Buncher at 11,000 feet although haze had restricted visibility to 3 miles on take-off.

A good formation was maintained upon leaving the buncher and the route over England was flown according to schedule and on course. The English coast was crossed at 0913 and our position was eighth in the Division. Entering Belgium near Ostend, the Wing gradually found itself flying about 40 miles south of course due to a 50 degree difference in the winds from those briefed. As individual wing navigators realized the situation and began to cut back north, a 50-mile front of combat wings soon resulted. The 457th however, reached the I.P. on time (1035) and on course.

Thick altostratus and cumulus to 12,000 feet had been gathering over Belgium, and by the time the wing reached the I.P. the ground was completely obscured by altostratus reaching to 20,000 feet. The formation flew at 26,000 feet as it turned into the bomb run on a magnetic heading of 146 degrees. The Wing Leader gave the box leaders a PFF target and asked them to trail him in visual bombing formation so as not to risk the target being uncovered at the last minute. Another wing turned at the I.P. behind "B" Wing and both were on the bomb run at the same time, the other wing being 2,000 feet higher. The group found it impossible to bomb without being hit by bombs falling from the wing above, so it made a 360.

The second run in from the I.P. lasted 5 minutes and the Mickey Operator was able to pick up the target that had been agreed upon. The APG8 functioned smoothly and the bombs were dropped at 1102. At this point the enemy began putting up a moderate AA barrage, but it was low and south of the formation.

After bombs away, the Wing was reformed and since no Division formation could be seen, the group took off for Glatton again flying just south of the briefed course. The weather over the continent on the return trip was the same as that in, with light, non-persistent contrails above 18,000 feet. Solid undercast at the target had made bomb results unobservable.

A normal let-down was begun from the target and control of individual boxes was released to the box leaders over the English Coast. The Wing then proceeded to base without incident and landed at 1400 hours. Fighter support had been excellent and all planes returned without any battle damage whatsoever. One A/C had to drop half its bomb load on a T/O (Friedberg, Germany).

Mission #125, Frankfurt, 25 September, 1944

Thirty-six A/C were dispatched on this date to form the 94th "B" Combat Wing attacking the east M/Y in Frankfurt, Germany. The rail lines in the city were handling extra heavy traffic for the western front and our Ground Forces were anxious that they be knocked out. Carrying twelve 500-lb G.P.'s per A/C, the group took off at 0710 led by Lt. Col. Francis. No clouds hampered the assembly over Glatton Buncher at 11,000 feet although haze had restricted visibility to 3 miles of take-off.

A good formation was maintained upon leaving the buncher and the route over England was flown according to schedule and on course. The English coast was crossed at 0913 and our position was eighth in the Division. Entering Belgium near Ostend, the Wing gradually found itself flying about 40 miles south of course due to a 50 degree difference in the winds from those briefed. As individual wing navigators realized the situation and began to cut back north, a 50-mile front of combat wings soon resulted. The 457th however, reached the I.P. on time (1035) and on course.

Thick altostratus and cumulus to 12,000 feet had been gathering over Belgium, and by the time the wing reached the I.P. the ground was completely obscured by altostratus reaching to 20,000 feet. The formation flew at 26,000 feet as it turned into the bomb run on a magnetic heading of 146 degrees. The Wing Leader gave the box leaders a PFF target and asked them to trail him in visual bombing formation so as not to risk the target being uncovered at the last minute. Another wing turned at the I.P. behind "B" Wing and both were on the bomb run at the same time, the other wing being 2,000 feet higher. The group found it impossible to bomb without being hit by bombs falling from the wing above, so it made a 360.

The second run in from the I.P. lasted 5 minutes and the Mickey Operator was able to pick up the target that had been agreed upon. The AFCE functioned smoothly and the bombs were dropped at 1102. At this point the enemy began putting up a moderate AA barrage, but it was low and south of the formation.

After bombs away, the Wing was reformed and since no Division formation could be seen, the group took off for Glatton again flying just south of the briefed course. The weather over the continent on the return trip was the same as that in, with light, non-persistent contrails above 18,000 feet. Solid undercast at the target had made bomb results unobservable.

A normal let-down was begun from the target and control of individual boxes was released to the box leaders over the English Coast. The Wing then proceeded to base without incident and landed at 1400 hours. Fighter support had been excellent and all planes returned without any battle damage whatsoever. One A/C had to drop half its bomb load on a T/O (Friedberg, Germany).

Loading List—September 26, 1944 • My Mission #7

```
SUBJECT:  Loading List For This Date.

SHIP 638
P     P     CHARLES F BARRIER          1st Lt     0758515
CP    CP    LEROY H WATSON JR          Major      023798
N     N     WILLIAM H DUPONT           Capt       0691968
N     N     WILLIAM J MORROW           1st Lt     0866053
N     RN    EDWIN E MAYS               1st Lt     0569355
B     B     DAVID B JONES              Capt       0752680
E     TT    Kenneth L Christensen      T/Sgt      19090299
RO    RR    Donald J Fehrman           T/Sgt      35090375
      WG    Robert P Ingraham          S/Sgt      32938625
CP    TG    HUGH C SLOAN JR            2nd Lt     0764483

SHIP 161
P     P     RAY D HEDRICK JR           1st Lt     0742715
CP    CP    BASIL R DUNDAS JR          2nd Lt     0770978
N     N     JOHN B PARKER              2nd Lt     0722930
B     B     LEE C MOHN                 2nd Lt     0886580
E     TT    Reginald W Buxton          S/Sgt      16108123
RO    RR    Donald H Gravelle          S/Sgt      36597044
      BT    John J Sweeney             T/Sgt      11042459
      WG    Vincent J Fallon           Sgt        32238758
      TG    Harvey G Ray               Sgt        33564680

SHIP 064
P     P     ARNET L FURR               2nd Lt     0812789
CP    CP    STERLING H BOOK JR         2nd Lt     0714630
N     N     JOSEPH W ANDREWS JR        2nd Lt     0723260
B     B     LEON M PLAGIANOS           2nd Lt     0708040
E     TT    Alfredo J Raimo            T/Sgt      11101490
RO    RR    Edward Rambler             S/Sgt      13080765
      BT    Warren M Rankin            Sgt        33172779
      WG    Leory E Wetzel             Sgt        35235299
      TG    Robert E Wills             S/Sgt      13146166

SHIP 088
P     P     WILLIAM T ROBERTSON        1st Lt     0523177
CP    CP    CLIFFORD HENDRICKSON       2nd Lt     0812261
N     N     EIMER L MANKIN             2nd Lt     02057973
B     B     CHARLES W CARBERY          2nd Lt     40712271
E     TT    Louis A Dahle              Sgt        16034867
RO    RR    Bernard Stutman            Sgt        13052839
      BT    Clifford B Digre           Sgt        3756
      WG    Stanley P Szydlowski       Sgt        20108024
      TG    Julius Kornblatt           Sgt        35009460
```

Track Chart—September 26, 1944

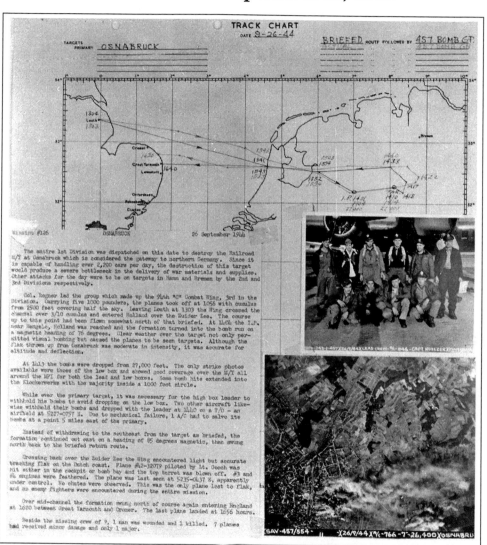

Mission #126, Osnabruck, 26 September, 1944

The entire 1st Division was dispatched on this date to destroy the Railroad M/Y at Osnabruck which is considered the gateway to northern Germany. Since it is capable of handling over 2,200 cars per day, the destruction of this target would produce a severe bottleneck in the delivery of war materials and supplies. Other attacks for the day were to be on targets in Hamm and Bremen by the 2nd and 3rd Divisions respectively.

Col. Rogner led the group which made up the 94th "C" Combat Wing, 3rd in the Division. Carrying five 1000 pounders, the planes took off at 1056 with cumulus from 2500 feet covering half the sky. Leaving Louth at 1303 the Wing crossed the channel over 3/10 cumulus and entered Holland over the Zuider Zee. The course up to this point had been flown somewhat north of that briefed. At 1404 the I.P. near Hengelo, Holland was reached and the formation turned into the bomb run on a magnetic heading of 76 degrees. Clear weather over the target not only permitted visual bombing but caused the planes to be seen targets. Although the flak thrown up from Osnabruck was moderate in intensity, it was accurate for altitude and deflection.

At 1413 the bombs were dropped from 27,000 feet. The only strike photos available were those of the low box and showed good coverage over the M/Y all around the MPI for both the lead and low boxes. Some bomb hits extended into the Klockerwerke with the majority inside a 1000 foot circle.

While over the primary target, it was necessary for the high box leader to withhold his bombs to avoid dropping on the low box. Two other aircraft likewise withheld their bombs and dropped with the leader at 1440 on a T/O—an airfield at 5227-0757 E. Due to mechanical failure, 1 A/C had to salvo its bombs at a point 5 miles east of the primary.

Instead of withdrawing to the southeast from the target as briefed, the formation continued out east on a heading of 85 degrees magnetic, then swung north back to the briefed return route.

Crossing back over the Zuider Zee the Wing encountered light but accurate tracking flak on the Dutch coast. Plane #42-32079 piloted by Lt. Gooch was hit either in the cockpit or bomb bay and the top turret was blown off. #3 and #4 engines were feathered. The plane was last seen at 5235-0437 E, apparently under control. No chutes were observed. This was the only plane lost to flak, and no enemy fighters were encountered during the entire mission.

Over mid-channel the formation swung north of course again entering England at 1620 between Great Yarmouth and Cromer. The last plan landed at 1656 hours.

Beside the missing crew of 9, 1 man was wounded and 1 killed. 7 planes had received minor damage and only 1 major.

Loading List—September 28, 1944 • My Mission #8

SHIP	574			
P	P	X. MELVIN	2nd Lt	0-822900
CP	CP	GUTHEIN, ROBERT E.	2nd Lt	0-709183
N	N	ALBERTSON, BEVERLY C.	2nd Lt	0-723746
B	B	WHIPPIE, HORACE W.	2nd Lt	0-557548
E	TT	ESLANGER, ADRIEN A.	Sgt	31072000
RO	RR	BLOOD, LLOYD J.	Sgt	32856964
	BT	VEVIER, ROLAND XXX	S/Sgt	11008710
	WG	PRUKOP, ALVIN B.	Sgt	38458969
	TG	ARNDT, HAROLD A.	Sgt	17118341
SHIP	633			
P	P	HAMPTON, LOREN	1st Lt	0-750981
CP	CP	HOCKER, ORVILLE K.	2nd Lt	0-761739
N	N	GASSMAN, JACK	2nd Lt	0-723346
B	B	FRIESEN, ANDREW	2nd Lt	0-769273
E	TT	DIEHL, MAURICE A.	S/Sgt	36746299
RO	RR	KARL, RUSSELL G.	S/Sgt	35483202
	BT	FARRELL, THOMAS V.	Sgt	32856644
	WG	FEITEL, IRVING	Sgt	12120163
	TG	FELDMAN, ARTHUR	Sgt	31532465
SHIP	088			
P	P	ROBERTSON, WILLIAM T.	1st Lt	0-525177
	CP	HENDRICKSON, CLIFFORD.	2nd Lt	0-812261
	N	PAGE, HERBERT	2nd Lt	0-717688
B	B	GARBERY, CHARLES W.	2nd Lt	0-712271
E	TT	DAHIE, LOUIS	Sgt	16034867
RO	RR	STUTMAN, BERNARD	Sgt	13053839
	BT	DIGHE, CLIFFORD	Sgt	3756
	WG	SZYDLOWSKI, STANLEY P.	Sgt	20108024
	TG	BROWN, JOHN F.	Sgt	12151503
SHIP	1161			
P	P	HEDRICK, RAYD.	1st Lt	0-724715
CP	CP	DUNDAS, BASIL R. JR	2nd Lt	0-770976
N	N	PARKER, JOHN B.	2nd Lt	0-722930
B	B	MOHN, LEE C.	2nd Lt	0-886580
E	TT	BUXTON, REGINALD	S/Sgt	16108132
RO	RR	GRAVELIE, DONALD H.	S/Sgt	36597044
	BT	SWEENEY, JOHN J.	T/Sgt	11042459
	WG	FALLON, VINCENT J.	Sgt	32258758
	TG	RAY, HARVEY G.	Sgt	33564680
SHIP	706			
P	P	HITCHIN, WILLIAM C.	2nd Lt	0-817215
CP	CP	REID, ROBERT C.	2nd Lt	0-822988
N	N	KLEIN, JAMES J.	2nd Lt	0-717337
B	B	BRICKMAN, LOUIS F.	2nd Lt	0-703555
E	TT	ELLSWORTH, HARLEY J.	T/Sgt	13171217
	RR	TURLEY, HILARY A.	T/Sgt	39038158
	BT	CRAIG, WILLIAM C.	Sgt	33737285
	WG	WEBER, RONALD A.	Sgt	19151792
	TG	THORMAN, NORMAN J.	Sgt	36868197

Track Chart—September 28, 1944

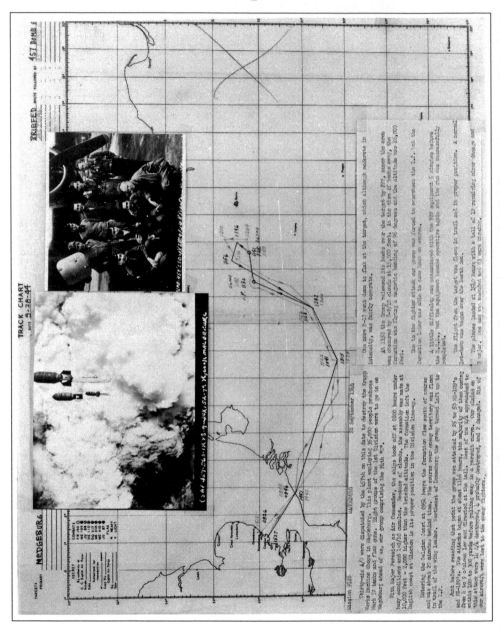

Mission #128, Magdeburg, 28 September, 1944

Thirty-six A/C were dispatched by the 457th on this date to destroy the Krupp Works Machine Shops in Magdeburg. This plant employing 35,000 people produces Mark IV tanks and flak guns. Eight groups of the 1st Division were to go in on Magdeburg ahead of us, our group comprising the 94th "C".

With Major Peresich as Air Commander, the ships took off at 0800 hours under hazy conditions and 1-2/10 cumulus. Because of clouds, the assembly was made at 10,000 feet—2,000 higher than the briefed altitude. The formation left the English coast at Clacton in its proper position in the Division line-up.

Entering the Belgian Coast at 0954 hours the formation flew south of course and was about 20 minutes behind time. The course over enemy territory was flown in trail of the wing leader. Northeast of Luxemburg the group turned left up to the I.P.

Just before reaching that point the group was attacked by 25 to 50 ME-109's and FW-190's. The attacks began at about 1146 hours, the majority of them coming from 4 to 9 o'clock low and directed at the tail. Most of the E/A approached to within 100 to 300 yards before pulling away in a pursuit curve. Our claims on this attack were 14 E/A destroyed, 4 probably destroyed, and 2 damaged. Six of our aircraft were lost to the enemy fighters.

One more B-17 went down to flak at the target, which although moderate in intensity, was fairly accurate.

At 1158 the Group released its bombs over the target by PFF, since the area was obscured by 8-9/10 clouds at 15,000 feet. At the time of bombs away, the formation was flying a magnetic heading of 96 degrees and the altitude was 26,000 feet.

Due to the fighter attack our group was forced to overshoot the I.P. but the formation later was able to come back on course.

A little difficulty was encountered with the PFF equipment 5 minutes before the B.R.L., but the equipment became operative again and the run was successfully completed.

The flight from the target was flown in trail and in proper position. A normal let-down was begun over the North Sea.

The planes landed at 1540 hours with a toll of 12 receiving minor damage and 3 major. One man was wounded and 63 were missing.

Loading List—September 30, 1944 • My Mission #9

My Mission #9

SHIP	534			
P	P	FOX, MELVIN M.	2nd Lt	O-822900
CP	CP	SOUTHERN, ROBERT E.	2nd Lt	O-709183
N	N	ROBERTSON, BEVERLY C.	2nd Lt	O-723746
B	B	WHIPPLE, HORACE	2nd Lt	O-557548
E	TT	BELANGER, ADRIEN A.	Sgt	31072000
RO	RR	BLOOD, LLOYD J.	Sgt	32856964
	BT	RIDGE, ROBERT H.	S/Sgt	34652805
	WG	PRUKOP, ALVIN B.	Sgt	38458969
	TG	ARNDT, HAROLD	Sgt	17118341
SHIP	088			
P	P	ROBERTSON, WILLIAM T.	1st Lt	O-533177
CP	CP	HENDRICKSON, CLIFFORD	2nd Lt	O-812251
N	N	CARBERY, CHARLES	2nd Lt	O-718271
CHIN		BANKS, ALBERT P.	S/Sgt	6077698
E	TT	DAHLE, LOUIS A.	Sgt	16034867
RO	RR	STUTMAN, BERNARD	Sgt	13052839
	BT	DIGHE, CLIFFORD V.	Sgt	3756
	WG	SZYDLOWSKI, STANLEY P	Sgt	20109026
	TG	BROWN, JOHN F.	Sgt	12151505
SHIP	164			
P	P	FISHER, WILLIAM S.	2nd Lt	O-819781
CP	CP	BONNELL, WILLIAM C.	2nd Lt	O-714528
N	N	EKBLOM, ROBERT	2nd Lt	O-723538
B	B	BENSON, EDWIN B.	2nd Lt	O-706671
E	TT	PETERSON, DAVID M.	S/Sgt	36818325
RO	RR	RATICA, HERMAN J.	S/Sgt	13086759
	BT	BRANTLEY, CECIL B.	Sgt	34854382
	WG	GILLESPIE, STANLEY P	Sgt	57578695
	TG	LAWSON, BUFORD	Sgt	34884913
SHIP	574			
P	P	HITCHIN, WILLIAM C.	2nd Lt	O-817215
CP	CP	REID, ROBERT C.	2nd Lt	O-822988
N	N	KLEIN, JAMES	2nd Lt	O-718337
B	B	BRICKMAN, LOUIS F.	2nd Lt	O-703555
E	TT	ELLSWORTH, HARLEY J.	T/Sgt	15171217
RO	RR	TURLEY, HILARY	T/Sgt	39038158
	BT	CRAIG, WILLIAM C.	Sgt	33737286
	WG	WEBER, RONALD	Sgt	19151792
	TG	THORMAN, NORMAN J.	Sgt	36866197
SHIP	828			
P	P	SHEAKLEY, ALLEN D.	2nd Lt	O-823969
CP	CP	YAVOROSKY, BERNARD	2nd Lt	O-
N	N	BUNKER, LEO B.	2nd Lt	O-757175
B	B	HOYT, MARSHALL H.	2nd Lt	O-757718
E	TT	NOLAN, EDWARD	T/Sgt	16054974
RO	RR	TOBEAN, MURRELL	T/Sgt	16063648
	BT	PAPAIANNI, ANTONIO	S/Sgt	32678360
	WG	SHARPE, ALLEN A.	S/Sgt	34109748
	TG	REICH, HOMER D.	S/Sgt	35254090

Track Chart—September 30, 1944

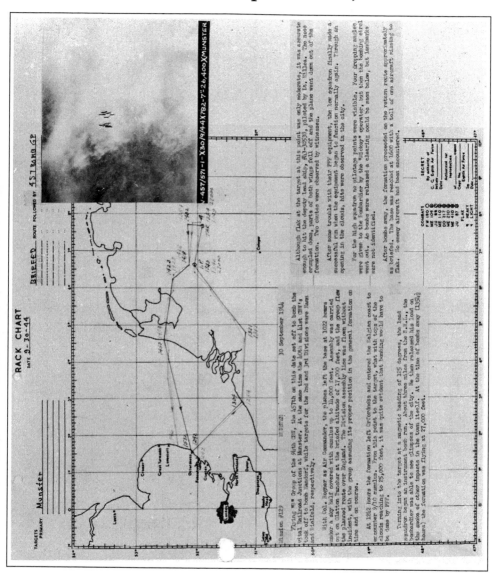

Mission #129, Munster, 30 September, 1944

Flying "B" Group of the 94th CBW, the 457th on this date set off to bomb the vital Railroad Junctions at Munster. At the same time the 40th and 41st CBW's took off to bomb Handorf, while targets for the 2nd and 3rd Divisions were Hamm and Bielfeld, respectively.

With Col. Rogner as Air Commander, the planes left the base at 1022 hours under a sky half covered with cumulus up to 14,000 feet. Assembly was carried out on Glatton Buncher at the briefed altitude of 17,000 feet, and the group flew the planned route over England. The Division assembly line was flown without incident, with the group assuming its proper position in the general formation on time and on course.

At 1242 hours the formation left Orfordness and entered the Belgian coast to encounter 9/10 cumulus. From this point to the target, what with tops of the clouds reaching to 25,000 feet, it was quite evident that bombing would have to be done by PFF.

Turning into the target at a magnetic heading of 125 degrees, the lead squadron began an instrument bomb run. About three miles from the B.R.L., the bombardier was able to see glimpses of the city. He then released his load on the smoke of other impacts in the town itself. At the time of bombs away (1354½ hours) the formation was flying at 27,000 feet.

Although flak at the target at this point was only moderate, it was accurate enough to hit the deputy lead ship, #43-38538, piloted by Lt. Millea. The nose crumpled down, parts of both wings fell off and the plane went down out of the formation. Two chutes were observed by witnesses.

After some trouble with their PFF equipment, the low squadron finally made a successful run when the equipment began to function normally again. Through an opening in the clouds, hits were observed in the city.

For the high squadron no pilotage points were visible. Four dropping angles were given to the Bombardier by the "Mickey" operator, but then the bombing circle went out. As bombs were released a clearing could be seen below, but landmarks were not identified.

After bombs away, the formation proceeded on the return route approximately as briefed. The base was reached at 1600 with a toll of one aircraft missing to flak. No enemy aircraft had been encountered.

Loading List—October 5, 1944 • My Mission #10

```
SHIP    574
P     P    HITCHINS, WILLIAM C.        2nd Lt     0-817215
CP    CP   NEIL, ROBERT G.             2nd Lt     0-822988
N     N    KLEIN, JAMES J.             2nd Lt     0-718337
B     B    BRICKMAN, LOUIS F.          2nd Lt     0-703555
E     TT   ELLSWORTH, HARLEY J.        T/Sgt      13171217
RO    RR   TURLEY, HILARY A.           T/Sgt      39058158
      BT   CRAIG, WILLIAM C.           S/Sgt      33737286
      WG   STRAHAN, ARCHIE C.          S/Sgt      38267454
      TG   NEHER, RONALD A.            S/Sgt      19151762

SHIP    034
P     P    FOX, MELVIN B.              2nd Lt     0-822900
CP    CP   BOIFFHAN, ROBERT H.         2nd Lt     0-709183
N     N    ROBERTSON, BEVERLY C.       2nd Lt     0-723746
B     B    WHIPPLE, HORACE             2nd Lt     0-557548
RO    RR   BLOOD, LLOYD J.             Sgt        32856964
E     TT   BELANGER, ADRIEN A.         Sgt        31072000
      BT   VEVIER, ROLAND F.           S/Sgt      11008710
      WG   PRUKOP, ALVIN B.            Sgt        38458969
      TG   ARNDT, HAROLD A.            Sgt        17118341

SHIP    038
P     P    ROBERTSON, WILLIAM T.       1ST Lt     0-523177
CP    CP   HENDRICKSON, CLIFFORD       2nd Lt     0-812261
N     N    CAREBRY, CHARLES            2nd Lt     0-712271
E CHINE    MOORE, ROBERT               S/Sgt      19068057
E     TT   DAHLE, LOUIS A.             S/Sgt      16034867
RO    RR   STUHMAN, BERNARD            S/Sgt      13052839
      BT   DIGHE, CLIFFORD V.          S/Sgt      3756
      WG   SZYDLOWSKI, STANLEY P       Sgt        30108025
      TG   BROWN, JOHN F.              S/Sgt      12151503

SHIP    051
P     P    HOOPER, ROBERT B.           1st Lt     0-757104
CP    CP   THOMPSON, WILLIAM E.        2nd Lt     0-822850
N     N    SCHROEDER, NEIL C.          2nd Lt     0-720017
B     B    CRAIG, CHARLES W.           1st Lt     0-749818
E     TT   CRAVEN, FRANCIS M.          T/Sgt      32829890
RO    RR   BILLINGTON, JOHN R.         T/Sgt      12203669
      BT   RIDGE, ROBERT               S/Sgt      32652805
      WG   BROCK, JOSEPH P.            Sgt        32607044
      TG   NILLS, ROBERT E.            S/Sgt      13146166

SHIP    591
P     P    SHEARLEY, ALLEN D.          1st Lt     0-835989
CP    CP   MCGUIRE, JAMES A.           Major      0-406440
N     N    BUNKER, LOE B.              1st Lt     0-717175
B     B    HOYT, MARSHALL              1st Lt     0-757718
E     TT   NOLAN, EDWARD               T/Sgt      16041973
RO    RR   TOBIAN, MURRELL N.          T/Sgt      16085648
      BT   GLEBS, RICHARD L.           S/Sgt      37504229
      WG   PAPAIANNI, ANTONIO          S/Sgt      32678360
      TG   REICH, HOMER D.             S/Sgt      35234090
```

Track Chart—October 5, 1944

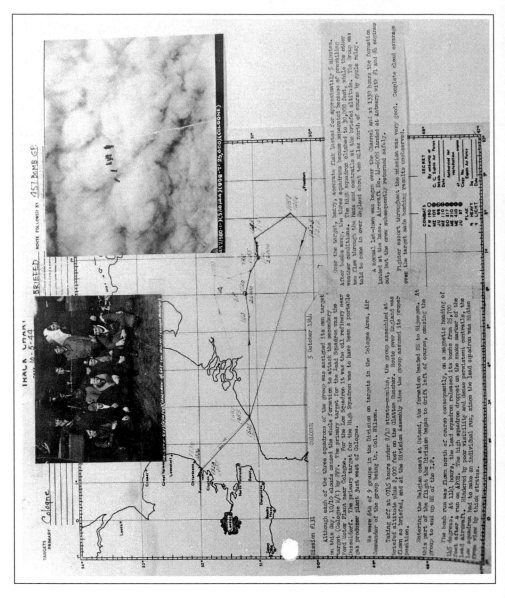

Mission #131, Cologne, 5 October, 1944

Although each of the three squadrons of the group was assigned its own target on this day, 10/10 clouds caused the whole formation to attack the secondary target (Cologne M/Y) by PFF. The primary target for the Lead Squadron was the Ford Motor Plant near Cologne. For the Low Squadron it was the oil refinery near Dusseldorf. The primary target for the High Squadron was to have been a portable gas producer plant just west of Cologne.

We were 6th of 9 groups in the Division on targets in the Cologne Area, Air Commander of the group being Lt. Col. Wilson.

Taking off at 0745 hours under 8/10 strato-cumulus, the group assembled at briefed altitude plus 2,000 feet on the Glatton Buncher. Route over England was flown as briefed, and at the Division Assemble Line the group assumed its proper position.

Entering the Belgian coast at Ostend, the formation headed NE to Nijmegen. At this part of the flight the Division began to drift left of course, causing the group to end up NE of the I.P.

The bomb run was flown north of course consequently, on a magnetic heading of 145 degrees. At 1141 hours, the lead squadron released its bombs from 25,700 feet after a run on AFCE. The high squadron dropped on the smoke marker of the lead aircraft. Hindered by poor visibility and dense persistent contrails, the low squadron had to make an individual run, since the lead squadron was hidden from view by thick stratus.

Over the target, heavy, accurate flak lasted for approximately 5 minutes. After bombs away, the three squadrons became separated because of prevailing weather conditions. The high squadron climbed to 30,000 feet, while the other two flew through the haze and contrails at the briefed altitude. The Group was told to come in over England about ten miles north of course by cycle relay.

A normal let-down was begun over the Channel and at 1330 hours the formation landed at the base. Aircraft No. 44-6088* was diverted to Antwerp with #1 and #4 engines out, but the crew subsequently returned safely.

Fighter escort throughout the mission was very good. Complete cloud coverage over the target made bombing results unobserved.

*My crew—the Lt. Wm. T. (Robbie) Robertson crew

Loading List—October 25, 1944 • My Mission #11

```
SHIP    164
P       P       BURGESS, OLIVER G. JR       2nd Lt    0-764870
CP      CP      TEUTSCHEL, ALBERT V. JR     2nd Lt    0-767685
N       N       PIKE, LOUIS                 2nd Lt    0-720004
B       B       ELWOOD, JOHNE               2nd Lt    0-769021
E       TT      MOLESTATORE, ELDO           T/Sgt     33102264
RO      RR      PARSONS, GEORGE             T/Sgt     31319167
        BT      BURKE, ROBERT J.            S/Sgt     32401099
        WG      DOLLAR, HERBERT E.          S/Sgt     38509207
        TG      RAY. HARVEY G.              S/Sgt     33564680

SHIP    161
P       P       COLEMAN, JOE D.             1st Lt    0-760991
CP      CP      SLAMAN, EDWARD F.           1st Lt    0-814576
N       N       CROWLEY, THOMAS S.          1st Lt    0-771901
CHIN            WRIGHT, WILLIAM C.          S/Sgt     10675366
E       TT      SNOW, FRANCIS E.            T/Sgt     39116574
RO      RR      HARRISON, ROBERT L.         T/Sgt     32767685
        BT      MARTIN, GEORGE JR           S/Sgt     39187124
        WG      CROCKETT, GEORGE B.         S/Sgt     39043628
        TG      SMITH, ROBERT C.            S/Sgt     33511600

SHIP    051
P       P       HOOPER, ROBERT B.           1st Lt    0-767104
CP      CP      MAGUIRE, JAMES A.           Major     0-406440
N       N       CRAIG, CHARLES W.           1st Lt    0-749818
BHIN    N       VEVIER, ROLAND F.           S/Sgt     11008710
E       TT      SNYDER, PHILIP H.           S/Sgt     12176625
RO      RR      BILLINGTON   JOHN R.        T/Sgt     12203669
        BT      MAHENSKE, JOHN W.           S/Sgt     16159459
        WG      BROCK, JOSEPH P             S/Sgt     32607044
        TG      DICKINGSON,                 2nd Lt    0-

SHIP    594
P       P       ROBERTSON, WILLIAM T.       Lst Lt    0-823177
CP      CP      HENDRICKSON, CLIFFORD       2nd Lt    0-812261
N       N       CARBERY, CHARLES.           2nd Lt    0-712271
CHIN            KORNBLATT, JULIUS           S/Sgt     32689450
E       TT      DAHLE, LOUIS                S/Sgt     16034867
RO      RR      STUTMAN, BERNARD            T/Sgt     13052839
        BT      DIGRE, CLIFFORD V.          S/Sgt     3756
        WG      SZYDLOWSKI, STANLEY P       S/Sgt     20108025
        TG      BROWN, JOHN F.              S/Sgt     12151503

SHIP    034
P       P       WHITMAN, HARRY J.           1st Lt    0-761230
CP      CP      GILBERTSON, ALBERT O        F/O       T-62919
N       N       STONER, HAROLD A            1st Lt    0-772767
CHIN            BYERS, ROBERT C             Sgt       35607172
E       TT      MELLY, JOSEPH P             T/Sgt     11119434
RO      RR      MUNGER, HOWARD B.           T/Sgt     17150363
        BT      SITEK, BERNARD F.           S/Sgt     31284358
        WG      SCHARNSHORST, WILLAIM A.    S/Sgt     37671842
        TG      MCGRIFF, KENNETH E.         S/Sgt     39704936
RADAR           ARNOLD, JACK                S/Sgt     36543055
```

Track Chart—October 25, 1944

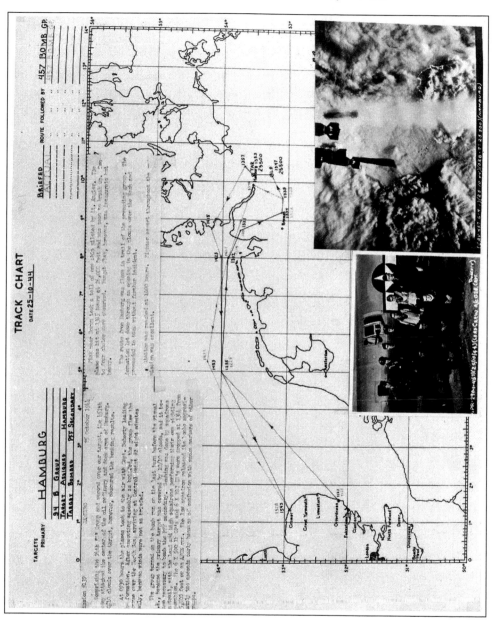

Mission #139, Hamburg, 25 October, 1944

Comprising the 94th "B" Group and second over our target, the 457th today attacked the center of the oil refinery and dock area of Hamburg. 10/10 clouds over the target, however, obscured the bombing results.

At 0930 hours the planes took to the air with Capt. Doherty leading the formation. After executing assembly as briefed, the group flew the course over the North Sea, arriving at Control Point #2 eight minutes early, because winds were not as briefed.

The group turned on the bomb run on the last turn before the visual I.P., because the primary target was covered by 10/10 clouds, and it became necessary to bomb the PFF secondary. Bombing was done by squadrons in trail, with the lead and high squadrons performing their own sighting operation. The 6 x 500 lb GP's and 6 x M17 IB's were dropped at 1344 from 25,500 feet on the AFCE run. The low squadron released its bombs approximately two seconds early because of confusion with smoke markers of other groups.

Flak near Dorum took a toll of one ship piloted by Lt. Angier. The plane was hit at 1315 hours at 26,000 feet and was soon to break up. Two to four chutes were observed. Target flak, however was inaccurate but heavy.

The route from Hamburg was flown in trail of the preceding group. The formation let down through an opening in the clouds over the Wash and proceeded to base without further incident.

Glatton was reached at 1600 hours. Fighter escort throughout the mission was excellent.

Loading List—October 28, 1944 • My Mission #12

SUBJECT: Combat Crew Loading List.

SHIP 540

P	P	HEDRICK, RAY D.	1ST Lt	0-742715
CP	CP	MAGUIRE, JAMES A.	Major	0-406440
N	N	PARKER, JOHN B.	2ND Lt	0-722930
N	N	MARTIN, JOHN W.	2ND Lt	0-2058524
B	B	BENSON, EDWIN B.	2ND Lt	0-706671
E	TT	WILLS,, ROBERT E.	S/Sgt	13146166
RO	RR	GRAVELLE, DONALD H.	T/Sgt	35597044
	BT	SWEENEY, JOHN J.	T/Sgt	11042459
	WG	FALLON, VINCENT J.	S/Sgt	32238758
CP	TG	DUNDAS, BASIL R. JR.	2ND Lt	0-770978

SHIP 255

P	P	FIEDLER, WILLIAM F.	1ST Lt	0-761579
CP	CP	ERNEST, FREDERICK	2ND Lt	0-693457
N	N	PACE, HERBERT W.	2ND Lt	0-717688
B	B	ELWOOD, JOHN E.	2ND Lt	0-769021
MO	N	BASUIL, FELECISIMO	2ND Lt	0-552175
E	TT	ATTAWAY, MICHAEL E.	T/Sgt	18116002
RO	RR	STELTZER, GEORGE A.	T/Sgt	32042843
	BT	STEGEMAN, RUDOLPH	S/Sgt	12191719
	TG	STEVENS, GERALD D.	S/Sgt	35874618

SHIP 034

P	P	ROBERTSON, WILLIAM T.	1ST Lt	0-523177
CP	CP	HENDRICKSON, CLIFFORD	2ND Lt	0-812261
N	N	CARBERY, CHARLES	2ND Lt	0-712271
CHIN		KORNBLATT, JULIUS	S/Sgt	32689450
E	TT	DAHLE, LOUIS	S/Sgt	16034867
RO	RR	STUTMAN, BERNARD	T/Sgt	13052839
	BT	DIGRE, CLIFFORD V.	S/Sgt	3756-----
	WG	SZYDLOWSKI, STANLEY P.	S/Sgt	20108025
	TG	BROWN, JOHN F.	S/Sgt	12151503

SHIP 064

P	P	MC CALL, WILLIAM R.	2ND Lt	0-756295
CP	CP	GREGORY, THOMAS L.	2ND Lt	0-823505
N	N	LIVINGSTONE, ARTHUR	2ND Lt	0-712618
CHIN		COOKE, GEORGE A.	S/Sgt	6975178
E	TT	PERRY, GEORGE W.	T/Sgt	7001463
RO	RR	HAYES, ROBERT J.	T/Sgt	20952240
	BT	WILLS, LINVILLE	S/Sgt	35872372
	WG	SLATE, WALTER L.	S/Sgt	12033727
	TG	BATTISTI, LARIDO A.	S/Sgt	16127713

SHIP #051

P	P	HITCHEN, WILLIAM C.	2ND Lt	0-817215
CP	CP	REID, ROBERT C.	2ND Lt	0-822988
N	N	KLEIN, JAMES J.	2ND Lt	0-718337
B	D	BRICKMAN, LOUIS F.	2ND Lt	0-703555
E	TT	ELLSWORTH, HARLEY J.	T/Sgt	13171217
RO	RR	TKURLEY, HILARY A.	T/Sgt	39038158
	BT	CRAIG, WILLIAM C.	S/Sgt	33737286
	WG	WEBER, RONALD A.	S/Sgt	19151782
	TG	THORAN, NORMAN J.	S/Sgt	36868197

Track Chart—October 28, 1944

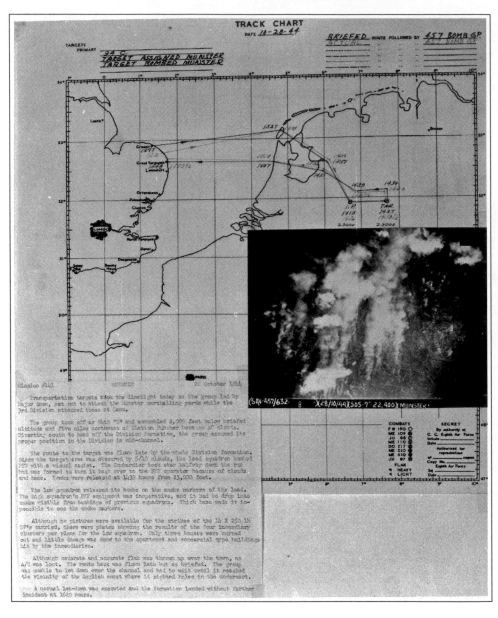

Mission #141, Munster, 28 October, 1944

Transportation targets took the limelight today as the group led by Major Snow, set out to attack the Munster marshalling yards while the 3rd Division attacked those at Hamm.

The group took off as 94th "C" and assembled 2,000 feet below briefed altitude and five miles northwest of Glatton Buncher because of clouds. Diverting south to head off the Division formation, the group assumed its proper position in the Division in mid-channel.

The route to the target was flown late by the whole Division formation. Since the target area was obscured by 5/10 clouds, the lead squadron bombed PFF with a visual assist. The Bombardier took over halfway down the run but was forced to turn it back over to the PFF operator because of clouds and haze. Bombs were released at 1439 hours from 23,000 feet.

The low squadron released its bombs on the smoke markers of the lead. The high squadron's PFF equipment was inoperative, and it had to drop into smoke visible from bombings of previous squadrons. Thick haze made it impossible to see the smoke markers.

Although no pictures were available for the strikes of the 14 x 250 lb GP's carried, there were photos showing the results of the four incendiary clusters per plane for the low squadron. Only three houses were burned out and little damage was done to the apartment and commercial type buildings hit by the incendiaries.

Although moderate and accurate flak was thrown up over the town, no A/C was lost. The route back was flown late but as briefed. The group was unable to let down over the channel and had to wait until it reached the vicinity of the English coast where it sighted holes in the undercast.

A normal let-down was executed and the formation landed without further incident at 1620 hours.

Loading List—October 30, 1944 • My Mission #13

SHIP	594			
P	P	BURGESS. OLIVER G. JR	1st Lt	0-764870
CP	CP	TEUTSCHEL. ALBERT V.	2nd Lt	0-767685
N	N	PIKE. LOUIS	2nd Lt	0-720004
CHIN		MAHINSKE. JOHN W.	S/Sgt	16159459
E	TT	MOLESTATORE. ALDO	T/Sgt	33102264
RO	RR	PARSONS. GEORGE A.	T/Sgt	31319167
	BT	BURKE. ROBERT J.	S/Sgt	32401099
	WG	DOLIAR. HERBERT E.	S/Sgt	38509207
	TG	REICH. HOMER D.	S/gt	35234090
SHIP	051			
P	P	ROBERTSON. WILLIAM T.	1st Lt	0-523177
CP	CP	HENDRICKSON. CLIFFORD	2nd Lt	0-812261
N	N	CARBERY. CHARLES	2nd Lt	0-712271
CHIN		KORNBLATT. JULIUS	S/Sgt	32689450
E	TT	DAHLE. LOUIS.	S/Sgt	16034867
RO	RR	STUTMAN. BERNARD	T/Sgt	13052839
	BT	DIGRE. CLIFFORD V.	S/Sgt	3756
	WG	SZYDLOWSKI. STANLEY.	S/Sgt	20108025
	TG	SNYDER. PHILIP H.	S/Sgt	12176625
SHIP	518			
P	P	MCCALL. WILLIAM R	2nd Lt	0-756295
CP	CP	GREGORY. THOMAS L	2nd Lt	0-823504
N	N	LIVINGSTONE. ARTHUR M	2nd Lt	0-712518
CHIN		COOKE. GEORGE A	S/Sgt	6975178
E	TT	MOLESTA PERRY. GEORGE W	T/Sgt	7001463
RO	RR	HAYES. ROBERT L	T/Sgt	20952240
	BT	WILLS. LINVILLE	S/Sgt	35872372
	WG	SLATE. WALTER L	S/Sgt	12033727
	TG	BATTISTI. LARIDO A	S/Sgt	16127713
SHIP	161			
P	P	BOYES. WALLACE F JR.	2nd Lt	0-826086
CP	CP	FEIGENHAUER. EIMER W	2nd Lt	0-828131
N	N	FURST. KENNETH L	2nd Lt	0-2064561
B	B	TURNER. MERRITT D	2nd Lt	0-782986
E	TT	HORAN. FRANCIS J	Sgt	32852015
RO	RR	FELDMAN. ABRAHAM	Sgt	33508742
	BT	TRAPANI. FRANK	Sgt	38544408
	WG	DUITMAN. ROY S	Sgt	19124898
	TG	DILLEY. ROBERT A	Sgt	37534270

Track Chart—October 30, 1944

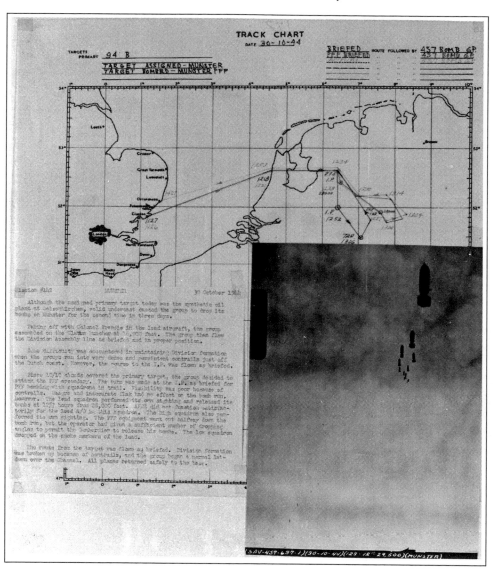

Mission #142, Munster, 30 October, 1944

Although the assigned primary target today was the synthetic oil plant at Gelsenkirchen, solid undercast caused the group to drop its bombs on Munster for the second time in three days.

Taking off with Colonel Francis in the lead aircraft, the group assembled on the Glatton Buncher at 16,000 feet. The group then flew the Division Assembly line as briefed and in proper position.

Some difficulty was encountered in maintaining Division formation when the groups ran into very dense and persistent contrails just off the Dutch coast. However, the course to the I.P. was flown as briefed.

Since 10/10 clouds covered the primary target, the group decided to attack the PFF secondary. The turn was made at the I.P. as briefed for PFF bombing with squadrons in trail. Visibility was poor because of contrails. Meager and inaccurate flak had no effect on the bomb run, however. The lead squadron performed its own sighting and released its bombs at 1257 hours from 28,000. AFCE did not function satisfactorily for the lead A/C in this squadron. The high squadron also performed its own sighting. The PFF equipment went out halfway down the bomb run, but the operator had given a sufficient number of dropping angles to permit the Bombardier to release his bombs. The low squadron dropped on the smoke markers of the lead.

The route from the target was flown as briefed. Division formation was broken up because of contrails, and the group began a normal let-down over the Channel. All planes returned safely to the base.

Loading List—November 5, 1944 • My Mission #14

SUBJECT: LOADING LIST FOR THIS DATE.

SHIP NO 028

P	P	CHARLES BARRIER	CAPTAIN	0758515
CP	CP	RAYMOND STYPAK	MAJOR	0409778
N	N	GEORGE S. INMAN	1ST LT	0716450
N	N	WILLIAM C. WATTS	1ST LT	0722235
N	N	EDWIN E. MAYES	1ST LT	0569355
B	B	CLINTON E. WELLS	1ST LT	0703546
E	TT	KENNETH L. CHRISTENSON	TS/GT	19090299
RO	RR	DONALD J. FAHRAN	T/SGT	35090375
	BT	WILBUR A. KURTZ	S/SGT	79041197
CP	TG	HUGH C. SLOAN	1ST LT	0764483

SHIP NO 064

P	P	ARNET L. FURR	1ST LT	0819780
CP	CP	STERLING H. BOOK JR	2ND LT	0714630
N	N	JOSEPH W. ANDREWS JR	2ND LT	0723260
B	B	LEON M. PLAGIANOS	2ND LT	0708040
E	TT	DONALD D. BRUNSVOLD	S/SGT	17071215
RO	RR	RICHARD C. WEAVER	S/SGT	12109761
	BT	WARREN M. RANKIN	S/SGT	32172779
	WG	GLENN M. WISDOM	S/SGT	25123388
	TG	LEROY E. WETZEL	S/SGT	36235399

SHIP NO 828

P	P	WILLIAM T. ROBERTSON	1ST LT	0523177
CP	CP	CLIFFORD HENDRICKSON	2ND LT	0612261
N	N	CHARLES CARBERY	2ND LT	0712271
CHIN		JULIUS KORNBLATT	S/SGT	32689450
E	TT	LOUIS DAHLE	T/SGT	16034867
RO	RR	BERNARD STUTMAN	T/SGT	13052839
	BT	CLIFFORD V. DIGRE	S/SGT	3758
	WG	STANLEY SZYDLOWSKI	S/SGT	20108025
	TG	JOHN F. BROWN	S/SGT	1215150

SHIP NO. 534

P	P	OLIVER G. BURGESS JR	1ST LT	0764870
CP	CP	ALBERT V. TEUTSCHEL	2ND LT	0767685
N	N	LOUIS PIKE	2ND LT	0720004
CHIN		PHILIP H. SNYDER JR	S/SGT	12176625
E	TT	ALDO MOLESTATORE	T/SGT	33102264
RO	RR	GEORGE A. PARSONS JR	T/SGT	31319167
	BT	ROBERT J. BURKE	S/SGT	32401099
	WG	HERBERT E. DOLLAR	S/SGT	38509207
	TG	C. T. SNYDER	S/SGT	37536683

Track Chart—November 5, 1944

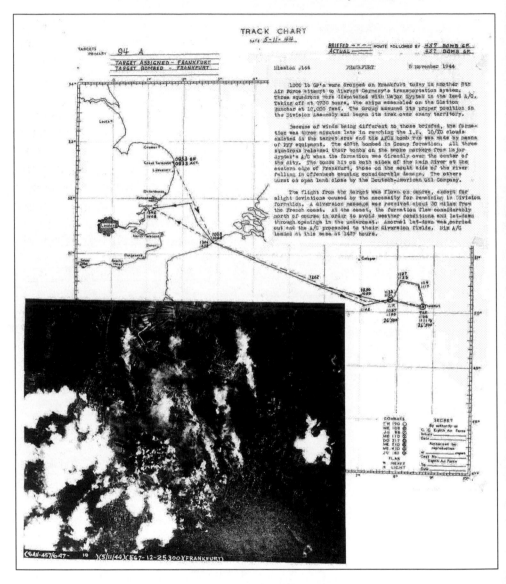

Mission #144, Frankfurt, 5 November 1944

1000 lb GP's were dropped on Frankfurt today in another 8th Air Force attempt to disrupt German's transportation system. Three squadrons were dispatched with Major Syptak in the lead A/C. Taking off at 0730 hours, the ships assembled on the Glatton Buncher at 10,000 feet. The group assumed its proper position in the Division assembly and began its trek over enemy territory.

Because of winds being different to those briefed, the formation was three minutes late in reaching the I.P. 10/10 clouds existed in the target area and the AFCE bomb run was made by means of PFF equipment. The 457th bombed in Group formation. All three squadrons released their bombs on the smoke markers from Major Syptak's A/C when the formation was directly over the center of the city. The bombs hit on both sides of the Main River at the eastern edge of Frankfurt, those on the south side of the river falling in Offenbach causing considerable damage. The others burst on open land close by the Deutsch-American Oil Company.

The flight from the target was flown on course, except for slight deviations caused by the necessity for remaining in Division formation. A diversion message was received about 30 miles from the French coast. At the coast, the formation flew considerably north of course in order to avoid weather conditions and let-down through openings in the undercast. A normal let-down was carried out and the A/C proceeded to their diversion fields. Six A/C landed at this base at 1437 hours.

Loading List—November 6, 1944 • My Mission #15

```
SHIP 530
P      P      WILLIAM R McCAIL          2nd Lt     0756295
CP     CP     THOMAS L GREGORY          2nd Lt     0322504
N-B    N-B    ARTHUR L LIVINGSTONE      2nd Lt     0712518
CHN           George A Cooke            S/Sgt      6978178
E      TT     George W Perry            T/Sgt      7001463
RO     RR     Robert L Hayes            T/Sgt      20952240
BT     BT     Linville Wills            S/Sgt      35872372
       WG     Walter L Slate            S/Sgt      12033727
       TG     Iarido A Battisti         S/Sgt      16127713


SHIP 574
P      P      ROBERT W KELLY            1st Lt     0705242
CP     CP     ALBERT O GILBERTSON JR    F/O        T62919
N-B    N-B    LEONARD G STONER          1st Lt     0772767
CHN           Albert P Banks            S/Sgt      6099698
E      TT     Joseph W Melly            T/Sgt      11119434
RO     RR     Howard B Munger           T/Sgt      17150363
       BT     Bernard F Sitek           S/Sgt      31284358
       WG     William J Prettyman       Sgt        39138917
       TG     Kenneth E McGriff         S/Sgt      39704936


SHIP 064
P      P      ARNET L FURR              1st Lt     0819789
CP     CP     STERLING H BOOK JR        2nd Lt     0714650
N      N      JOSEPH W ANDREWS JR       2nd Lt     0723260
B      B      LEON M PLAGIANOS          2nd Lt     0708040
E      TT     Donald D Brunsvold        T/Sgt      17071215
RO     RR     Richard C Weaver          T/Sgt      15109761
       BT     Warren M Rankin           S/Sgt      33172779
       WG     Glenn M Wisdom            S/Sgt      35123338
       TG     Leroy E Wetzel            S/Sgt      35235299


SHIP 828
P      P      WILLIAM T ROBERTSON       1st Lt     0523177
CP     CP     CLIFFORD HENDRICKSON      2nd Lt     0812261
N-B    N-B    CHARLES C  BERY           2nd Lt     0712271
CHN           Julius Kornblatt          S/Sgt      32689450
E      TT     Louis Dahle               T/Sgt      16034867
RO     RR     Bernard Stutman           T/Sgt      13052839
       BT     Clifford V Digre          S/Sgt      37561501
       WG     Stanley Szydolwski        S/Sgt      20108025
       TG     John F Brown              S/Sgt      12151503
```

Track Chart—November 6, 1944

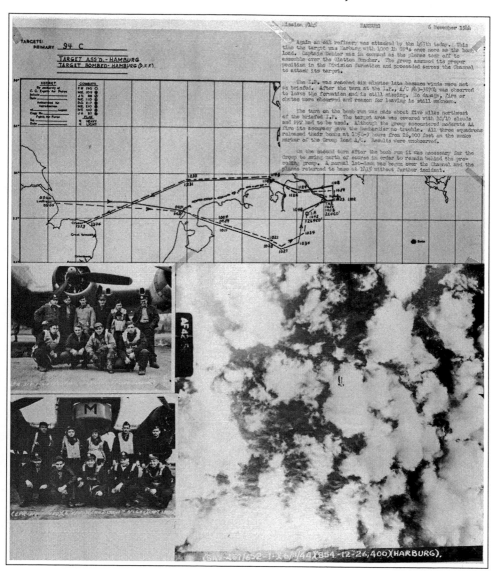

Mission #145, Harburg, 6 November, 1944

Again an oil refinery was attacked by the 457th today. This time the target was Harburg with 1000 lb GP's once more as the bomb load. Captain Dozier was in command as the planes took off to assemble over the Glatton Buncher. The group assumed its proper position in the Division formation and proceeded across the Channel to attack its target.

The I.P. was reached six minutes late because winds were not as briefed. After the turn at the I.P., A/C #43-38904 was observed to leave the formation and is still missing. No damage, fire or chutes were observed and reason for leaving is still unknown.

The turn on the bomb run was made about five miles northwest of the briefed I.P. The target area was covered with 10/10 clouds and PFF had to be used. Although the group encountered moderate AA fire its accuracy gave the Bombardier no trouble. All three squadrons released their bombs at 1058-9 hours from 26,000 feet on the smoke marker of the Group Lead A/C. Results were unobserved.

On the second turn after the bomb run it was necessary for the Group to swing north off course in order to remain behind the preceding group. A normal let-down was begun over the Channel and the planes returned to base at 1415 without further incident.

Loading List—November 8, 1944 • My Mission #16

SUBJECT: LOADING LIST FOR THIS DATE.

SHIP# 540		SHIP# 706		SHIP# 594	
P	HURDIS	P	HAMPTON	P	COLEMAN
CP	MITTWOCH	CP	HOCKER	CP	SLAMAN
N	POND	N	SCHROEDER	N	CROWLEY
N	PIKE	B	FRESIER	CHIN	WRIGHT
B	MILLER	TT	DIEHL	TT	SNOW
TT	MAYO	RO	KARL	RO	HARRISON
RO	RICHMOND	BT	FARRELL	BT	MARTIN
BT	MCEWEN	WG	MCGILLIAN	WG	CROCKETT
WG	JOHNSTON	TG	FRITEL	TG	SMITH
TG	LT. PALM				

SHIP# 152		SHIP# 418		SHIP# 574	
P	FEIBLER	P	ELDUFF	P	BURGESS
CP	ERNEST	CP	JENKINS	CP	TEUTSHELL
N	PACE	N	GEREN	N	ELWOOD
N	KELLY	B	COOKLEY	CHIN	BYERS
B	SAGE	TT	SCHULLER	TT	MOLESTATORE
MO	QUARRY	RO	STEIN	RO	PARSONS
TT	ATTAWAY	BT	ANDERSON	BT	BURKE
RO	STELTZER	WG	CAPSALLIS	WG	DOLLAR
BG	STEGEMAN	TG	ROTHBARD	TG	VEVIER
TG	STEVENS				

SHIP# 034		SHIP# 828	
		P	ROBERTSON
		CP	HENDRICKSON
P	LACKEY	N	CARBERY
CP	PARK	CHIN	KORNBLATT
N	LISS	TT	DAILE
CHIN	WARD	RO	STUTMAN
TT	GARRISON	BT	DIGRE
RO	MADGETT	WG	SZYALOWSKI
BT	CAPELLE	TG	BROWN
WG	RABIDEAUX		
TG	SOBIESKI	SHIP# 534	
RADAR	KINSLER		
		P	FISHER
		CP	BONNELL
SHIP# 064		N	EKBLOM
		CHIN	GILLESPIE
P	FURR	TT	PETERSON
CP	BOOK	RO	RATICA
N	ANDREWS	BT	LEVONIAN
B	PLAGIANOS	WG	BRANTLEY
TT	BRUNSVOLD	TG	LAWSON
RO	WEAVER		
BT	RANKIN		
WG	WISDOM		
TG	WETZEL		

Track Chart—November 8, 1944

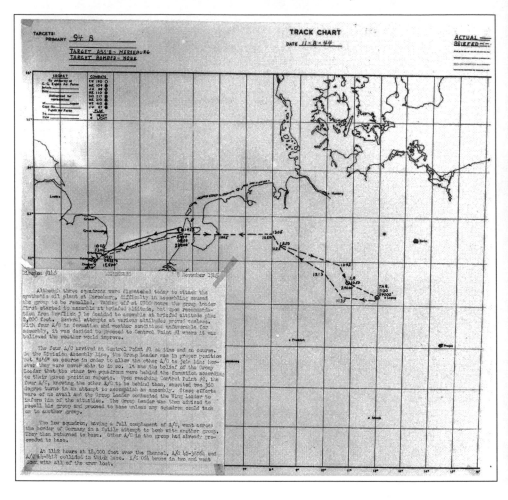

Mission #146, Merseburg, 8 November, 1944

Although three squadrons were dispatched today to attack the synthetic oil plant at Merseburg, difficulty in assembling caused the group to be recalled. Taking off at 0700 hours the group leader first started to assemble at briefed altitude, but upon recommendation from Newflick 3 he decided to assemble at briefed altitude plus 2,000 feet. Several attempts at various altitudes proved useless. With four A/C in formation and weather conditions unfavorable assembly, it was decided to proceed to Control Point #1 where it was believed the weather would improve.

The four A/C arrived at Control Point #1 on time and on course. On the Division Assembly Line, the Group Leader was in proper position but "S'd" on course in order to allow the other A/C to join him; however they were never able to do so. It was the belief of the Group Leader that the other two squadrons were behind the formation according to their given position reports. Upon reaching Control Point #2, the four A/C, knowing the other A/C to be behind them, executed two 360 degree turns in an attempt to accomplish an assembly. These efforts were of no avail and the Group Leader contacted the Wing Leader to inform him of the situation. The Group Leader was then advised to recall his group and proceed to base unless any squadron could tack on to another group.

The low squadron, having a full complement of A/C, went across the border into Germany in a futile attempt to bomb with another group. They then returned to base. Other A/C in the group had already proceeded to base.

At 1142 hours at 18,000 feet over the Channel, A/C 42-38064 and A/C 44-8418 collided in thick haze. AC 064 broke in two and went down with all of the crew lost.

Loading List—November 9, 1944 • My Mission #17

SHIP 828

P	P	WILLIAM T. ROBERTSON	1ST Lt	0523177
CP	CP	CLIFFORD HENDRICKSON	2ND Lt	0812261
N-B	N-B	CHARLES CARBERRY	2ND Lt	0712271
CHIN		Julius Kornblatt	S/Sgt	32689450
E	TT	Louis Dahle	T/Sgt	16034867
RO	RR	Bernard Stutman	T/Sgt	13052839
	BT	Clifford V. Degre	S/Sgt	37561501
	WG	Stanley Szydlowski	S/Sgt	20108025
	TG	John F. Brown	S/Sgt	12151503

SHIP 161

P	P	ROBERT B. HOOPER	1ST Lt	0757104
CP	CP	WILLIAM E. THOMPSON	1ST Lt	0822850
N-B	N-B	DOMINICK J. GIANNICO	2ND Lt	0769029
CHIN		Robert V. Moore	S/Sgt	19068057
E	TT	David C. Foltz	T/Sgt	13058218
RO	RR	Raymond D. Conway	T/Sgt	35696049
	BT	John W. Mahinski	S/Sgt	16159459
	WG	Joseph P. Brock	S/Sgt	32607044
	TG	Homer D. Reich	S/Sgt	35234090

SHIP 706

P	P	WILLIAM R. McCALL JR	2ND Lt	0756295
CP	CP	THOMAS L. GREGORY	2ND Lt	0823492
N-B	N-B	ARTHUR M. LIVINGSTONE	2ND Lt	0712618
CHIN		George A. Cooke	S/Sgt	6974178
E	TT	George W. Perry	T/Sgt	7001463
RO	RR	Robert J. Hays	T/Sgt	20952240
	BT	Linville Wills	S/Sgt	35872372
	WG	Walter L. Slate	S/Sgt	12033727
	TG	Larido A. Battisti	S/Sgt	16127713

SHIP 164

P	P	WALLACE F. BOYES JR	2ND Lt	0826086
CP	CP	ELMER W. HELGENHAUER	2ND Lt	0828131
N	N	KENNETH F. FURST	2ND Lt	02064561
B	B	MERITT E. TURNER	2ND Lt	0782986
E	TT	Francis J. Horan	Sgt	35852015
RO	RR	Abraham Feldman	Sgt	33508742
	BT	Frank Trapani	Sgt	38544408
	WG	William J. Prettyman	Sgt	39138917
	TB	Robert A. Dilley	Sgt	37534270

Track Chart—November 9, 1944

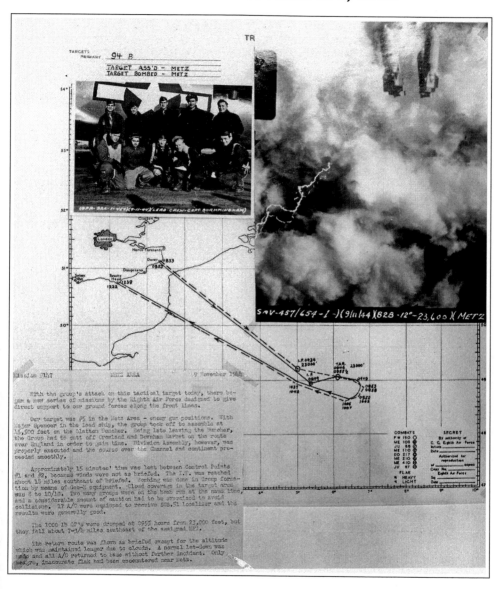

Mission #147, Metz Area, 9 November, 1944

With the group's attack on this tactical target today, there began a new series of missions by the 8th Air Force designed to give direct support to our ground forces along the front lines.

Our target was #5 in the Metz Area—enemy gun positions. With Major Spencer in the lead ship, the group took off to assemble at 15,500 feet on the Glatton Buncher. Being late leaving the Buncher, the Group had to cut off Crowland and Downham Market on the route over England in order to gain time. Division Assembly, however, was properly executed and the course over the Channel and continent proceeded smoothly.

Approximately 15 minutes time was lost between Control Points #1 and #2, because winds were not as briefed. Bombing was done in Group formation by means of Gee-H equipment. Cloud coverage in the target area was 8 to 10/10. Too many groups were on the bomb run at the same time, and a considerable amount of caution had to be exercised to avoid collisions. 17 A/C were equipped to receive SCS.51 localizer and the results were generally good.

The 1000 lb GP's were dropped at 0955 hours from 23,000 feet, but they fell about 7 ¾ miles southeast of the assigned MPI.

The return route was flown as briefed except for the altitude which was maintained longer due to clouds. A normal let-down was made and all A/C returned to base without further incident. Only meager, inaccurate flak had been countered near Metz.

Loading List—November 16, 1944 • My Mission #18

```
SUBJECT:  LOADING LIST FOR THIS DATE.

SHIP    152
P       P       FULTON, RAYMOND A.        Capt      O-756520
AC      AC      SNOW, WILBUR              Major     O-24737
N       N       FONDA, JOHN C.            1st Lt    O-716295
B       B       PEARMAN, FRANK            Capt      O-752694
N       N       VAUGHN, ROY I.            Capt      O-561680
MO      MO      DOLPH, HERBERT A.         1st Lt    O-720041
E       TT      GARDNER, RICHARD B.       T-Sgt     11068804
RO      RO      GUETARA, FRANK N.         T-Sgt     32202788
        WG      TAYLOR, CALVIN W.         S/Sgt     32755116
CP      TG      ERNEST, FREDRICK          2nd Lt    O-693467


SHIP    881
P       P       McCALL, WILLIAM R. JR     1st Lt    O-756245
CP      CP      GREGORY, THOMAS L.        2nd Lt    O-823442
N       N       LIVINGSTONE, ARTHUR       2nd Lt    O-712416
CHIN    CHIN    COOKE, GEORGE A.          S-Sgt     6922495
E       TT      PERRY, GEORGE W.          T-Sgt     7021505
RO      RR      HAYES, ROBERT J.          T-Sgt     20162240
        BT      WILLS, LINVILLE           S-Sgt
        WG      SIATE, WALTER L.          S-Sgt
        TG      BATTISTI, LARIDO A.       S-Sgt     16167415


SHIP    534
P       P       PARK, EVERETT             2nd Lt    O-
CP      CP      PALM, EDWARD G.           2nd Lt    O-
N       N       LISS, BERNARD (NMI)       2nd Lt    O-
CHIN    WARD, DONALD G.                   Sgt
E       TT      GARRISON, KENNETH M.      Sgt
RO      RR      MADGETT, RAYMOND J.       Sgt
        BT      CAPELLE, JOY J.           Sgt
        WG      RABIDEAUX, CLIFTON J.     Sgt
        TG      SOBIESKI, STEVE (NMI)     Sgt


SHIP    828
P       P       ROBERTSON, WILLIAM J.     1st Lt    O-
CP      CP      HENDRICKSON, CLIFFORD     2nd Lt
N       N       RANKIN, ELMER L.          2nd Lt
B       B       GARRETT, CHARLES V.       2nd Lt
E       TT      DAHLE, LOUIS (NMI)        T-Sgt
RR      RO      STUIMAN, BERNARD          S-Sgt
        BT      DEGEN, CLIFFORD V.        S-Sgt
        WG      SZYDLOWSKI, STANLEY       S-Sgt
        TG      BROWN, JOHN J.            S-Sgt
```

Track Chart—November 16, 1944

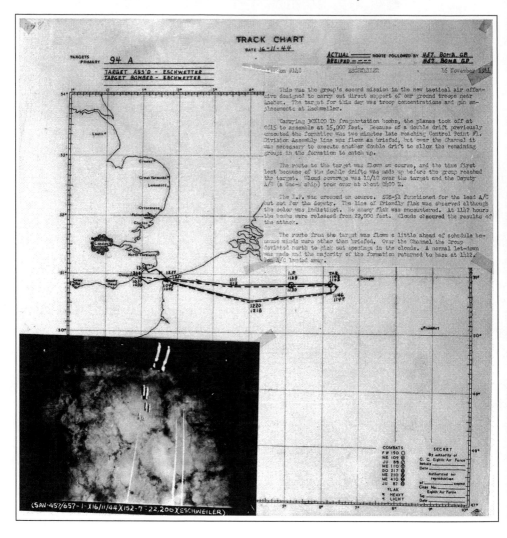

Mission #148, Eschweiler, 16 November, 1944

This was the group's second mission in the new tactical air offensive designed to carry out direct support of our ground troops near Aachen. The target for this day was troop concentrations and gun emplacements at Eschweiler.

Carrying 30 x 100 lb fragmentation bombs, the planes took off at 0815 to assemble at 15,000 feet. Because of a double drift previously executed the formation was two minutes late reaching Control Point #1. Division Assembly Line was flown as briefed, but over the Channel it was necessary to execute another double drift to allow the remaining groups in the formation to catch up.

The route to the target was flown on course, and the time first lost because of the double drifts was made up before the group reached the target. Cloud coverage was 10/10 over the target and the Deputy A/C (a Gee-H ship) took over at about 0400 E.

The I.P. was crossed on course. SCS-51 functioned for the lead A/C but not for the deputy. The line of friendly flak was observed although the color was indistinct. No enemy flak was encountered. At 1142 hours the bombs were released from 22,000 feet. Clouds obscured the results of the attack.

The route from the target was flown a little ahead of schedule because winds were other than briefed. Over the Channel the Group deviated north to pick out openings in the clouds. A normal let-down was made and the majority of the formation returned to base at 1412. Ten A/C landed away.

Loading List—November 29, 1944 • My Mission #19

SHIP 115				
P	P	NOWLING, RUSSELL A.	2ND LT	0-768642
CP	CP	BRAUN, EDWIN C.	2ND LT	0-82193
N	N	BALWIN, DALE F.	2ND LT	0-777118
CHIN		GUNN, ALLISON J.	S-Sgt	395583
E	TT	SKULIE, STEPHEN	S-Sgt	35531856
RO	RR	HANDLER, JOHN M.	S-Sgt	13076141
	BT	STELIE, THEODORE F. JR.	S-Sgt	37724
	WG	STELL, WILLIAM M.	S-Sgt	38517534
	TG	RHONE, DONALD F.	S-Sgt	337568

SHIP 828				
P	P	ROBERTSON, WILLIAM T.	1ST LT	0-6523177
CP	CP	HENDRICKSON, CLIFFORD	2ND LT	0-812261
N	N	MANKIN, ELMER L.	2ND LT	0-2057973
B	B	CARBERY, CHARLES W.	2ND LT	0-712271
E	TT	DAHLE, LOUIS	T-Sgt	16034867
RO	RR	STUTMAN, BERNARD	T-Sgt	13052839
	BT	DIGRE, CLIFFORD V.	S-Sgt	37561501
	WG	SZYDLOWSKI, STANLEY	S-Sgt	20100025
	TG	BROWN, JOHN F.	S-Sgt	12151503

SHIP 164				
P	P	WESCOTT, JACK E.	2ND LT	0-826335
CP	CP	STEADMAN, FRED L.	2ND LT	0-828015
N	N	ROSS, MERRILL H.	2ND LT	0-2062703
B	B	DECUNZO, LOUIS P.	2ND LT	0-2063227
E	TT	MAKI, HOWARD L.	Sgt	31365639
RO	RR	DECOUX, ABER J.	Sgt	18641994
	BT	BERRY, BILLY K.	Sgt	39713988
	WG	GIANACOPOLIS, JAMES C.	Sgt	3127925
	TG	ADAMS, HAROLD A.	Sgt	39722822

SHIP 021				
P	P	BURGESS, OLIVER G. JR.	1ST LT	0-764870
CP	CP	SLOAN, HUGH C.	1ST LT	0-764483
N	N	ELWOOD, JOHN E.	1ST LT	0-769021
CHIN		BANKS, ALBERT P.	S-Sgt	6077698
E	TT	MOLESTATORE, ALDO	T-Sgt	33102264
RO	RR	PARSONS, GEORGE	S-Sgt	31316197
	BT	BURKE, ROBERT J.	S-Sgt	32401099
	WG	BUXTON, REGINALD	T-Sgt	16108132
	TG	DOLLAR, HERBERT E.	S-Sgt	38509207

Track Chart—November 29, 1944

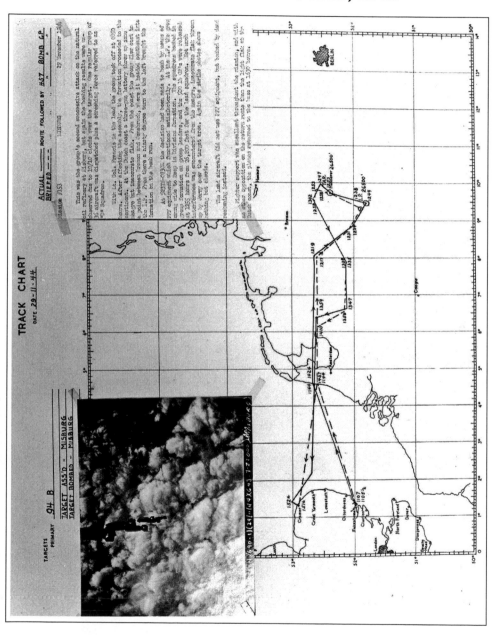

Mission #153, Misburg, 29 November, 1944

This was the group's second successive attack on the natural oil refinery at Misburg, but again the bombing results were unobserved due to 10/10 clouds over the target. One regular group of 36 aircraft was dispatched plus a screening force referred to as "D" Squadron.

With Lt. Col. Francis in the lead the group took off at 0850 hours. After affecting the assembly, the formation proceeded to the continent. At the Dutch coast a three-gun battery threw up some meager but inaccurate flak. From the coast the group flew east to a point between Bremen and Osnabruck, where it headed southeast into the I.P. From there a ninety degree turn to the left brought the formation on the bomb run.

At 5237N-0730E the decision had been made to bomb by means of PFF equipment which functioned satisfactorily. At the I.P. the group swung wide to keep in Division formation. The squadrons bombed in group formation on group leaders, and the 500 lb GP's were released at 1255 hours from 26,200 feet for the lead squadron. Not much interference was encountered from the meager, inaccurate flak thrown up by Jerry over the target area. Again the strike photos show nothing but clouds.

The lead aircraft did not use PFF equipment, but bombed by dead reckoning instead.

Fighter support was excellent throughout the mission, and with no other opposition on the return route than the light flak at the Dutch coast, the planes returned to the base at 1630 hours.

Loading List—December 19, 1944

This is the loading list from the day of the fateful Cliff Hendrickson crash. The track chart for this mission is missing.

SUBJECT:	LOADING LIST FOR THIS DATE			
SHIP #152				
P	P	ROBERTSON, WILLIAM T.	1ST LT	0-652317
CP	CP	MAGUIRE, JAMES A.	MAJOR	0-408440
N	N	WATTS, WILLIAM C.	1ST LT	0-722235
N	N	HOVEY, MARSH	1ST LT	0-695917
RN	RN	DOLPH, HERBERT A.	1ST LT	0-729541
B	B	PEARMAN, FRANK H.	CAPT.	0-752694
E	TT	DAHLE, LOUIS (NMI)	T-SGT	16034867
RO	RR	STUTMAN, BERNARD	T-SGT	13052839
	WG	SZYDLOWSKI, STANLEY	S-SGT	20406025
	TG	MAXEY, EDWARD C. JR.	2ND LT	0-833940
SHIP #539				
P	P	HERBOLD, JOHNATHAN M.	1ST LT	0-751998
CP	CP	SOUTHERN, ROBERT	2ND LT	0-709183
N	N	MARTIN, JOHN W.	2ND LT	0-8058524
B	B	WALLS, PATRICK A.	1ST LT	0-753088
N	N	PETERSON	379TH BOMB GP., 527TH BOMB SQ.	
E	TT	BUXTON, REGINALD W.	T-SGT	16108123
RO	RR	COOK, GERALD E.	T-SGT	35553582
	WG	GIBBS, RICHARD L.	S-SGT	37504229
	WG	ASTOR, NUBAR A.	S-SGT	39708542
	TG	INGRAHAM, ROBERT P.	S-SGT	32938625
SHIP #088				
P	P	FEIDLER, WILLIAM F.	1ST LT	0-761579
CP	CP	ERNEST, FREDERICK G.	2ND LT	0-693457
N	N	PACE, HERBERT W.	2ND LT	0-717688
RN	RN	ZELEKOFSKY, GERALD	F-O	T-125383
B	B	SAGE, EDWARD R.	2ND LT	0-771975
E	TT	ATTAWAY, MICHAEL E.	T-SGT	18116002
RO	RR	STELTZER, GEORGE A.	T/SGT	32042843
	WG	MOONEY, JOSEPH M.	S-SGT	33595287
	WG	STEGEMAN, RUDOLPH E.	S-SGT	12191719
	TG	STEVENS, GERALD D.	S-SGT	35874618
SHIP #812				
P	P	HENDRICKSON, CLIFFORD	2ND LT	0-812261
CP	CP	GRAVES, WALTER B.	2ND LT	0-825619
N	N	KILMER, JOSEPH L.	F-O	T-129699
B	B	WILLIAMS, DAVID E.	F-O	T-129575
E	TT	BRUER, GEORGE H.	SGT	14058137
RO	RR	RIEDEL, ROBERT H.	SGT	35061926
	BT	HAWLEY, GEORGE B.	SGT	37625529
	WG	FITZGERALD, EDMUND T.	SGT	31366496
	TG	HEINRICH, CLIFFORD A.	SGT	3690142

Loading List—February 23, 1945 • My Mission #20

```
Crew #165   SHIP #570
P     Thompson      Thomas    P. Jr.  0820104    2nd Lt.  P
CP    Jett          Murry     V.      0782294    2nd Lt.  CP
N     O'Brian       Anthony   A.      02068297   2nd Lt.  N
B     Kenyon        Ralph     S.      02068101   2nd Lt.  B
TT    Nose          Daniel    W.      13144290   T/Sgt.   AEG
RO    Digre         Cliford   B.      37561791   S/Sgt.   ROG
WG    Elliott       Thomas    C.      11116955   S/Sgt.   AAEG
BT    Johnson       Bennie    W.      18138428   S/Sgt.   AROG
TG    Nowak         Walter    C.      36903497   S/Sgt.   AAG

Crew #170   SHIP #190
P     Burk          Marion    K.      0777576    2nd Lt.  P
CP    Harris        Cecil     C.      0828790    2nd Lt.  CP
N     Freese        John      T.      02068645   2nd Lt.  N
TOG   Cunningham    Clifford  N.      15325502   Sgt.     AG
TT    Clark         Herbert   K. Jr.  39147908   Sgt.     AAEG
RO    Keyon         Earl      R. Jr.  31291423   Sgt.     Rog
BT    Buhrow        Harold    E.      37560669   Sgt.     AROG
TG    Floerke       Joe       E.      17136907   Sgt.     AAG
WG    McDuffie      Frederick A.      38539698   Sgt.     AEG

Crew #164   SHIP #072
P     Southwood     Duane     E.      0775169    2nd Lt.  P
CP    Keran         Lyle      H.      0782301    2nd Lt.  CP
N     Reed          Wallace   (NMI)   02068747   2nd Lt.  N
TOG   Van Wagner    Raymond   D.      35556610   S/Sgt.   AG
TT    Parmeter      Warren    H.      38404201   T/Sgt.   AEG
RO    Clark         Orville   D.      35148605   T/Sgt.   ROG
WG    Radakovich    George    N.      33421864   S/Sgt.   AAEG
BT    Kelley        R.        B.      38548440   S/Sgt.   AROG
TG    Maira         Santo     V.      42086554   S/Sgt.   AAG

Crew #143   SHIP #506
P     McChesney     Ben       W.      0828726    2nd Lt.  P
CP    Manspeaker    William   C.      0835796    2nd Lt.  CP
N     Siler         William   W.      02064343   2nd Lt.  N
TOG   Byoff         George    S.      18142965   S/Sgt.   AAG
TT    Gubino        Joseph    H.      33603906   T/Sgt.   AAEG
RO    Madsen        Chester   C.      37555990   T/Sgt.   ROG
WG    Saylor        Wilbert   M.      37566366   S/Sgt.   AG
BT    Young         Robert    H.      39215688   S/Sgt.   CG
TG    Wilt          Charles   A.      35870639   S/Sgt.   AAEG
```

Track Chart—February 23, 1945

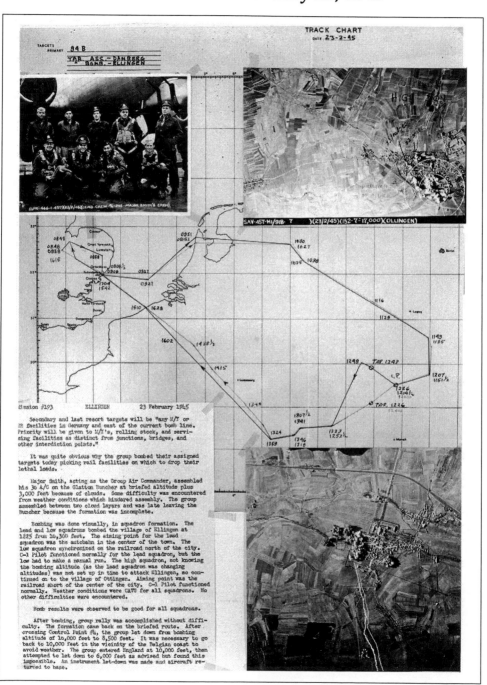

Mission #193, Ellingen, 23 February, 1945

Secondary and last resort targets will be "any M/Y or RR facilities in German and east of the current bomb line. Priority will be given to M/Y's, rolling stock, and servicing facilities as distinct from junctions, bridges, and other interdiction points."

It was quite obvious why the group bombed their assigned targets today picking rail facilities on which to drop their lethal loads.

Major Smith, acting as the Group Air Commander, assembled his 36 A/C on the Glatton Buncher at briefed altitude plus 3,000 feet because of clouds. Some difficulty was encountered from weather conditions which hindered assembly. The group assembled between two cloud layers and was late leaving the Buncher because the formation was incomplete.

Bombing was done visually, in squadron formation. The lead and low squadrons bombed the village of Ellingen at 1225 from 16,300 feet. The aiming point for the lead squadron was the autobahn in the center of the town. The low squadron synchronized on the railroad north of the city. C-1 Pilot functioned normally for the lead squadron, but the low had to make a manual run. The high squadron, not knowing the bombing altitude (as the lead squadron was changing altitudes) was not set up in time to attack Ellingen, so continued on to the village of Ottingen. Aiming point was the railroad short of the center of the city. C-1 Pilot functioned normally. Weather conditions were CAVU for all squadrons. No other difficulties were encountered.

Bomb results were observed to be good for all squadrons.

After bombing, group rally was accomplished without difficulty. The formation came back on the brief route. After crossing Control Point #4, the group let down from bombing altitude of 16,000 feet to 8,500 feet. It was necessary to go back to 10,000 feet in the vicinity of the Belgian coast to avoid weather. The group entered England at 10,000 feet, then attempted to let down to 6,000 feet as advised but found this impossible. An instrument let-down was made and aircraft returned to base.

Loading List—March 1, 1945 • My Mission #21

```
CREW #162   SHIP #902
P     Hottle      George     L. Jr.   0774661    2nd Lt.   P
CP    Racine      Emile      E.       0814551    2nd Lt.   CP
NB    Ellis       David      W.       02065343   2nd Lt.   B
TOG   Zucker      George              32719207   S/Sgt.    AG
TT    Holden      Roger      R.       16076712   T/Sgt.    AEG
RO    Bell        James      T. Jr.   15372438   T/Sgt.    ROG
WG    Buck        Walter     L.       32938639   Sgt.      Gun. Inst
BT    Dufford     William    J.       17064929   S/Sgt.    AROG
TG    Cupp        Francis    C.       39568582   S/Sgt.    AAEG
RCM   Astor       Nubar      A.       39708542   S/Sgt     RCM

CREW #143   SHIP #072
P     McChesney   Ben        W        0828726    2nd Lt    P
CP    Manspeaker  William    C        0835796    2nd Lt    CP
NB    Siler       William    W        02064343   1st Lt    N
TT    Gubino      Joseph     H        33603906   T/Sgt     AEG
RO    Digree      Clifford   B        37561701   S/Sgt     ROG
TOG   Byoff       George     S        19142965   S/Sgt     AAG
WG    Wilt        Charles    A        35870639   S/Sgt     AAEG
BT    Young       Robert     H        39216588   S/Sgt     CG
TG    Tedder      Franklin   P   Jr   14049582   Sgt       Gun Inst

CREW #171   SHIP #506
P     Lindholm    John       C        0780641    2nd Lt    P
CP    Parker      George     E        0784933    2nd Lt    CP
N     Barr        Albert     D        02073299   2nd Lt    N
B     Panematos   Ted        D        02065413   2nd Lt    B
TT    Choc        Abraham             12151655   Sgt       AEG
RO    Friedman    Daniel              16098639   Sgt       ROG
WG    Trace       Laffetti            33546265   S/Sgt     AAG
BT    Miller      Baron      E        39280403   Sgt       AAEG
TG    Levine      Edwin               36736078   Sgt       AAG

CREW #159   SHIP #203
P     Jacobs      Kelly      P.       0561353    1st Lt    P
CP    Sellon      Donald     G.       0775157    2nd Lt    CP
N     Czarnowski  Albert     F.       01634651   1st Lt    B
TOG   Haby        George     H. Jr.   38453198   S/Sgt.    AG
TT    Gee         Robert     E.       38401833   S/Sgt.    AEG
RO    Finnerty    Jacob      L.       33727472   T/Sgt.    ROG
WG    Means       James      T.       18110418   S/Sgt.    AAEG
BT    Brown       Charles    F.       33711907   S/Sgt.    AROG
TG    Carey       James      A.       35808835   S/Sgt.    AAEG
```

Track Chart—March 1, 1945

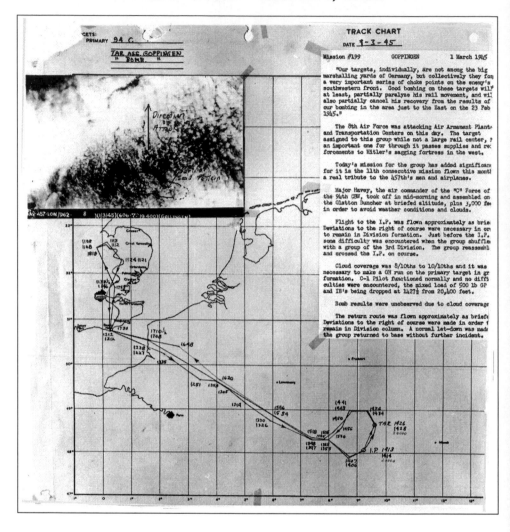

Mission #199, Goppingen, 1 March, 1945

"Our targets, individually, are not among the big marshalling yards of German, but collectively they form a very important series of choke points on the enemy's southwestern front. Good bombing on these targets will at least, partially paralyze his rail movement, and will also partially cancel his recovery from the results of our bombing in the area just to the East on the 23 Feb 1945."

The 8th Air Force was attacking Air Armament Plants and Transportation Centers on this day. The target assigned to this group while not a large rail center, is an important one for through it passes supplies and reinforcements to Hitler's sagging fortress in the west.

Today's mission for the group had added significance for it is the 11th consecutive mission flown this month, a real tribute to the 457th's men and airplanes.

Major Havey, the air commander of the "C" Force of the 94th CBW, took off in mid-morning and assembled on the Glatton Buncher at briefed altitude, plus 3,000 feet in order to avoid weather conditions and clouds.

Flight to the I.P. was flow approximately as briefed. Deviations to the right of course were necessary in order to remain in Division formation. Just before the I.P. some difficulty was encountered when the group shuffled with a group of the 3rd Division. The group reassembled and crossed the I.P. on course.

Cloud coverage was 8/10ths to 10/10ths and it was necessary to make a GH run on the primary target in group formation. C-1 Pilot functioned normally and no difficulties were encountered, the mixed load of 500 lb GP's and IB's being dropped at 1427½ from 20,400 feet.

Bomb results were unobserved due to cloud coverage.

The return route was flown approximately as briefed. Deviations to the right of course were made in order to remain in Division column. A normal let-down was made and the group returned to base without further incident.

Loading List—April 8, 1945 • My Mission #22

```
A/C 167
P      2nd Lt.  Hall          James      L   O-894193    P
CP     F/O      Fortner       Robert     L   T-6709      CP
N      2nd Lt.  Dykes         Gordon     W   O-2071881   N
B      2nd Lt.  Ambrose       Edward     F   O-2065224   B
RO     S-Sgt    MiddlebrooksJohn         R   14181364    RO
TT     S-Sgt    Morton        Alan       (NMI)35067693   AEG
BTG    S-Sgt    Colin         Anthony    (NMI)36660651   AG
TG     S-Sgt    Sempf         Harry      A   36036330    AAG
LWG    S-Sgt    Fischer       Robert     L   37736275    AAG

A/C 863
P      1st Lt.  Buettner      Harlan     (NMI)O-776227   P
CP     2nd Lt.  Grau          George     J   O-827143    CP
NB     1st Lt.  DuPont        Philip     A   O-2068195   NB
CH     S-Sgt    Hawkins       Ray        F   33516060    CH
RO     S-Sgt    Dodds         Richard    A   33788831    RO
TT     S-Sgt    Hungate       Gerald     W   37519040    AEG
BTG    S-Sgt    Westbrook     James      R   18242712    AG
TG     S-Sgt    Rendina       Leo        (NMI)36897071   AAG
LWG    S-Sgt    Vann          Kenneth    R   38072719    AAG

A/C 551
P      1st Lt.  Stevenson     Fred       M   O-517967    P
CP     2nd Lt.  Sanders       Jack       E   O-834664    CP
NB     2nd Lt.  Rattray       Robert     E   O-207031    NB
CH     S-Sgt    Hughes        Harry      M   36897228    CH
RO     S-Sgt    Smith         Stanley    E   38533692    RO
TT     S-Sgt    Dressler      Jerome     C   18009692    AEG
BTG    S-Sgt    McMahon       Larry      B   36467651    AG
TG     S-Sgt    Tiedemann     Alfred     F   38662412    AAG
LWG    S-Sgt    Hoots         Clyde      (NMI)33662412   AAG

A/C 749
P      2nd Lt.  Sopocy        Richard    S   O-834905    P
CP     2nd Lt.  McManus       William    J   O-781627    CP
N      2nd Lt.  Mitchell      Elmo       J   O-200575    N
B      2nd Lt.  Miller        Melvin     (NMI)O-703277   B
RO     Sgt      Hennebry      Floyd      T   37578935    RO
TT     Sgt      Staff         Francis    J   38460110    AEG
BTG    Sgt      Dobson        Wayne      O   36483847    AG
TG     Sgt      Blakeley      James      E   36880060    AAG
LWG    S-Sgt    Reynolds      HaroldDale W   37536344    AAG

A/C 535
P      2nd Lt.  Latimer       James      H   O-782759    P
CP     2nd Lt.  Eymann        Leon       D   O-706260    CP
NB     2nd Lt.  Christensen   Swen       A   O-722279    NB
CH     S-Sgt    Roe           Norman     (NMI)37570253   CH
RO     S-Sgt    Digre         Clifford   B   37561701    RUG
RO     S-Sgt    Anthony       Harold     B   18072849    AEG
BTG    S-Sgt    Petcoff       Boris      W   16190022    AG
TG     S-Sgt    Roeder        Harry      E   32979858    AAG
LWG    S-Sgt    Hale          Ramsey     E   14176412    AAG
```

Track Chart—April 8, 1945

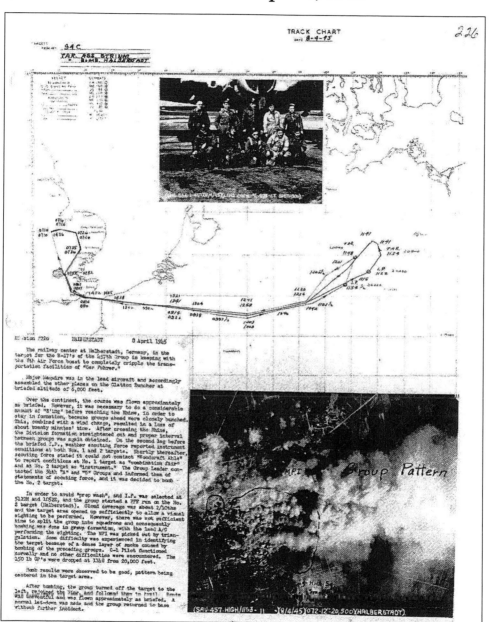

Mission #226, Halberstadt, 8 April, 1945

The railway center at Halberstadt, Germany, is the target for the B-17's of the 457th Group in keeping with the 8th Air Force boast to completely cripple the transportation facilities of "Der Fuhrer."

Major Maguire was in the lead aircraft and accordingly assembled the other planes on the Glatton Buncher at briefed altitude of 6,000 feet.

Over the continent, the course was flown approximately as briefed. However, it was necessary to do a considerable amount of "S-ing" before reaching the Rhine, in order to stay in formation, because groups ahead were closely bunched. This, combined with a wind change, resulted in a loss of about twenty minutes' time. After crossing the Rhine, the Division formation straightened out and proper interval between groups was again obtained. On the second leg before the briefed I.P., weather scouting force reported instrument conditions at both Nos. 1 and 2 targets. Shortly thereafter, scouting force stated it could not contact "Woodcraft Able" to report conditions at No. 1 target as "combination fair" and at No. 2 target as "instrument." The Group Leader contacted the 94th "A" and "B" Groups and informed them of statements of scouting force, and it was decided to bomb the No. 2 target.

In order to avoid "prop wash", and I.P. was selected at 5122M and 1052E, and the group started a PFF run on the No. 2 target (Halberstadt). Cloud coverage was about 2/10ths and the target area opened up sufficiently to allow a visual sighting to be performed. However, there was not sufficient time to split the group into squadrons and consequently bombing was done in group formation, with the lead A/C performing the sighting. The MPI was picked out by triangulation. Some difficulty was experienced in identifying the target because of a dense layer of smoke caused by bombing of the preceding groups. C-1 Pilot functioned normally and no other difficulties were encountered. The 150 lb GP's were dropped at 1140 from 20,000 feet.

Bomb results were observed to be good, pattern being centered in the target area.

After bombing, the group turned off the target to the left, rejoining the Wing, and followed them in trial. Route was uneventful and was flown approximately as briefed. A normal let-down was made and the group returned to base without further incident.

Loading List—April 9, 1945 • My Mission #23

A/C 167
P	2nd Lt.	Coons	Ralph	W	'O-831666	P
CP	F/O	Blakebrough	Kenneth	(NMI)	T-63559	CP
NB	2nd Lt.	Beran	Jennings	B	O-	NB
CH	S-Sgt	Cokorogianis	Stephen	S	31423717	CH
RO	T-Sgt	Crescio	Joseph	D	36420555	RO
TT	T-Sgt	Peschen	George	F	33593996	AEG
BTG	S-Sgt	Wraig	Conrad	E	42082264	AG
TG	S-Sgt	Whiteaker	Robert	D	33655320	AAG
LWG	S-Sgt	Tatman	Woodrow	W	16016562	AAG

A/C 195
P	1st Lt.	Starnes	John	P	0-828516	P
CP	2nd Lt.	McCurry	George	D	0-835467	CP
NB	2nd Lt.	Robbin	Sheldon	J	0-2069123	NB
CH	S-Sgt	Altmaier	Robert	E	36832027	CH
RO	T-Sgt	Johanson	Victor	C	39331465	RO
TT	S-Sgt	Bleck	Edward	A	17156063	AEG
BTG	S-Sgt	Qualls	Louis	A	39923306	AG
TG	S-Sgt	Esterholdt	Stephen	T	39702762	AAG
LWG	S-Sgt	Reynolds	Harold	H	12150344	AAG
SJ	S-Sgt	Coleman	Charles	W	34842236	SJ

A/C 694
P	2nd Lt.	Latimer	James	H	0-782759	P
CP	2nd Lt.	McMillen	Jack	O	0-929387	CP
NB	2nd Lt.	Brower	Orien	C	0-2073038	NB
CH	S-Sgt	Roe	Norman	(NMI)	37570253	CH
RO	T-Sgt	Crain	Lewis	J	35797754	RO
TT	T-Sgt	Anthony	Harold	B	18072849	AEG
BTG	S-Sgt	Petcoff	Boris	W	16190022	AG
TG	S-Sgt	Roeder	Harry	E	32979858	AAG
LWG	S-Sgt	Hale	Ramsey	F	14176412	AAG

A/C 881
P	1st Lt.	Buettner	Harlan	(NMI)	0-776227	P
Cp	2nd Lt.	Grau	George	J	0-827143	CP
NB	1st Lt.	Dupont b	Philip	A	0-2068195	NB
CH	S-Sgt	Hawkins	Ray	F	35160601	CH
RO	T-Sgt	Digre	Clifford	B	37563471	RO
TT	T-Sgt	Haynes	Charles	R	13169567	AEG
BTG	S-Sgt	Westbrook	James	R	18242712	AG
TG	S-Sgt	Rendina	Leo	(NMI)	36897071	AAG
LWG	S-Sgt	Vann	Kenneth	R	38072719	AAG

A/C 528
P	2nd Lt.	Hey	Robert	H	0-822436	P
CP	2nd Lt.	Owens	William	S	0-779565	Cp
NB	2nd Lt.	Zissler	Christopher	(NMI)	0-2075354	NB
CH	S-Sgt	Druder	Edward	A	12205541	CH
RO	T-Sgt	Payne	Robert	T	14148400	RO
TT	T-Sgt	Gately	George	C	33187121	AEG
BTG	S-Sgt	Clark	Andrew	V	32920214	AG
TG	S-Sgt	Packingham	Robert	W	16139719	AAG
LWG	S-Sgt	Smith	Edward	A	37542118	AAG
SJ	S-Sgt	Ottorphol	Robert	B	17038376	SJ

Track Chart—April 9, 1945

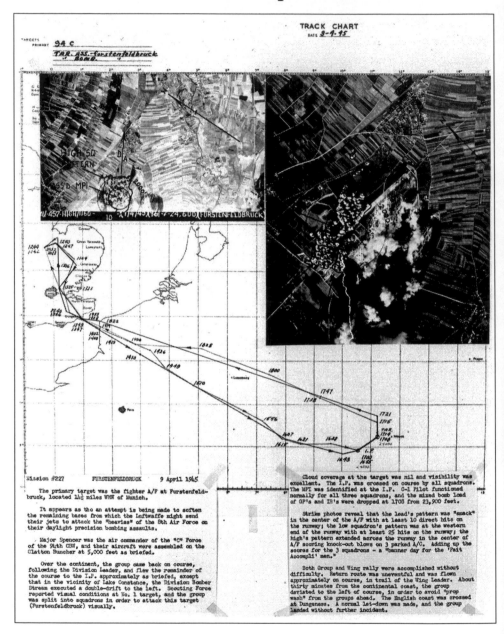

TRACK CHART
DATE 9-4-45

TARGETS
PRIMARY 94 C

TAR. ASS. Furstenfeldbruck
BOMB

Mission #227   FURSTENFELDBRUCK   9 April 1945

The primary target was the fighter A/F at Furstenfeld-bruck, located 14½ miles WNW of Munich.

It appears as tho an attempt is being made to soften the remaining bases from which the Luftwaffe might send their jets to attack the "heavies" of the 8th Air Force on their daylight precision bombing assaults.

Major Spencer was the air commander of the "C" Force of the 94th CBW, and their aircraft were assembled on the Clatton Buncher at 5,000 feet as briefed.

Over the continent, the group came back on course, following the Division Leader, and flew the remainder of the course to the I.P. approximately as briefed, except that in the vicinity of Lake Constance, the Division Bomber Stream executed a double-drift to the left. Scouting Force reported visual conditions at No. 1 target, and the group was split into squadrons in order to attack this target (Furstenfeldbruck) visually.

Cloud coverage at the target was nil and visibility was excellent. The I.P. was crossed on course by all squadrons. The MPI was identified at the I.P. C-1 Pilot functioned normally for all three squadrons, and the mixed bomb load of GP's and IB's were dropped at 1706 from 23,900 feet.

Strike photos reveal that the lead's pattern was "smack" in the center of the A/F with at least 10 direct hits on the runway; the low squadron's pattern was at the western end of the runway with at least 25 hits on the runway; the high's pattern extended across the runway in the center of A/F scoring knock-out blows on 3 parked A/C. Adding up the scores for the 3 squadrons - a "banner day for the 'Fait Accompli' men."

Both Group and Wing rally were accomplished without difficulty. Return route was uneventful and was flown approximately on course, in trail of the Wing Leader. About thirty minutes from the continental coast, the group deviated to the left of course, in order to avoid "prop wash" from the groups ahead. The English coast was crossed at Dungeness. A normal let-down was made, and the group landed without further incident.

Mission #227, Furstenfeldbruck, 9 April, 1945

The primary target was the fighter A/F at Furstenfeldbruck, located 14½ miles WNW of Munich.

It appears as though an attempt is being made to soften the remaining bases from which the Luftwaffe might send their jets to attack the "heavies" of the 8th Air Force on their daylight precision bombing assaults.

Major Spencer was the air commander of the "C" Force of the 94th CBW, and their aircraft were assembled on the Glatton Buncher at 5,000 feet as briefed.

Over the continent, the group came back on course, following the Division Leader, and flew the remainder of the course to the I.P. approximately as briefed, except that in the vicinity of Lake Constance, the Division Bomber Stream executed a double-drift to the left. Scouting Force reported visual conditions at No. 1 target, and the group was split into squadrons in order to attack this target (Frsutenfeldbruck) visually.

Cloud coverage at the target was nil and visibility was excellent. The I.P. was crossed on course by all squadrons. The MPI was identified at the I.P. C-1 Pilot functioned normally for all three squadrons, and the mixed bomb load of GP's and IB's were dropped at 1708 from 23,900 feet.

Strike photos reveal that the lead's pattern was "smack" in the center of the A/F with at least 10 direct hits on the runway; the low squadron's pattern was at the western end of the runway with at least 25 hits on the runway; the high's pattern extended across the runway in the center of A/F scoring knock-out blows on 3 parked A/C. Adding up the scores for the 3 squadrons—a "banner day for the 'Fait Accompli' men."

Both Group and Wing rally were accomplished without difficulty. Return route was uneventful and was flown approximately on course, in trail of the Wing Leader. About thirty minutes from the continental coast, the group deviated to the left of course, in order to avoid "prop wash" from the groups ahead. The English coast was crossed at Dungeness. A normal let-down was made, and the group landed without further incident.

Loading List—April 14, 1945 • My Mission #24

```
A/C 863
P     1st Lt.  Holden        James      R      O-721752   P
CP    F/O      Pitts         Vaden      S      T-126295   CP
NB    2nd Lt.  LeVar         John       E      O-2009386  NB
CH    S-Sgt    Kleinpeter    Leo        J      38487234   CH
RO    T-Sgt    McCombs       Leo        I      37661348   RO
TT    T-Sgt    Esvanko       Paul       A      35058848   AEG
BTG   S-Sgt    Bradley       Lila       B      37622566   AG
TG    S-Sgt    Johnson       Bertram    G      33699280   AAG
LWG   S-Sgt    Campbell      Jackson    R      16013309   AAE

A/C 694
P     2nd Lt.  Coons         Ralph      W      O-831666   P
CP    F/O      Blakebrough   Kenneth   (NMI)   T-63559    CP
NB    2nd Lt.  Beran         Jennings   B      O-2009146  NB
CH    S-Sgt    Cokoroglanis  Stephen   (NMI)   314237171  CH
RO    T-Sgt    Crescio       Joseph     D      36420555   RO
TT    T-Sgt    Peschen       George     F      33593996   AEG
BTG   S-Sgt    Craig         Conrad     E      42082264   AG
TG    S-Sgt    Whiteaker     Robert     D      33655320   AAG
LWG   S-Sgt    Westbrook     James      R      18242712   AAG

A/C 855
P     1st Lt.  Starnes       John       P      O-828516   P
CP    1st Lt.  Medvin        John      (NMI)   O-836625   CP
NB    F/O      Schuller      Frederick (NMI)   T-1374     NB
CH    S-Sgt    Altmaier      Robert     E      36832027   CH
RO    T-Sgt    Digre         Clifford   B      37561701   RO
TT    S-Sgt    Bleck         Edward     A      17156063   AEG
BTG   S-Sgt    Qualls        Louis      A      39923306   AG
TG    S-Sgt    Rendina       Leo       (NMI)   36897071   AAG
LWG   S-Sgt    Seastrand     Robert     F      37684223   AAG

A/C 195
P     2nd Lt.  McMillen      Jack       O      O-929387   P
CP    F/O      Leath         Clarence   E      T-4432     CP
NB    2nd Lt.  Sangar        Harold     H      O-2074809  NB
CH    S-Sgt    Radak         Sam       (NMI)   15400677   CH
RO    T-Sgt    Doherty       Daniel     A      14187260   RO
TT    T-Sgt    Haynes        Charles    R      13169567   AEG
BTG   S-Sgt    Lewandowski   Leonard   (NMI)   33920996   AG
TG    S-Sgt    Spahr         Myron      S      35874333   AAG
LWG   S-Sgt    Giacobbi      Anthony    S      31306341   AAG
SJ    S-Sgt    Branch        Jacobs    (NMI)   14160179   SJ
```

Track Chart—April 14, 1945

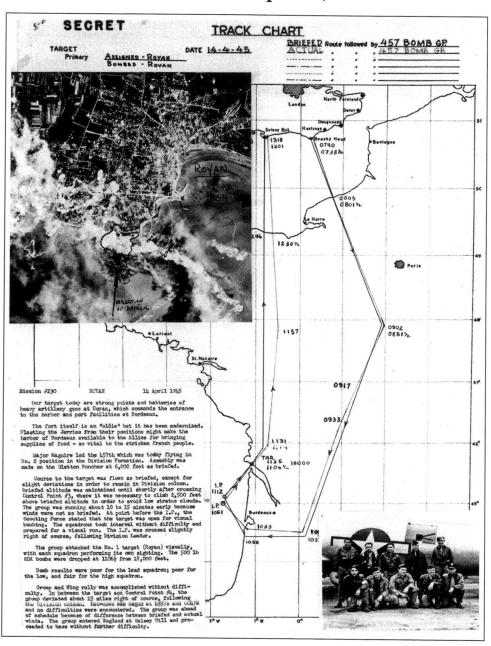

Mission #230, Royan, 14 April, 1945

Our target today are strong points and batteries of heavy artillery guns at Royan, which commands the entrance to the harbor and part facilities at Bordeaux.

The fort itself is an "oldie" but it has been modernized. Blasting the Jerries from their positions might make the harbor of Bordeaux available to the Allies for bringing supplies of food—so vital to the stricken French people.

Major Maguire led the 457th which was today flying in No. 2 position in the Division Formation. Assembly was made on the Glatton Buncher at 6,000 feet as briefed.

Course to the target was flown as briefed, except for slight deviations in order to remain in Division column. Briefed altitude was maintained until shortly after crossing Control Point #3, where it was necessary to climb 2,500 feet above briefed altitude in order to avoid low stratus clouds. The group was running about 10 to 15 minutes early because winds were not as briefed. At point before the I.P., the Scouting Force stated that the target was open for visual bombing. The squadrons took interval without difficulty and prepared for a visual run. The I.P. was crossed slightly right of course, following Division Leader.

The group attacked the No. 1 target (Royan) visually, with each squadron performing its own sighting. The 500 lb RDX bombs were dropped at 1106½ from 18,000 feet.

Bomb results were poor for the lead squadron; poor for the low, and fair for the high squadron.

Group and Wing rally was accomplished without difficulty. In between the target and Control Point #4, the group deviated about 15 miles right of course, following the Division column. Let-down was begun at 4557N and 0047W and no difficulties were encountered. The group was ahead of schedule because of difference between briefed and actual winds. The group entered England at Selsey Bill and proceeded to base without further difficulty.

APPENDIX D
Glossary of Terms

Abbreviation	Definition
AC, A/C, ac	Aircraft
A/F	Air Field
AFCE	Automatic Flight Control Equipment
BBC	British Broadcasting Corporation
B.R.L.	Bomb Release Line
C-1	Designation of the B-17 auto pilot
CAVU	Ceiling and Visibility Unlimited
CBW	Combat Bomb Wing
CO	Commanding Officer
EIA	Enemy Aircraft
FOTE	Friends of the Eighth (Eighth Army Air Corps)
G.P.	General Purpose Bomb
GEE.H	Same as GH
GH	Intersection of two pre-computed arcs
IB	Incendiary Bomb
I.P.	Initial Point—Ground position over which bombing run was begun
M.I.A.	Missing in Action
MY	Marshalling Yards
MPI	Main Point of Impact
NCO	Noncommissioned Officer
PFF	Pathfinder Force
P.O.W.	Prisoner of War
RR	Railroad
SCS.51	Designation of the B-17 mapping radar
S'd	Stayed
T.O.	Target of Opportunity

About the Book

World War II vet Cliff Digre takes us on an adventure from two years before he goes to England with the 8th Air Force through early jobs, induction, and basic training. The pace picks up when Digre is chosen by the discerning and confident pilot William T. Robinson to be a member of his crew. We learn about each of the crew members who are from all around the United States and from many different social and religious backgrounds.

High drama occurs when the Robertson crew goes into battle over Germany in B-17 bombers from the 457th Bomb Group, 8th Air Force, from 1944 until the end of the war. The final chapter recounts the transition from "Life's School" to "Life" as the author shares the lessons he learns about friendship, teamwork, thinking flexibly, learning new skills, and making commitments to both a career and to his beloved wife.

You will laugh and you will cry as Digre takes us through real human drama, and what it was like for a young man to take on the responsibilities of military training, flying missions, and struggling to get on with his life.